Betty Crocker's
Ultimate
cake mix
COOKBOOK

Create Sweet Magic from a Mix

Wiley Publishing, Inc.

Copyright © 2002 General Mills, Inc., Minneapolis, MN

Published by Wiley Publishing, Inc., New York, NY

Library of Congress Cataloging-in-Publication Data
Crocker, Betty.
  Betty Crocker's ultimate cake mix cookbook : create sweet magic from a mix.
    p. cm.
Includes index.
  ISBN 0-7645-6635-0 (hardcover : alk. paper)
  1. Cake. I. Title.
  TX771 .C6997 2002
  641.8'653—dc21
2002008222

Manufactured in China
10   9   8   7   6   5   4   3   2   1

Cover photo: Chocolate Velvet Cream Cake (variation of Lemon Velvet Cream Cake, page 84)

Table of contents photo: Brown Sugar Crunch Torte (page 67)

General Mills, Inc.

DIRECTOR, BOOKS AND ELECTRONIC PUBLISHING: Kim Walter

MANAGER, BOOKS: Lois L. Tlusty

EDITOR: Kelly A. Kilen

RECIPE DEVELOPMENT AND TESTING: Betty Crocker Kitchens

FOOD STYLING: Betty Crocker Kitchens

PHOTOGRAPHY: General Mills Photo Studios

Wiley Publishing, Inc.

PUBLISHER: Jennifer R. Feldman

EDITOR: Caroline Schleifer

PRODUCTION EDITOR: Tammy Ahrens

COVER AND BOOK DESIGN: Amy Trombat and Edwin Kuo

MANUFACTURING MANAGER: Kevin Watt

PHOTOGRAPHY ART DIRECTION: Becky Landes

For more great ideas visit **www.bettycrocker.com**

Dear Friends,

For any occasion, big or small, there's nothing like a home-baked dessert to make the moment memorable. Now, with *Betty Crocker's Ultimate Cake Mix Cookbook*, all it takes is a box of your favorite Betty Crocker cake mix and just a few ingredients to create the desserts you've always dreamed of baking.

Whether you're a novice or an experienced baker, there are plenty of recipes to inspire you to bake. You'll enjoy tempting treats ranging from potluck-ready cakes to spectacular showstoppers to super-easy cookies, and even a Classic Wedding Cake (page 94) you can make! There are fun cut-up cakes for any occasion, like a Gingerbread Cake Cottage (page 140) for the holidays or a Housewarming Cake (page 112) that says welcome home. Plus, every recipe comes with a helpful *Betty's Tip* of extra baking information, such as time-saving hints, super substitutions and easy ways to add a fabulous finishing touch. *Betty's Baking Secret* pages in each chapter are jammed full of clever ideas, from creative decorating to best bake-sale tactics to making kids' birthday parties extra-special.

To celebrate more than fifty years of Betty Crocker cake mix history, we've gathered all of our favorite recipes, along with lots of fresh new ideas. Look for the **All-Time FAVORITE** symbol to easily find the most requested recipes. So, treat your family and friends to the best with *Betty Crocker's Ultimate Cake Mix Cookbook*— the best cakes, cookies, bars and desserts you've ever baked!

Betty Crocker

PS: Whip up a delicious dessert with cake mix today—no one will guess your secret ingredient!

Contents

Over 50 Years of Cake Mix Success

Cake mix, one of the first convenience foods, reflects five decades of American history. Developed shortly after the end of World War II, cake mix was welcomed by consumers who were looking for ways to make cooking, and especially baking, easier and more convenient. By listening to what consumers want, Betty Crocker has made baking fun for many generations!

1940s: It takes almost a decade to develop cake mix.

Beginning in 1943, the Betty Crocker labs and kitchens spent four intensive years creating and researching cake mixes. Layer cake mixes were sent to consumer kitchens for additional testing. An unexpected result: consumer testers preferred to add some of their own fresh ingredients in order to make the cake more genuine. Powdered eggs were removed from the mixes, and the cake mix directions called for adding two fresh eggs instead.

A (Cake) Walk through Betty Crocker's Cake Mix History:

1949	1951	1953

Even in the beginning, Betty Crocker Cake Mix was always the life of the party!

Ask Betty a question, and you're sure to get the right answer—every time!

Betty's "eggs-cellent" answer was to add fresh eggs to the mix!

Consumers also wanted multiple flavors. Betty Crocker responded by creating Party Cake layer cake mix. This versatile box of cake mix could turn out yellow, white or spice cake depending on whether whole eggs, egg whites only, or spices and whole eggs were added. In 1948, Betty Crocker Devil's Food and Party Cake layer cake mixes were distributed nationally and sold for $.35 to $.37 each.

1950s and 1960s: Cake mix variety is the spice of life.

The first layer cake flavors introduced in the fifties were Yellow (1952), White (1952), Marble (1954) and Chocolate Malt (1955). Spice layer cake mix created a challenge. After months of taste tests, a special blend of natural spices—fresh cinnamon, cloves, allspice and ginger—was selected. But the taste was still too pungent and sharp. Honey to the rescue! It mellowed the spices and, even better, added moistness and a fine texture to the cake. Honey Spice cake mix was introduced in 1953 and was available until 1973.

Angel food cake was considered a luxury in the American home because it was costly and tricky to make. Betty Crocker Angel Food cake mix was first introduced in 1953, followed by a one-step mix in 1960.

Answer Cake, a unique all-in-one package, complete with cake mix, aluminum foil baking pan and frosting, entered the cake mix scene in 1954. Tailored for individuals and small families, it could be cut into six generous pieces or up to 12 tea-size servings. Flavors included white, yellow, devil's food and peanut butter. Answer Cake remained on the shelves until 1968.

1957

1958

1959

Bakers have been having fun with cake mixes for generations! These great ideas are just as deliciously enjoyable today.

In the 1950s you asked, "What's a fast cake for tonight?" Answer: Cake!

Finally, a cake that was just like Grandma used to bake (only better!).

Harry Baker divulged the recipe for his famous chiffon cake to Betty Crocker in 1948, revealing for the first time its secret ingredient: salad oil. Consumers wrote in requesting a mix, so after extensive testing, Betty Crocker Chiffon cake mix appeared on the market in 1958.

The same year, Betty Crocker responded to a national family opinion survey that identified moistness and tenderness as the most desired qualities in cake by developing Country Kitchen cake mixes. Made with a softer flour, finer sugar and new homogenized shortening, this mix produced a tender crumb and moister cake. "New Improved—adds new moistness to the best taste in cakes." This flag appeared on all Betty Crocker layer cakes after the mix recipe was changed in 1964.

1970s: Consumers want it all—convenience and more moistness.

In 1975, Betty Crocker developed the most convenient cake mix yet: Stir 'n Frost™, which contained cake mix, a foil-lined baking pan and ready-to-spread frosting all in one package.

Later in the decade, General Mills responded to a grassroots baking trend for denser, extra-moist cakes. By adding pudding to the mix, Betty Crocker created the present-day SuperMoist® cake mixes.

As the definition of fitness changed, so did cake mix. With polls showing 50 percent of Americans avoiding or cutting down on sugar and desserts, Betty Crocker answered the call with Light Style layer cake mix in 1979 that had 30 percent fewer calories. As Betty Crocker discovered, what people said they wanted wasn't what they *really* wanted. Consumers preferred the regular mixes, so Light Style layer cake mixes were discontinued in 1981.

1964	1966	1976

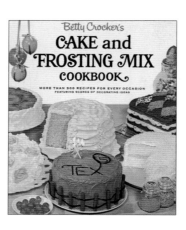

Richer, moister, tastier than ever before!

The first, the original, cake mix cookbook.

All in one box—everything you needed to whip up a fabulous dessert!

1980s: Decadent desserts steal center stage.

Indulgent baking made its debut in 1986 with Betty Crocker Cake Lovers' Collection®, a line of deluxe mixes. Rich-tasting and extra-moist, each of the four featured flavors contained nearly three times the flavoring ingredients of regular cake mixes.

Microwave ovens became the latest popular appliance, and Betty Crocker's microwavable cake mix line, MicroRave™ cake mixes, came out in 1988. In the end, the old-fashioned oven method proved more popular and this line was discontinued in 1992.

1990s: From healthy to indulgent—all in one decade.

The health craze took over, and Betty Crocker SuperMoist Light cake mix, 94 percent fat free and with 50 percent less fat than the average cake, was introduced in 1990. It was renamed Betty Crocker Sweet Rewards® cake mix in 1996.

Renewed demand for convenience led to the introduction of Stir 'n Bake® cake mix in 1997: Just add water, bake it in its own pan and top with the enclosed frosting or topping. With less time to bake, everyone depended more and more on mixes that guaranteed quality. To celebrate the 50th Anniversary of cake mix and to enhance texture and taste, Betty Crocker reformulated SuperMoist layer cake mix to make it the moistest cake ever.

2000 and beyond: The future of cake mix is bright!

With delicious flavors in the double digits, Betty Crocker has what everyone wants in a cake mix today: quality, ease, convenience, and most important of all, the best taste ever!

1979	1980	1999

What made Christmas more magical than cake mix? Fruit-flavored gelatin and imagination mixed together.

If you loved cake before, with new and improved SuperMoist you loved it even more.

Still delicious, still easy, and still a great idea after all these years.

Bake a Perfect Cake Every Time

From special occasions to everyday celebrations, a home-baked cake takes the cake! For years, Betty Crocker cake mixes have taken the guesswork out of baking and given you a head start on memorable homemade creations. It's your secret that these marvelous cakes start with a mix and look fabulous without taking lots of time to make!

Baking Equipment

The right equipment makes cake baking easy and fun. Look for these equipment features when stocking your kitchen.

Pans It's important to use the size of pan called for in a recipe. Standard pan sizes are usually marked on the back of the pan; if not, measure the length and width across the top of the pan from inside edge to inside edge. If the pan is too large, your cake will be flat and dry; if the pan is too small, it will bulge or overflow the pan.

Choose shiny metal pans for baking cakes. They reflect heat away from the cake for a tender, light-brown crust. If you use dark nonstick or glass baking pans, follow the manufacturer's directions, which may call for reducing the baking temperature by 25 degrees. These pans absorb heat; therefore, cakes will bake and brown faster.

Mixer You will need a handheld electric or stand mixer. Heavy-duty commercial mixers are too powerful for mixing package cake mixes. It is possible to mix cake mixes by hand with a wire whisk, but an electric mixer makes it easier!

Bowls Choose stainless-steel or glass bowls. Plastic doesn't work very well when beating egg whites. Stock your kitchen with a few in each size—small, medium and large.

Cooling Racks You will need wire racks for cooling your cakes. Stainless steel is a wise choice, because it won't rust and will last a lifetime.

✳ Your Pan Plan ✳

To bake most of the cakes in this book, you will want to have these standard-sized pans on hand.

- ✳ 13 x 9 x 2-inch rectangular pan
- ✳ Two or three 8 x 1 1/2- or 9 x 1 1/2-inch round pans
- ✳ 9 x 9 x 2-inch square pan
- ✳ 12-cup bundt cake pan
- ✳ 10 x 4-inch angel food cake (tube) pan
- ✳ Two 8 1/2 x 4 1/2 x 2 1/2-inch or 9 x 5 x 3-inch loaf pans
- ✳ Muffin pan with medium cups, 2 1/2 x 1 1/4 inches
- ✳ 15 1/2 x 10 1/2 x 1-inch jelly roll pan
- ✳ Shiny aluminum cookie sheets (at least 2 inches narrower and shorter than the inside dimensions of your oven so the heat will circulate around them)

Knives For layer cakes, choose a sharp, long, thin knife for splitting cakes into layers and to slice cakes into serving pieces. Choose a serrated or electric knife for angel food and pound cakes.

Ready, Set, Bake!

Rack Position and Oven Temperature For most cakes, position the oven rack in the middle of the oven. Since angel food cake rises so high, it should be baked at the lowest oven rack position. If the rack is placed too high, angel food cake will brown too quickly on top and will test done before it is completely baked.

If you are making a layer cake, check to see how your cake pans will fit on the oven rack before you heat the oven. Some layer cake recipes call for three round pans. To see if they all will fit, stagger the pans on the middle rack in the cold oven, leaving 1 inch between pans and the sides of the oven. Make sure the door will close completely. What if three pans don't fit or you have only two layer pans? You can cover and refrigerate the batter in the third pan or in the mixing bowl while the first two layers are baking.

Preheat the oven 10 to 15 minutes before you plan to bake to allow time for it to heat to baking temperature. It's a good idea to have your oven heat control checked for accuracy by your local utility company. If this service is not available or is too costly, judge for yourself based on whether baked goods are already golden brown at the minimum bake time (oven may run high) or not yet done at the maximum bake time (oven may run low).

Preparing Pans Correctly greased and floured pans will keep cakes from sticking. In most cases, you will want to grease the bottom and side of the pan with about 1 tablespoon solid vegetable shortening. Then, dust the pan with about 1 tablespoon flour and tap out the excess. You may use baking cocoa to dust the pan for a chocolate cake. Be sure to follow the recipe directions carefully. Some recipes may call for greasing the bottom only of the pan or for leaving the pan ungreased. For nonstick pans, follow the manufacturer's directions; greasing is usually recommended.

Cooking spray may also be used; however, the cake may rise with high sides and a lip. If using cooking spray, coat only the bottom of the pan; do not dust the pan with flour.

Angel food cake is an exception. Leave the pan ungreased so the cake will cling to the side as it rises during baking.

✳ Serve It Up! ✳

Ever wondered how many servings each kind of cake can yield?

Size and Type of Cake	Number of Servings
One-layer 8- or 9-inch round	8
Two-layer 8- or 9-inch round	12 to 16
8- or 9-inch square	9
13 x 9 x 2-inch rectangular	12 to 15
10 x 4-inch angel food	12 to 16
12-cup bundt or pound cake	16 to 24

Measuring Be sure to measure carefully. To measure liquid, place a liquid measuring cup on your counter, pour in the liquid, bend down and check the amount at eye level. Too little liquid can cause a heavy, low-volume cake. Too much liquid can cause a cake to fall. To measure a dry ingredient, gently spoon the ingredient into a dry-ingredient measuring cup and level off with a straight spatula or knife. Do not shake the cup or pack down the ingredients. Brown sugar is the exception; pack it firmly into a dry-ingredient measuring cup, then level off. Use measuring spoons for small amounts of both liquid and dry ingredients.

Mixing All of the cake recipes in this cookbook were tested with handheld electric mixers. Because mixers vary in power, you may need to adjust the speed, especially when first combining ingredients. If using a powerful stand mixer, be careful not to overmix the batter, which can cause tunnels (large air holes) or a sunken center.

You can also mix cakes by hand with a wire whisk. Stir the ingredients until they are combined, then beat 150 strokes for each minute of beating time given in a recipe. Take care not to overbeat. This actually breaks down the cake, and it may not rise as high or it may shrink as it cools.

Baking Time Follow the recommended baking time in the recipe as a guideline. Begin checking at the minimum time. If using a dark or nonstick pan, you may need to decrease the baking time by 2 to 3 minutes. You may need to experiment a bit with the baking time, especially if your oven isn't quite accurate.

Testing for Doneness Follow the test for doneness indicated in the recipe or on the package directions. Typically, cakes are done when a toothpick inserted in the center comes out clean. If a cake contains a lot of "gooey" ingredients, however, this test may not be accurate. You can also judge if a cake is done if the top springs back when touched lightly in the center and the cake starts to pull away from the sides of the pan.

Cooling and Splitting Cakes

Cooling Layer Cakes Cool layer cakes in the pans on wire racks about 10 minutes before removing them from the pans. This helps prevent the cake from breaking apart, which can happen when it is too warm and tender. To remove a layer cake from the pan, run a knife around the side of the pan to loosen the cake. Cover a wire rack with a towel. Place rack, towel side down, on top of cake layer. Turn pan and rack upside down; carefully remove pan.

Place a second wire rack over the inverted cake layer; turn both racks upside down so cake layer is upright.

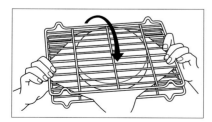

Remove towel and top wire rack. Repeat with remaining layer(s). Allow layers to cool completely, about 1 hour, on racks.

Cooling Specialty Cakes For deeper cakes, such as bundt cakes, cool in the pan for 15 to 20 minutes. To remove a bundt cake from the pan, place a wire rack on top of the cake. Turn pan and rack upside down; carefully remove pan.

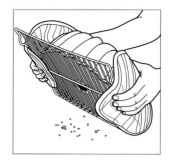

Cooling Angel Food Cake Angel food cake must cool while hanging upside down or it will sink and collapse. To cool an angel food cake, immediately after baking, turn the pan upside down onto a glass bottle or metal funnel and let hang at least 2 hours. The cake should be completely cool.

To remove an angel food cake from the pan, loosen cake by running a knife between the cake and pan in a sawing motion around edges. If the pan has a removable bottom, hold pan by the center tube and lift the cake from the pan. Loosen cake from the bottom with a knife; remove cake and turn cake upside down. If the pan is one piece, use your fingers to loosen the cake from the pan.

Splitting Cake Layers First mark middle points on the side of a cake layer with toothpicks. To split layer, use a knife or the thread technique. Using thread and toothpicks as a guideline, split the cake layer by pulling a piece of heavy sewing thread back and forth through the layer. Or, using a long, thin, sharp knife and toothpicks as a guideline, cut horizontally through the layer.

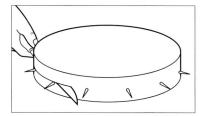

Splitting Angel Food Cake An angel food cake can be split into three layers. Measure the cake with a ruler, and mark into equal widths the number of desired layers with toothpicks. Using a serrated knife and toothpicks as a guideline, cut horizontally across the cake with a light, sawing motion.

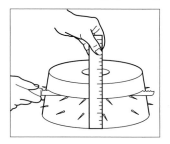

Frosting and Glazing Cakes

Frosting a Layer Cake Start out by lining the edge of the cake plate with 4 strips of waxed paper. Brush any loose crumbs from the cooled cake layer. Place the layer, rounded side down, on the plate. (The waxed paper will protect the plate as you frost and can be removed later.)

To frost, spread about 1/3 cup creamy frosting (or 1/2 cup fluffy frosting) over the top of the first layer to about 1/4 inch from the edge.

Place the second layer, rounded side up, on the first layer so that the two flat sides of the layers are together with frosting in between. Coat the side of

✳ Fabulous Frosting ✳

Here are some simple success tips for frosting layer cakes.

✳ Freeze the cake for 30 to 60 minutes to make it easier to frost.

✳ Place a dab of frosting under the cake on the serving plate to keep the cake from sliding.

✳ Try a flexible metal spatula that allows you to spread the frosting in a larger area.

✳ Use a light touch to prevent layers from sliding and the filling from squishing out between layers.

the cake with a very thin layer of frosting to seal in the crumbs.

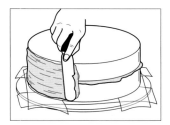

Frost the side of the cake in swirls, making a rim about 1/4 inch above the top of the cake to prevent the top from appearing sloped.

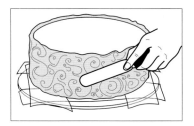

Spread the remaining frosting on top, just to the built-up rim. Remove waxed paper strips.

Glazing a Cake Glazing is a good option for pound cakes and cakes that are too rich for frosting. To glaze a cake, pour or drizzle glaze over top of cake. Immediately spread with a spatula or the back of a spoon, allowing some glaze to drizzle down the side.

Storing Cakes

Cakes may be stored at room temperature, refrigerated or frozen. To store at room temperature, cool the cake thoroughly on a wire rack to keep the top from becoming sticky. Store frosted or unfrosted cakes loosely covered at room temperature for up to two days. To loosely cover, place aluminum foil, plastic wrap or waxed paper over cake, or place a cake safe or large inverted bowl over the cake.

Refrigerate cakes with custard, whipped cream or cream cheese toppings or fillings. During humid weather or in humid climates, refrigerate cakes containing very moist ingredients such as chopped apples, applesauce, shredded carrots or zucchini, mashed bananas or pumpkin. These cakes tend to mold quickly if stored at room temperature.

Freeze frosted or unfrosted cake up to two months. Cool cake completely before freezing. Place cake in a rigid container (such as a cardboard bakery box) to prevent crushing, then cover with aluminum foil, plastic wrap or large freezer bag. Cakes frosted with a creamy frosting freeze best. Fluffy or whipped cream frosting freezes well but tends to stick to the wrapping. To prevent sticking, freeze cake uncovered 1 hour, insert toothpicks around the top and side of cake, and wrap.

To thaw cakes, loosen wrap on frozen unfrosted cakes, and thaw at room temperature 2 to 3 hours. Loosen wrap on frozen frosted cakes, and thaw overnight in refrigerator.

Baking Cakes at High Altitude

As the altitude increases, air pressure decreases, which calls for some baking adjustments. Because the rate of evaporation is faster at high altitude, cakes often require more liquid and longer bake times. Also, the lighter air at high altitude allows cake batter to expand more and faster, often making it necessary to increase the oven temperature by 25° and to use larger baking pans. And remember to generously grease and flour pans, because cakes have a greater tendency to stick to pans.

Baking cakes at high altitude can be trickier than other baked goods. There are no hard and fast rules to follow—changes to cake recipes depend upon the type of cake and the proportion of ingredients. For all your baking, we suggest you use only recipes that have been tested and adjusted for high altitude. All of the recipes in this book have been tested at high altitude.

✳ Saucy Secrets ✳

Here's how to substitute unsweetened applesauce for oil in cake mix recipes.

Cake Mix Flavor	Ingredients
butter recipe yellow, chocolate fudge, devil's food, German chocolate or yellow cake	3/4 cup water 3/4 cup applesauce 3 eggs
carrot cake	1/2 cup water 3/4 cup applesauce 3 eggs
lemon cake	2/3 cup water 3/4 cup applesauce 3 eggs
white cake	3/4 cup water 3/4 cup applesauce 3 egg whites

Consumer Q & A

Every day, consumers like you ask the experts in the Betty Crocker Kitchens all their baking questions. Here are some of the questions that can help all bakers learn more about cake mix!

Question: *Can I substitute butter or margarine for the vegetable oil in SuperMoist cakes? What about canola or olive oil for the vegetable oil?*

Answer: The good news is that butter, margarine, shortening and all types of vegetable oil can be used interchangeably for the vegetable oil called for in SuperMoist package directions. Although there may be slight differences in texture and flavor, all cakes will have satisfactory baking results.

Measure the same amount of butter, margarine and shortening called for in package directions, then melt and cool the butter, margarine or shortening before preparing the cake mix. Since the amount of oil in a cake mix is small in proportion to all of the combined ingredients, there is very little flavor difference among different types of vegetable oils. Go ahead and use oil labeled vegetable, corn, canola, all types of olive, peanut, sunflower oil and oil blends.

Question: *I usually grease and flour my cake pans, but SuperMoist cake mix package directions say to grease only the bottom of the pan. Is flour necessary?*

Answer: With our latest cake mix formula, when adding only water, oil and eggs, the cake releases well from the pan without flouring the pan. What a convenience! However, if additional ingredients are added to the cake mix or if you are baking at high altitude, the chances of the cake sticking to the pan increase, and we recommend greasing and flouring the cake pan. In addition, run a knife around the side of the pan before removing the cake to help the cake release easily.

Question: *Can I use applesauce in place of the oil in SuperMoist cake mixes? I like to reduce fat in my baking whenever possible.*

Answer: Although the appearance and texture of a SuperMoist layer cake is slightly different when made with applesauce instead of oil, results will be satisfactory. You'll need to follow directions for each specific cake mix flavor (see Saucy Secrets on page 14). Then the amount of water you add needs to be lower than that called for on standard package directions to make up for the extra moisture in the applesauce. Also, you'll need to use *unsweetened* applesauce so you aren't adding more sugar to the cake mix. Just mix cake mix with applesauce in the same way as directed on package.

Question: *Can I add pudding mix to my favorite cake mix recipe?*

Answer: Pudding is already included in SuperMoist cake mixes, so adding extra pudding is not recommended; in some cases, the cake would be too moist. There are some recipes in this book that contain extra pudding mix as an ingredient—these cakes have been tested with delicious results.

Bake-and-Take

Cherry–Chocolate Chip Cake (page 44) and S'mores Cake (page 40)

Chocolate Turtle Cake

Prep: 15 min * Bake: 55 min * Cool: 1 hr

15 SERVINGS

1 package Betty Crocker SuperMoist devil's food cake mix

1 1/3 cups water

1/2 cup vegetable oil

3 eggs

1 bag (14 ounces) caramels

1/2 cup evaporated milk

1 cup chopped pecans

1 bag (6 ounces) semisweet chocolate chips (1 cup)

1 Heat oven to 350°. Grease bottom and sides of rectangular pan, 13 x 9 x 2 inches, with shortening; lightly flour.

2 Make cake mix as directed on package, using water, oil and eggs. Pour half of the batter into pan. Bake 25 minutes.

3 Meanwhile, heat caramels and milk in 1-quart saucepan over medium heat about 10 minutes, stirring frequently, until caramels are melted. (Or place caramels and milk in 4-cup glass measuring cup. Microwave uncovered on High 2 minutes to 3 minutes 30 seconds, stirring once or twice.) Pour and spread caramel over warm cake in pan. Sprinkle with pecans and chocolate chips. Spread with remaining batter.

4 Bake 30 minutes. Run knife around side of pan to loosen cake. Cool completely, about 1 hour. Store covered at room temperature.

High Altitude (3500 to 6500 feet): Decrease oil to 1/3 cup. Beat cake mix on low speed 2 minutes.

1 Serving: Calories 430 (Calories from Fat 200); Fat 22g (Saturated 7g); Cholesterol 45mg; Sodium 350mg; Carbohydrate 58g (Dietary Fiber 2g); Protein 5g. **% Daily Value:** Vitamin A 2%; Vitamin C 0%; Calcium 8%; Iron 10%.

Betty's Tip It's hard to resist this popular cake, especially if you serve it with ice cream. Make it extra special by drizzling chocolate and caramel syrups over the ice cream and sprinkling with a few additional chopped pecans.

Chocolate Turtle Cake

Chocolate Graham Streusel Cake

Prep: 15 min * Bake: 38 min * Cool: 1 hr

15 SERVINGS

1 1/2 cups graham cracker crumbs (21 squares)

1/2 cup chopped nuts

1/2 cup packed brown sugar

1 1/4 teaspoons ground cinnamon

1/2 cup butter or margarine, melted

1 package Betty Crocker SuperMoist devil's food cake mix

1 1/3 cups water

1/2 cup vegetable oil

3 eggs

1/4 cup Easy Vanilla Glaze (page 242) or 1/2 recipe Vanilla Glaze (page 242)

1 Heat oven to 350°. Grease bottom only of rectangular pan, 13 x 9 x 2 inches, with shortening. Mix cracker crumbs, nuts, brown sugar, cinnamon and butter; set aside.

2 Make cake mix as directed on package, using water, oil and eggs. Pour about 2 1/3 cups batter into pan; sprinkle with about 1 1/2 cups crumb mixture. Pour remaining batter into pan; sprinkle with remaining crumb mixture.

3 Bake 33 to 38 minutes or until toothpick inserted in center comes out clean. Run knife around side of pan to loosen cake. Cool completely, about 1 hour. Drizzle with Easy Vanilla Glaze. Store covered at room temperature.

High Altitude (3500 to 6500 feet): If using devil's food cake mix, heat oven to 375°; make cake mix following high-altitude directions on package for 13 x 9 x 2-inch rectangle. If using yellow cake mix, heat oven to 350°; make cake mix following high-altitude directions on package for 13 x 9 x 2-inch rectangle.

1 Serving: Calories 390 (Calories from Fat 180); Fat 20g (Saturated 7g); Cholesterol 60mg; Sodium 360mg; Carbohydrate 50g (Dietary Fiber 0g); Protein 3g. **% Daily Value:** Vitamin A 6%; Vitamin C 0%; Calcium 4%; Iron 8%.

Yellow Graham Streusel Cake: Substitute SuperMoist yellow cake mix for the devil's food cake mix. Make cake mix using 1 1/4 cups water, 1/3 cup vegetable oil and 3 eggs.

Betty's Tip Vanilla glaze gives this special cake a dressed-up look. If you like, you can leave off the glaze and serve slices of cake with whipped topping or Sweetened Whipped Cream (page 243).

Dad and daughter enjoy a yummy bite of togetherness in the 1970s.

Easy Red Velvet Cake

Prep: 10 min * Bake: 35 min * Cool: 1 hr

15 SERVINGS

1 package Betty Crocker SuperMoist German chocolate cake mix

3/4 cup buttermilk

1/4 cup water

1/4 cup vegetable oil

3 eggs

1 bottle (1 ounce) red food color

1 tub Betty Crocker Rich & Creamy vanilla ready-to-spread frosting or Vanilla Buttercream Frosting (page 236)

1 Heat oven to 350°. Grease bottom and sides of rectangular pan, 13 x 9 x 2 inches, with shortening.

2 Beat all ingredients except frosting in large bowl with electric mixer on low speed 30 seconds; beat on medium speed 1 minute. Pour into pan.

3 Bake 30 to 35 minutes or until toothpick inserted in center comes out clean. Run knife around side of pan to loosen cake. Cool completely, about 1 hour. Spread frosting over top of cake. Store loosely covered at room temperature.

High Altitude (3500 to 6500 feet): Heat oven to 375°. Add 1/4 cup all-purpose flour to dry cake mix. Increase water to 1/2 cup.

1 Serving: Calories 310 (Calories from Fat 100); Fat 11g (Saturated 6g); Cholesterol 45mg; Sodium 270mg; Carbohydrate 51g (Dietary Fiber 0g); Protein 3g. **% Daily Value:** Vitamin A 2%; Vitamin C 0%; Calcium 4%; Iron 2%.

Betty's Tip Believe it or not, to get the intense red color that is characteristic of this special cake, you will need to use the whole 1-ounce bottle of red food color.

Better-than-Almost-Anything Cake

Prep: 10 min • Bake: 35 min • Cool: 15 min • Chill: 2 hr

15 SERVINGS

1 package Betty Crocker
SuperMoist German chocolate
cake mix

1 1/3 cups water

1/2 cup vegetable oil

3 eggs

1 can (14 ounces) sweetened
condensed milk

1 jar (16 to 17 ounces) caramel,
butterscotch or fudge topping

1 container (8 ounces) frozen
whipped topping, thawed,
or 3 cups Sweetened Whipped
Cream (page 243)

1 bag (8 ounces) toffee chips
or bits

1 Heat oven to 350°. Generously grease bottom only of rectangular pan, 13 x 9 x 2 inches, with shortening.

2 Make cake mix as directed on package, using water, oil and eggs. Pour into pan.

3 Bake 30 to 35 minutes or until toothpick inserted in center comes out clean. Cool 15 minutes.

4 Poke top of warm cake every 1/2 inch with handle of wooden spoon. Drizzle milk evenly over top of cake; let stand until milk has been absorbed into cake. Drizzle with caramel topping. Run knife around side of pan to loosen cake. Cover and refrigerate about 2 hours or until chilled.

5 Spread whipped topping over top of cake. Sprinkle with toffee chips. Store covered in refrigerator.

High Altitude (3500 to 6500 feet): Heat oven to 375°. Add 2 tablespoons all-purpose flour to dry cake mix. Increase water to 1 1/2 cups; decrease oil to 1 tablespoon. Beat cake mix on low speed 30 seconds; beat on medium speed 4 minutes. Bake 35 to 40 minutes.

1 Serving: Calories 535 (Calories from Fat 190); Fat 21g (Saturated 9g); Cholesterol 60mg; Sodium 310mg; Carbohydrate 80g (Dietary Fiber 1g); Protein 7g. **% Daily Value:** Vitamin A 6%; Vitamin C 0%; Calcium 18%; Iron 4%.

Betty's Tip Mmmm! This sinfully decadent cake of the 1980s received its name for obvious reasons. The rich combination of ingredients produces an intense sugar high that rivals all other pleasures!

Better-than-Almost-Anything Cake

Triple-Fudge Cake

Prep: 15 min * Bake: 50 min * Cool: 2 hr

15 SERVINGS

1/3 cup sweetened condensed milk

1 bag (6 ounces) semisweet chocolate chips (1 cup)

1 package Betty Crocker SuperMoist chocolate fudge cake mix

1/2 cup vegetable oil

1 cup applesauce

2 eggs

1/2 cup chopped pecans

1 Heat oven to 350°. Grease bottom only of rectangular pan, 13 x 9 x 2 inches, with shortening; lightly flour.

2 Microwave milk and 1/2 cup of the chocolate chips in small microwavable bowl uncovered on Medium (50%) about 1 minute or until chocolate is softened; stir until smooth and set aside.

3 Beat cake mix and oil in large bowl with electric mixer on low speed 30 seconds (mixture will be crumbly); reserve 1 cup. Beat applesauce and eggs into remaining cake mixture on low speed 30 seconds (batter will be thick and grainy); beat on medium speed 2 minutes. Spread in pan.

4 Drop melted chocolate mixture by teaspoonfuls over batter, dropping more around edge than in center. Stir remaining 1/2 cup chocolate chips and the pecans into reserved cake mixture; sprinkle over batter. Bake 45 to 50 minutes or until center is set. Run knife around side of pan to loosen cake. Cool completely, about 2 hours. Store covered at room temperature.

High Altitude (3500 to 6500 feet): No changes.

1 Serving: Calories 330 (Calories from Fat 155); Fat 17g (Saturated 5g); Cholesterol 30mg; Sodium 290mg; Carbohydrate 41g (Dietary Fiber 1g); Protein 4g. **% Daily Value:** Vitamin A 0%; Vitamin C 0%; Calcium 6%; Iron 6%.

Betty's Tip If you have milk chocolate or white baking chips on hand, you can use them as part of the 1/2 cup chocolate chips stirred into the reserved cake mixture.

Triple-Fudge Cake

Chocolate Pudding Cake

Prep: 10 min * Bake: 35 min * Cool: 1 hr * Chill: 2 hr

15 SERVINGS

1 package Betty Crocker SuperMoist chocolate fudge cake mix

1 1/3 cups water

1/2 cup vegetable oil

3 eggs

1 package (4-serving size) chocolate instant pudding and pie filling mix

2 cups cold milk

1 Heat oven to 350°. Grease bottom only of rectangular pan, 13 x 9 x 2 inches, with shortening.

2 Make cake mix as directed on package, using water, oil and eggs. Pour into pan.

3 Bake 30 to 35 minutes or until toothpick inserted in center comes out clean. Cool completely, about 1 hour.

4 Poke cake every 1/2 inch with handle of wooden spoon. Beat pudding mix and milk in medium bowl with wire whisk about 2 minutes. Pour pudding evenly over cake. Run knife around side of pan to loosen cake. Refrigerate about 2 hours until chilled. Store covered in refrigerator.

High Altitude (3500 to 6500 feet): Heat oven to 375°. Add 2 tablespoons all-purpose flour to dry cake mix. Increase water to 1 1/2 cups; decrease oil to 1 tablespoon. Bake 35 to 40 minutes. Chocolate-Banana Pudding Cake variation not recommended.

1 Serving: Calories 240 (Calories from Fat 90); Fat 10g (Saturated 2g); Cholesterol 45mg; Sodium 380mg; Carbohydrate 35g (Dietary Fiber 1g); Protein 4g. **% Daily Value:** Vitamin A 0%; Vitamin C 0%; Calcium 8%; Iron 6%.

Chocolate-Banana Pudding Cake: Decrease water to 3/4 cup. Beat in 1 cup mashed, very ripe bananas (about 2 medium) with the cake mix, water, oil and eggs.

Betty's Tip This is a great all-family recipe that can also be used for casual entertaining. To make it more special, top with whipped cream and chopped nuts or a scoop of fudge swirl ice cream.

Chocolate Pudding Cake

Stir-in-the-Pan Applesauce Cake

Prep: 10 min ✳ Bake: 40 min ✳ Cool: 1 hr

9 SERVINGS

1 package Betty Crocker SuperMoist yellow cake mix

1 1/2 cups applesauce

1/2 cup chopped nuts

1/2 cup raisins

1 1/2 teaspoons ground cinnamon

3 eggs

Powdered sugar, if desired

1 Heat oven to 350°. Mix cake mix and remaining ingredients except powdered sugar in ungreased square pan, 9 x 9 x 2 inches, with fork, scraping corners frequently, until blended (some lumps may remain). Scrape sides with rubber spatula; spread batter evenly.

2 Bake 35 to 40 minutes or until toothpick inserted in center comes out clean. Run knife around side of pan to loosen cake. Cool completely, about 1 hour. Sprinkle with powdered sugar. Store covered in refrigerator.

High Altitude (3500 to 6500 feet): Heat oven to 375°. Use rectangular pan, 13 x 9 x 2 inches. Decrease applesauce to 1 1/4 cups; add 1 tablespoon all-purpose flour.

1 Serving: Calories 360 (Calories from Fat 90); Fat 10g (Saturated 2g); Cholesterol 70mg; Sodium 380mg; Carbohydrate 63g (Dietary Fiber 2g); Protein 4g. **% Daily Value:** Vitamin A 2%; Vitamin C 0%; Calcium 12%; Iron 10%.

Betty's Tip What could be easier than this stir-in-the-pan cake? It makes a great snack for picnics and potlucks. Serve it straight from the pan, or top it with Caramel Frosting (page 240) for a decadent treat.

Mini-Cakes and Cupcakes

What's even more fun than a great big cake? Lots of little cakes! And they're easy to decorate, too! So the next time your celebration or mood calls for a cake, make small cakes, then break out the frosting, sprinkles and candies and get family or friends involved in adding some finishing touches.

Mini Party Cakes

Start with 1 package Betty Crocker SuperMoist cake mix (any flavor). Each package makes about 50 little cakes. Heat oven to 350°. Spread batter in greased and floured jelly roll pan. Bake 25 to 30 minutes or until toothpick inserted in center comes out clean; cool completely. Frost the cake, then cut into smaller shapes. First cut cake into thirds, then cut into triangles, squares or diamonds.

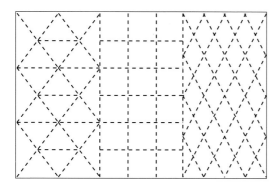

A variety of pretty decorations give your little cakes a personal touch. Here are just a few ideas:

* Top with mini chocolate chips, candies, pastel mints or jelly beans.

* Sprinkle the tops of cakes with colored sugar or sprinkles.

* Drizzle zigzag lines with melted chocolate. Use dark chocolate on white frosting; white chocolate on chocolate frosting.

* Add a garden-fresh touch by topping with edible flowers such as violets, primroses and rose petals (make sure they're pesticide free).

Cupcakes

Cupcakes are easy to transport, making them perfect for parties and picnics. And because they're individual, they're more fun to hold and eat! You can make a batch from any cake batter; you'll get about 24 cupcakes. Here are some quick tips for making party-perfect cupcakes:

* Line medium muffin cups with paper baking cups. Look for festive cups in colors and special designs at your supermarket, party store or paper supply store.

* Fill each cup about 2/3 full with batter. Bake according to package directions.

* If you have only one 12-cup muffin pan, cover and refrigerate the rest of the batter while the first batch is baking.

* For mini-cupcakes, use small muffin cups, 1 3/4 x 1 inch. Heat oven to 350°, and bake 10 to 15 minutes. You'll get about 48 small cupcakes.

Pineapple Upside-Down Cake

All-Time FAVORITE

Prep: 15 min * Bake: 45 min * Cool: 30 min

15 SERVINGS

1/4 cup butter or margarine

1 cup packed brown sugar

1 can (20 ounces) sliced pineapple in juice, drained and juice reserved

1 jar (6 ounces) maraschino cherries without stems, drained

1 package Betty Crocker SuperMoist yellow or butter recipe yellow cake mix

1/3 cup vegetable oil

3 eggs

1 Heat oven to 350°. Melt butter in rectangular pan, 13 x 9 x 2 inches, in oven. Sprinkle brown sugar evenly over butter. Arrange pineapple slices on brown sugar; place cherry in center of each pineapple slice and arrange remaining cherries around slices; press gently into brown sugar.

2 Add enough water to reserved pineapple juice to measure 1 1/4 cups. Beat cake mix, pineapple juice mixture, oil and eggs in large bowl with electric mixer on low speed 30 seconds; beat on medium speed 2 minutes. Pour batter over pineapple and cherries.

3 Bake 40 to 45 minutes or until toothpick inserted in center comes out clean. Immediately run knife around side of pan to loosen cake. Turn pan upside down onto heatproof serving plate; leave pan over cake 1 minute so topping can drizzle over cake. Cool 30 minutes. Serve warm or cool. Store covered in refrigerator.

High Altitude (3500 to 6500 feet): Grease sides of pan with shortening. Add 3 tablespoons all-purpose flour to dry cake mix. Use 3 egg whites instead of 3 eggs. Bake 45 to 50 minutes.

1 Serving: Calories 315 (Calories from Fat 100); Fat 11g (Saturated 5g); Cholesterol 50mg; Sodium 260mg; Carbohydrate 52g (Dietary Fiber 1g); Protein 2g. **% Daily Value:** Vitamin A 2%; Vitamin C 0%; Calcium 8%; Iron 6%.

Peach Upside-Down Cake: Substitute 1 can (20 ounces) sliced peaches in juice, drained and juice reserved, for the sliced pineapple. Omit cherries.

Even movie stars had their favorite cake mix recipes, like Bob Hope's luscious Peach Upside-Down Cake in this 1950 ad.

Betty's Tip SuperMoist white cake mix can also be used to make this popular cake. Make the cake batter according to package directions, using pineapple juice as part of the total water measurement.

Pineapple Upside-Down Cake

Bananas Foster Cake

Prep: 15 min * Bake: 35 min * Cool: 30 min

15 SERVINGS

1/4 cup butter or margarine

1 tablespoon dark rum or
1/2 teaspoon rum extract

1 cup packed brown sugar

2 medium ripe bananas, sliced
(2 cups)

1 cup chopped pecans

1 package Betty Crocker
SuperMoist yellow cake mix

3/4 cup water

1/2 cup dark rum or 1 tablespoon rum extract plus enough
water to measure 1/2 cup

1/3 cup butter or margarine,
melted

1 teaspoon ground cinnamon

3 eggs

1 Heat oven to 350°. Heat 1/4 cup butter and 1 tablespoon rum in rectangular pan, 13 x 9 x 2 inches, in oven, until butter is melted. Sprinkle brown sugar evenly over butter. Arrange bananas evenly over brown sugar; sprinkle evenly with pecans.

2 Beat cake mix, water, 1/2 cup rum, 1/3 cup butter, the cinnamon and eggs in large bowl with electric mixer on low speed 30 seconds; beat on medium speed 2 minutes. Pour batter over pecan mixture.

3 Bake 30 to 35 minutes or until toothpick inserted in center comes out clean. Immediately run knife around side of pan to loosen cake. Turn pan upside down onto heatproof serving plate; leave pan over cake 1 minute so topping can drizzle over cake. Cool 30 minutes. Serve warm or cool. Store covered in refrigerator.

High Altitude (3500 to 6500 feet): Increase water to 1 cup; decrease melted butter to 2 tablespoons. Add 1 tablespoon all-purpose flour to dry cake mix. Bake 38 to 43 minutes.

1 Serving: Calories 345 (Calories from Fat 145); Fat 16g (Saturated 6g); Cholesterol 60mg; Sodium 280mg; Carbohydrate 48g (Dietary Fiber 1g); Protein 3g. **% Daily Value:** Vitamin A 6%; Vitamin C 0%; Calcium 8%; Iron 6%.

Betty's Tip Serve this ooey-gooey cake with a scoop of vanilla ice cream or a generous dollop of whipped cream.

Sweet Potato Cake

Prep: 15 min ✳ Bake: 32 min ✳ Cool: 1 hr

15 SERVINGS

1 package Betty Crocker SuperMoist yellow cake mix

1/2 cup chopped pecans, if desired

1 teaspoon ground cinnamon

1/4 teaspoon ground nutmeg

3 eggs

1 can (18 ounces) vacuum-packed sweet potatoes or 2 medium sweet potatoes, cooked and mashed (1 3/4 cups)

Browned Butter Frosting (page 240)

Additional chopped pecans, if desired

1 Heat oven to 350°. Grease bottom and sides of rectangular pan, 13 x 9 x 2 inches, with shortening; lightly flour.

2 Beat all ingredients except Browned Butter Frosting and additional pecans in large bowl with electric mixer on low speed 30 seconds. Beat on medium speed 2 minutes, scraping bowl frequently. Pour into pan.

3 Bake 28 to 32 minutes or until toothpick inserted in center comes out clean. Run knife around side of pan to loosen. Cool completely, about 1 hour. Spread frosting over top of cake. Sprinkle with pecans. Store covered in refrigerator.

High Altitude (3500 to 6500 feet): Bake 33 to 38 minutes.

1 Serving: Calories 315 (Calories from Fat 70); Fat 8g (Saturated 4g); Cholesterol 55mg; Sodium 270mg; Carbohydrate 59g (Dietary Fiber 1g); Protein 3g. **% Daily Value:** Vitamin A 92%; Vitamin C 6%; Calcium 8%; Iron 6%.

Betty's Tip It's hard to beat the rich flavor of Browned Butter Frosting, but if you don't want to make frosting from scratch, you can serve the cake plain or topped with a drizzle of caramel sauce.

Mandarin Orange Cake

Prep: 15 min * Bake: 35 min * Cool: 1 hr

15 SERVINGS

1 package Betty Crocker SuperMoist yellow cake mix

1/2 cup vegetable oil

1/2 cup chopped walnuts

4 eggs

1 can (11 ounces) mandarin orange segments, undrained

Pineapple Topping (below)

Pineapple Topping

1 can (20 ounces) crushed pineapple, undrained

1 package (4-serving size) vanilla instant pudding and pie filling mix

1/2 to 1 teaspoon grated orange peel, if desired

1 cup frozen (thawed) whipped topping

1 Heat oven to 350°. Grease bottom only of rectangular pan, 13 x 9 x 2 inches, with shortening; lightly flour.

2 Beat cake mix, oil, walnuts, eggs and orange segments (with juice) in large bowl with electric mixer on low speed 30 seconds; beat on medium speed 2 minutes. Pour into pan.

3 Bake 30 to 35 minutes or until toothpick inserted in center comes out clean. Run knife around side of pan to loosen cake. Cool completely, about 1 hour. Spread Pineapple Topping over top of cake. Store covered in refrigerator.

Pineapple Topping

Mix pineapple, pudding mix (dry) and orange peel. Gently stir in whipped topping.

High Altitude (3500 to 6500 feet): Heat oven to 375°. Add 1/3 cup all-purpose flour to dry cake mix. Decrease oil to 2 tablespoons. Beat on low speed 4 minutes.

1 Serving: Calories 325 (Calories from Fat 135); Fat 15g (Saturated 3g); Cholesterol 60mg; Sodium 330mg; Carbohydrate 44g (Dietary Fiber 1g); Protein 4g. **% Daily Value:** Vitamin A 2%; Vitamin C 8%; Calcium 8%; Iron 4%.

Betty's Tip For an extra-special touch, adorn this sensational cake with curly strips of orange peel. Or sprinkle with toasted coconut (page 36) to enhance the tropical flavors of the cake and frosting.

Mandarin Orange Cake

Tres Leches Cake

Prep: 15 min * Bake: 35 min * Stand: 5 min * Chill: 3 hr

15 SERVINGS

1 package Betty Crocker SuperMoist yellow cake mix

1 cup water

1/3 cup vegetable oil

3 eggs

1 cup whipping (heavy) cream

1 cup whole milk

1 can (14 ounces) sweetened condensed milk

1/3 cup rum or 1 tablespoon rum extract plus enough water to measure 1/3 cup

1 cup whipping (heavy) cream

2 tablespoons rum or 1 teaspoon rum extract

1/2 teaspoon vanilla

1 cup flaked coconut, toasted*

1/2 cup chopped pecans, toasted**

1 Heat oven to 350°. Grease bottom only of rectangular pan, 13 x 9 x 2 inches, with shortening.

2 Beat cake mix, water, oil and eggs in large bowl on low speed 30 seconds; beat on medium speed 2 minutes. Pour into pan.

3 Bake 30 to 35 minutes or until toothpick inserted in center comes out clean. Let stand 5 minutes. Pierce top of hot cake every 1/2 inch with long-tined fork, wiping fork occasionally to reduce sticking. Mix 1 cup whipping cream, the whole milk, sweetened condensed milk and 1/3 cup rum in large bowl. Carefully pour whipping cream mixture evenly over top of cake. Cover and refrigerate about 3 hours or until chilled and most of whipping cream mixture has been absorbed into cake.

4 Beat 1 cup whipping cream, 2 tablespoons rum and the vanilla in chilled large bowl with electric mixer on high speed until soft peaks form. Frost cake with whipped cream mixture. Sprinkle with coconut and pecans. Store covered in refrigerator.

High Altitude (3500 to 6500 feet): Make cake mix following high-altitude directions on package for 13 x 9 x 2-inch rectangular pan. Bake 33 to 38 minutes.

1 Serving: Calories 465 (Calories from Fat 235); Fat 26g (Saturated 12g); Cholesterol 90mg; Sodium 310mg; Carbohydrate 52g (Dietary Fiber 1g); Protein 7g. **% Daily Value:** Vitamin A 10%; Vitamin C 0%; Calcium 20%; Iron 4%.

To toast coconut, bake uncovered in ungreased shallow pan in 350° oven 5 to 7 minutes, stirring occasionally, until golden brown. Or cook in ungreased heavy skillet over medium-low heat 6 to 14 minutes, stirring frequently until browning begins, then stirring constantly until golden brown.

**To toast nuts, bake uncovered in ungreased shallow pan in 350° oven about 10 minutes, stirring occasionally, until golden brown. Or cook in ungreased heavy skillet over medium-low heat 5 to 7 minutes, stirring frequently until browning begins, then stirring constantly until golden brown.*

Betty's Tip Triple your cake-eating pleasure with this easy variation of the traditional Latin American dessert. Translated, *tres leche* means "three milks," and this rich, extra-moist cake includes whipping cream, whole milk and sweetened condensed milk.

Golden Butterscotch Cake

Prep: 10 min * Bake: 35 min * Cook: 17 min * Cool: 1 hr

15 SERVINGS

1 package Betty Crocker
SuperMoist yellow cake mix

1 cup milk

1/2 cup butter or margarine,
melted

1/4 cup sugar

1 teaspoon vanilla

1/8 teaspoon baking powder

3 eggs

Butterscotch Icing (below)

Butterscotch Icing

1/2 cup butter or margarine

1 cup powdered sugar

1/2 cup reserved cake batter

1/2 cup evaporated milk

1 teaspoon vanilla

1 Heat oven to 350°. Grease bottom and sides of rectangular pan, 13 x 9 x 2 inches, with shortening; lightly flour.

2 Beat all ingredients except Butterscotch Icing in medium bowl with electric mixer on low speed 1 minute, scraping bowl constantly. Beat 2 minutes longer. Remove 1/2 cup batter; cover and refrigerate. Pour remaining batter into pan.

3 Bake 30 to 35 minutes or until toothpick inserted in center comes out clean. Run knife around side of pan to loosen cake. Cool completely, about 1 hour. Spread Butterscotch Icing over top of cake. Store covered in refrigerator.

Butterscotch Icing

Heat butter in 1-quart saucepan over low heat about 10 minutes, stirring constantly, until brown; remove from heat. Stir in powdered sugar, cake batter and milk. Cook over medium heat about 7 minutes, stirring constantly with wire whisk, until bubbly, smooth and almost thick; remove from heat. Stir in vanilla. Cool slightly.

High Altitude (3500 to 6500 feet): Add 1 tablespoon all-purpose flour to dry cake mix. For cake, increase milk to 1 1/2 cups; decrease butter to 2 tablespoons. Omit sugar and baking powder.

1 Serving: Calories 320 (Calories from Fat 145); Fat 16g (Saturated 9g); Cholesterol 80mg; Sodium 330mg; Carbohydrate 41g (Dietary Fiber 0g); Protein 3g. **% Daily Value:** Vitamin A 12%; Vitamin C 0%; Calcium 10%; Iron 4%.

Betty's Tip It's important to cook the icing long enough, until thickened and spreadable. If the icing is undercooked, it looks like syrup— and it will run off the cake.

Chocolate Chip Cookie Surprise Cake

Prep: 15 min * Bake: 55 min * Cool: 1 hr

15 SERVINGS

1 package Betty Crocker SuperMoist yellow cake mix

1 cup whole milk

1/2 cup butter or margarine, melted

3 eggs

1 pouch Betty Crocker chocolate chip cookie mix

1/2 cup butter or margarine, softened

1 egg

1 tub Betty Crocker Rich & Creamy chocolate ready-to-spread frosting or Creamy Chocolate Frosting (page 238)

1 Heat oven to 350°. Generously grease bottom only of rectangular pan, 13 x 9 x 2 inches, with shortening; lightly flour.

2 Beat cake mix, milk, melted butter and 3 eggs in large bowl with electric mixer on low speed 30 seconds; beat on medium speed 2 minutes. Pour into pan.

3 Make cookie mix as directed on package, using softened butter and 1 egg. Drop dough by teaspoonfuls evenly over batter in pan.

4 Bake 50 to 55 minutes or until toothpick inserted in center comes out clean. Run knife around side of pan to loosen cake. Cool completely, about 1 hour. Spread frosting over top of cake. Store loosely covered at room temperature.

High Altitude (3500 to 6500 feet): For cake mix, increase milk to 1 1/2 cups; decrease butter to 2 tablespoons; add 1 tablespoon all-purpose flour. For cookie mix, add 1 tablespoon all-purpose flour.

1 Serving: Calories 565 (Calories from Fat 260); Fat 29g (Saturated 17g); Cholesterol 90mg; Sodium 400mg; Carbohydrate 72g (Dietary Fiber 1g); Protein 5g. **% Daily Value:** Vitamin A 10%; Vitamin C 0%; Calcium 6%; Iron 6%.

Betty's Tip Surprise! The cookie dough that you drop on top of the cake will sink to the bottom and form a chewy cookie layer underneath the cake.

Chocolate Chip Cookie Surprise Cake

S'mores Cake

Prep: 15 min * Bake: 40 min * Cool: 2 hr 15 min

15 SERVINGS

1 package Betty Crocker
SuperMoist yellow cake mix

1 cup graham cracker crumbs
(14 squares)

1 1/4 cups water

1/3 cup vegetable oil

3 eggs

1 jar (16 to 17 ounces) hot
fudge or chocolate topping

1 jar (7 ounces) marshmallow
creme

1 Heat oven to 350°. Grease bottom only of rectangular pan,
13 x 9 x 2 inches, with shortening.

2 Beat cake mix, cracker crumbs, water, oil and eggs in large bowl
with electric mixer on low speed 30 seconds; beat on medium
speed 2 minutes. Pour into pan.

3 Reserve 1/4 cup hot fudge topping. Drop remaining hot fudge
topping by generous tablespoonfuls randomly in 12 to 14 mounds
onto batter in pan.

4 Bake 30 to 40 minutes or until toothpick inserted in center
comes out clean. Run knife around side of pan to loosen cake.
Cool 15 minutes.

5 Spoon teaspoonfuls of marshmallow creme onto warm cake; carefully spread with knife dipped in hot water. Drop small dollops of
reserved hot fudge topping randomly over marshmallow creme.
Swirl topping through marshmallow creme with knife for marbled
design. Cool 2 hours. Store uncovered at room temperature.
(Once cut, store cake in the pan, uncovered, with plastic wrap
pressed against cut sides.)

High Altitude (3500 to 6500 feet): Increase water to 1 1/2 cups; decrease oil to 2
tablespoons. Add 1 tablespoon all-purpose flour to dry cake mix. Bake 33 to 40
minutes.

1 Serving: Calories 370 (Calories from Fat 110); Fat 12g (Saturated 3g); Cholesterol 45mg; Sodium
370mg; Carbohydrate 62g (Dietary Fiber 1g); Protein 4g. **% Daily Value:** Vitamin A 2%; Vitamin C
0%; Calcium 8%; Iron 6%.

Betty's Tip The marshmallow creme topping makes this cake sticky, so
it can be tricky to cut. To make it easier, use a knife that has been
dipped in hot water. To store the cake once it has been cut, gently press
plastic wrap against the cut edges of the cake, leaving the top uncovered so the plastic wrap doesn't stick.

Photo on page 16

Strawberries and Cream Cake

Prep: 15 min * Bake: 35 min * Cool: 1 hr

15 SERVINGS

1 package Betty Crocker
SuperMoist white cake mix

1 package (0.14 ounce) straw-
berry-flavored unsweetened
soft drink mix

3/4 cup water

3 eggs

1 package (10 ounces) frozen
sliced strawberries, thawed
and undrained

1 tub Betty Crocker Rich &
Creamy cream cheese ready-to-
spread frosting or Whipped
Cream Cheese Frosting
(page 236)

1 Heat oven to 350°. Grease bottom only of rectangular pan,
13 x 9 x 2 inches, with shortening; lightly flour.

2 Beat cake mix, drink mix (dry), water, eggs and strawberries in
large bowl with electric mixer on low speed 30 seconds; beat on
medium speed 2 minutes. Pour into pan.

3 Bake 30 to 35 minutes or until toothpick inserted in center
comes out clean. Run knife around side of pan to loosen cake.
Cool completely, about 1 hour. Spread frosting over top of cake.
Store covered in refrigerator.

High Altitude (3500 to 6500 feet): No changes.

1 Serving: Calories 400 (Calories from Fat 80); Fat 9g (Saturated 3g); Cholesterol 50mg; Sodium
560mg; Carbohydrate 76g (Dietary Fiber 1g); Protein 3g. **% Daily Value:** Vitamin A 6%; Vitamin C
6%; Calcium 8%; Iron 6%.

Betty's Tip A patchwork design makes a pretty decoration on top of
this cake. Visually divide the cake into serving pieces, and place strawberries on half of the servings. Whole, halved, diagonal cut and strawberry
berry fans all would work well. Add a few washed strawberry leaves or
mint leaves for a colorful contrast.

Photo on page 237

Raspberry Poke Cake

Prep: 10 min ✳ Bake: 33 min ✳ Cool: 1 hr ✳ Chill: 2 hr

15 SERVINGS

1 package Betty Crocker SuperMoist white cake mix

1 1/4 cups water

1/3 cup vegetable oil

3 egg whites

1 package (4-serving size) raspberry-flavored gelatin

1 cup boiling water

1/2 cup cold water

2 cups frozen (thawed) whipped topping or Sweetened Whipped Cream (page 243)

Fresh raspberries, if desired

1 Heat oven to 350°. Grease bottom only of rectangular pan, 13 x 9 x 2 inches, with shortening.

2 Make cake mix as directed on package, using water, oil and egg whites. Pour into pan.

3 Bake 28 to 33 minutes or until toothpick inserted in center comes out clean. Cool completely, about 1 hour.

4 Pierce cake every 1/2 inch with fork. Stir gelatin and boiling water in small bowl until smooth; stir in cold water. Pour over cake. Run knife around side of pan to loosen cake. Refrigerate 2 hours. Spread whipped topping over top of cake; garnish with raspberries. Store covered in refrigerator.

High Altitude (3500 to 6500 feet): Make cake mix following high-altitude directions on package for 13 x 9 x 2-inch rectangle.

1 Serving: Calories 240 (Calories from Fat 90); Fat 10g (Saturated 2g); Cholesterol 10mg; Sodium 240mg; Carbohydrate 34g (Dietary Fiber 0g); Protein 3g. **% Daily Value:** Vitamin A 0%; Vitamin C 0%; Calcium 2%; Iron 2%.

Strawberry Poke Cake: Substitute strawberry gelatin for the raspberry gelatin and garnish the cake with fresh strawberries.

Betty's Tip In the 1980s, the Poke Cake peaked in popularity. Why is it called poke cake? Because that's just what you do—poke the cake, then pour a liquid such as gelatin, ice-cream syrup or a lemonade-sugar mixture over the top. This very-berry version is delicious, easy—and pretty enough for a springtime party!

Raspberry Poke Cake

Cherry–Chocolate Chip Cake

Prep: 15 min * Bake: 33 min * Cool: 1 hr

15 SERVINGS

1 package Betty Crocker
SuperMoist white cake mix

1 container (8 ounces) sour
cream

1/2 cup vegetable oil

1 teaspoon almond extract

3 egg whites

2 jars (10 ounces each)
maraschino cherries, well
drained and chopped (1 cup)

1 cup miniature semisweet
chocolate chips

1 tub Betty Crocker Rich &
Creamy cherry ready-to-spread
frosting or Cherry Buttercream
Frosting (page 236)

1 Heat oven to 350°. Generously grease bottom only of rectangular pan, 13 x 9 x 2 inches, with shortening; lightly flour.

2 Beat cake mix, sour cream, oil, almond extract and egg whites in large bowl with electric mixer on low speed 30 seconds; beat on medium speed 2 minutes (batter will be thick). Drain chopped cherries on paper towels; pat dry. Stir cherries and chocolate chips into batter. Pour into pan.

3 Bake 25 to 33 minutes or until cake springs back when touched lightly in center. Run knife around side of pan to loosen cake. Cool completely, about 1 hour. Spread frosting over top of cake. Store loosely covered at room temperature.

High Altitude (3500 to 6500 feet): Decrease oil to 2 tablespoons. Add 1/4 cup water and 1 tablespoon all-purpose flour. Bake 35 to 40 minutes.

1 Serving: Calories 400 (Calories from Fat 190); Fat 21g (Saturated 10g); Cholesterol 10mg; Sodium 260mg; Carbohydrate 51g (Dietary Fiber 1g); Protein 3g. **% Daily Value:** Vitamin A 2%; Vitamin C 0%; Calcium 8%; Iron 4%.

Betty's Tip Cherry chip cake lovers will cry for more when they taste this scrumptious take-off on the popular cake mix flavor. Be sure to use miniature chocolate chips in this recipe because regular chocolate chips will sink to the bottom.

Photo on page 16

A cheery Cherry Chip Cake was the perfect picnic finale, as this 1967 ad shows.

Grasshopper Fudge Cake

Prep: 15 min * Bake: 33 min * Cool: 1 hr

15 SERVINGS

3 tablespoons white crème de menthe or crème de menthe–flavored syrup

1 package Betty Crocker SuperMoist white cake mix

1/3 cup vegetable oil

3 egg whites

3 drops green food color

1 can (16 to 17 ounces) hot fudge topping

1 container (8 ounces) frozen whipped topping, thawed

1/4 cup white crème de menthe or crème de menthe–flavored syrup

4 drops green food color

Chocolate Curls (page 183), if desired

1 Heat oven to 350°. Grease bottom only of rectangular pan, 13 x 9 x 2 inches, with shortening.

2 Add enough water to 3 tablespoons crème de menthe to measure 1 1/4 cups. Make cake mix as directed on package, using crème de menthe mixture, oil and egg whites. Reserve 1 cup batter. Stir 3 drops food color into reserved batter; set aside. Pour remaining batter into pan.

3 Drop green batter by generous tablespoonfuls randomly in 12 to 14 mounds onto batter in pan. Cut through batters with spatula or knife in S-shaped curves in one continuous motion. Turn pan 1/4 turn, and repeat cutting for swirled design.

4 Bake 28 to 33 minutes or until toothpick inserted in center comes out clean. Run knife around side of pan to loosen cake. Cool completely, about 1 hour.

5 Carefully spread fudge topping evenly over cake. Stir whipped topping, 1/4 cup crème de menthe and 4 drops food color until blended. Spread whipped topping mixture evenly over fudge. Garnish with Chocolate Curls. Store covered in refrigerator.

High Altitude (3500 to 6500 feet): Bake 33 to 38 minutes.

1 Serving: Calories 305 (Calories from Fat 100); Fat 11g (Saturated 3g); Cholesterol 0mg; Sodium 350mg; Carbohydrate 49g (Dietary Fiber 1g); Protein 4g. **% Daily Value:** Vitamin A 0%; Vitamin C 0%; Calcium 8%; Iron 4%.

Betty's Tip If you don't have white crème de menthe, you can substitute 3 tablespoons milk plus 1/4 teaspoon peppermint extract for the 3 tablespoons white crème de menthe. Use 1/4 cup milk plus 1/2 teaspoon peppermint extract for the 1/4 cup white crème de menthe in the topping.

Chocolate Chip Marble Cake

Prep: 15 min * Bake: 40 min * Cool: 1 hr

15 SERVINGS

1 package Betty Crocker
SuperMoist white cake mix

1 1/4 cups water

1/3 cup vegetable oil

3 egg whites

3/4 cup miniature semisweet
chocolate chips

1/4 cup chocolate-flavor syrup

1 tub Betty Crocker Rich &
Creamy vanilla ready-to-spread
frosting or Vanilla Buttercream
Frosting (page 236)

Additional chocolate-flavor
syrup, if desired

1 Heat oven to 350°. Generously grease bottom only of rectangular
pan, 13 x 9 x 2 inches, with shortening.

2 Make cake mix as directed on package, using water, oil and egg
whites. Stir in 1/2 cup of the chocolate chips. Reserve 1 cup of
the batter. Pour remaining batter into pan.

3 Stir 1/4 cup chocolate syrup into reserved batter. Drop by generous tablespoonfuls randomly in 6 to 8 mounds onto batter in pan.
Cut through batters with spatula or knife in S-shaped curves in
one continuous motion. Turn pan 1/4 turn, and repeat cutting for
swirled design.

4 Bake about 40 minutes or until toothpick inserted in center
comes out clean. Run knife around side of pan to loosen cake.
Cool completely, about 1 hour. Stir remaining 1/4 cup chocolate
chips into frosting. Spread frosting over top of cake; drizzle
with additional chocolate syrup. Store loosely covered at room
temperature.

High Altitude (3500 to 6500 feet): No changes.

1 Serving: Calories 370 (Calories from Fat 135); Fat 15g (Saturated 7g); Cholesterol 0mg; Sodium
250mg; Carbohydrate 57g (Dietary Fiber 1g); Protein 3g. **% Daily Value:** Vitamin A 0%; Vitamin C
0%; Calcium 4%; Iron 4%.

Betty's Tip Check your chips—be sure to use only miniature semisweet
chocolate chips in this recipe. Larger chips in the batter will sink to the
bottom of the cake.

Chocolate Chip Marble Cake

Caramel Carrot Cake

Prep: 15 min ✳ Bake: 33 min ✳ Cool: 15 min ✳ Stand: 15 min ✳ Chill: 2 hr

15 SERVINGS

1 package Betty Crocker
SuperMoist carrot cake mix

1 cup water

1/3 cup butter or margarine,
melted

3 eggs

1 jar (16 to 17 ounces) caramel
or butterscotch topping

1 tub Betty Crocker Rich &
Creamy vanilla ready-to-spread
frosting

1 Heat oven to 350°. Grease bottom only of rectangular pan,
13 x 9 x 2 inches, with shortening.

2 Beat cake mix, water, butter and eggs in large bowl with electric
mixer on low speed 30 seconds; beat on medium speed
2 minutes. Pour into pan.

3 Bake 27 to 33 minutes or until toothpick inserted in center
comes out clean. Cool 15 minutes. Poke top of warm cake every
1/2 inch with handle of wooden spoon, wiping handle occasionally
to reduce sticking. Reserve 1/2 cup caramel topping. Drizzle
remaining caramel topping evenly over top of cake; let stand
about 15 minutes or until caramel topping has been absorbed
into cake. Run knife around side of pan to loosen cake. Cover
and refrigerate about 2 hours or until chilled.

4 Set aside 2 tablespoons of the reserved 1/2 cup caramel topping.
Stir remaining topping into frosting; spread over top of cake.
Drizzle with reserved 2 tablespoons caramel topping. Store
covered in refrigerator.

High Altitude (3500 to 6500 feet): Heat oven to 375°. Add 1/3 cup all-purpose
flour to dry cake mix. Add additional 2 tablespoons water. Beat on low speed
30 seconds, then beat on medium speed 3 minutes. Bake 30 to 35 minutes.

1 Serving: Calories 300 (Calories from Fat 110); Fat 12g (Saturated 8g); Cholesterol 55mg; Sodium
170mg; Carbohydrate 45g (Dietary Fiber 0g); Protein 3g. **% Daily Value:** Vitamin A 4%; Vitamin C
0%; Calcium 8%; Iron 2%.

Betty's Tip Some caramel ice-cream toppings are thicker and stickier
than others. If the type you purchased is too thick to pour, warm it in
the microwave just until it pours easily.

Hummingbird Cake

Prep: 15 min * Bake: 35 min * Cool: 1 hr

15 SERVINGS

1 can (8 ounces) crushed pineapple in juice, undrained

1 jar (10 ounces) maraschino cherries, well drained and chopped (1/2 cup)

1 package Betty Crocker SuperMoist lemon cake mix

1 cup mashed very ripe bananas (about 2 medium)*

1/3 cup vegetable oil

1 teaspoon ground cinnamon

3 eggs

Easy Vanilla Glaze (page 242) or Vanilla Glaze (page 242)

1 Heat oven to 350°. Generously grease bottom only of rectangular pan, 13 x 9 x 2 inches, with shortening; lightly flour.

2 Drain pineapple in colander set over a bowl, pushing pineapple against side and bottom of colander with back of wooden spoon to squeeze out as much juice as possible; reserve juice. Drain chopped cherries on paper towels; pat dry.

3 Add enough water, if necessary, to reserved pineapple juice to measure 1/3 cup. Beat cake mix, pineapple, bananas, oil, cinnamon, pineapple juice mixture and eggs in large bowl with electric mixer on low speed 2 minutes. Stir in cherries. Pour into pan.

4 Bake 30 to 35 minutes or until cake springs back when touched lightly in center. Run knife around side of pan to loosen cake. Cool completely, about 1 hour. Spread Easy Vanilla Glaze over top of cake. Store loosely covered at room temperature.

High Altitude (3500 to 6500 feet): Heat oven to 375°. Omit pineapple juice and oil. Add 1/2 cup water and 1/4 cup all-purpose flour. Bake 38 to 43 minutes.

1 Serving: Calories 250 (Calories from Fat 70); Fat 8g (Saturated 2g); Cholesterol 40g; Sodium 230mg; Carbohydrate 44g (Dietary Fiber 1g); Protein 2g. **% Daily Value:** Vitamin A 0%; Vitamin C 2%; Calcium 6%; Iron 4%.

Do not use frozen bananas. Frozen bananas contain too much moisture and may cause the cake to sink and become gummy.

Betty's Tip This cake is great to make ahead for a bake sale or potluck dessert party. Our taste testers agree, this cake not only tastes great the day it's made, it's even better the next day!

Lemonade Party Cake

Prep: 15 min * Bake: 35 min * Cool: 15 min * Chill: 2 hr

15 SERVINGS

1 package Betty Crocker
SuperMoist lemon cake mix

1 1/4 cups water

1/3 cup vegetable oil

3 eggs

1 can (6 ounces) frozen
lemonade concentrate, thawed
(3/4 cup)

3/4 cup powdered sugar

1 tub Betty Crocker Whipped
fluffy white or lemon ready-to-
spread frosting or Lemon
Buttercream Frosting (page 236)

1 Heat oven to 350°. Grease bottom only of rectangular pan,
   13 x 9 x 2 inches, with shortening.

2 Make cake mix as directed on package, using water, oil and eggs.
   Pour into pan.

3 Bake 30 to 35 minutes or until toothpick inserted in center
   comes out clean. Cool 15 minutes.

4 Mix lemonade concentrate and powdered sugar. Pierce top of
   warm cake every 1/2 inch with long-tined fork, wiping fork
   occasionally to reduce sticking. Drizzle lemonade mixture
   evenly over top of cake. Run knife around side of pan to loosen
   cake. Cover and refrigerate about 2 hours or until chilled.

5 Spread frosting over top of cake. Store covered in refrigerator.

High Altitude (3500 to 6500 feet): Make cake mix as directed on package for
13 x 9 x 2-inch rectangle.

1 Serving: Calories 350 (Calories from Fat 110); Fat 12g (Saturated 5g); Cholesterol 45mg; Sodium
220mg; Carbohydrate 58g (Dietary Fiber 0g); Protein 2g. **% Daily Value:** Vitamin A 0%; Vitamin C
0%; Calcium 6%; Iron 4%.

Betty's Tip For an extra-special touch, add a candy lemon wedge and
a sprig of fresh mint to each serving of cake. Or sprinkle yellow-colored
sugar over the top of the entire cake just before serving.

Lemonade Party Cake

2
Wonderfully
Indulgent

Brown Sugar Crunch Torte (page 67) and Neapolitan Cake (page 83)

Peanut-Caramel Candy Bar Cake

Prep: 20 min * Bake: 45 min * Cool: 1 hr 10 min * Chill: 2 hr

12 TO 16 SERVINGS

1/2 cup butter or margarine

1/4 cup whipping (heavy) cream

1 cup packed brown sugar

1/2 cup peanuts, coarsely chopped

1 package Betty Crocker SuperMoist devil's food cake mix

1 1/3 cups water

1/2 cup vegetable oil

3 eggs

4 bars (2.07 ounces each) chocolate-covered peanut, caramel and nougat candy, coarsely chopped

1 tub of Betty Crocker Whipped fluffy white ready-to-spread frosting or Creamy White Frosting (page 234)

1 Heat oven to 325°. Heat butter, whipping cream and brown sugar in heavy 1 1/2-quart saucepan over low heat, stirring occasionally, just until butter is melted. Pour into 2 ungreased round pans, 9 x 1 1/2 inches. Sprinkle evenly with peanuts.

2 Make cake mix as directed on package, using water, oil and eggs. Carefully spoon batter over peanuts.

3 Bake 35 to 45 minutes or until toothpick inserted in center comes out clean. Cool 10 minutes. Run knife around side of pans to loosen cakes; remove from pans to wire rack, placing cakes peanut side up. Cool completely, about 1 hour.

4 Fold candy into frosting. Place 1 cake layer, peanut side up, on serving plate. Spread with half the frosting mixture. Top with second layer, peanut side up. Spread top of cake with remaining frosting mixture. Cover and refrigerate at least 2 hours but no longer than 24 hours. Store covered in refrigerator.

High Altitude (3500 to 6500 feet): Heat oven to 350°. Add 2 tablespoons all-purpose flour to dry cake mix. Increase water to 1 1/2 cups; decrease oil to 1 tablespoon. Beat cake mix on low speed 30 seconds, then beat on medium speed 4 minutes.

1 Serving: Calories 670 (Calories from Fat 295); Fat 33g (Saturated 14g); Cholesterol 85mg; Sodium 470mg; Carbohydrate 89g (Dietary Fiber 2g); Protein 6g. **% Daily Value:** Vitamin A 8%; Vitamin C 0%; Calcium 10%; Iron 12%.

Betty's Tip Top off this decadent cake with a flourish of chocolate. Just melt 1/2 cup semisweet chocolate chips and 1 teaspoon shortening in 1-quart saucepan over low heat, stirring constantly. Drizzle the chocolate over the frosting.

Peanut-Caramel Candy Bar Cake

Cookies 'n Cream Torte

Prep: 15 min * Bake: 33 min * Cool: 1 hr

12 SERVINGS

1 package Betty Crocker SuperMoist devil's food cake mix

1 1/3 cups water

1/2 cup vegetable oil

3 eggs

6 regular-size or 25 miniature creme-filled chocolate sandwich cookies, crushed

1 container (12 ounces) frozen whipped topping, thawed, or 3 cups Sweetened Whipped Cream (page 243)

1. Heat oven to 350°. Grease bottom and sides of jelly roll pan, 15 1/2 x 10 1/2 x 1 inch, with shortening.

2. Make cake mix as directed on package, using water, oil and eggs. Pour into pan.

3. Bake 25 to 33 minutes or until toothpick inserted in center comes out clean. Run knife around sides of pan to loosen cake. Cool completely in pan on wire rack, about 1 hour.

4. Fold crushed cookies into whipped topping. Cut cake crosswise in half. Remove one cake half from pan, using wide spatula to lift cake; place on serving plate. Spread cake with half of the whipped topping mixture. Top with other half of cake; spread with remaining whipped topping mixture. Store covered in refrigerator.

High Altitude (3500 to 6500 feet): Heat oven to 375°. Add 2 tablespoons all-purpose flour to dry cake mix. Increase water to 1 1/2 cups; decrease oil to 1 tablespoon. Beat cake mix on low speed 30 seconds, then beat on medium speed 4 minutes. Bake 25 to 30 minutes.

1 Serving: Calories 365 (Calories from Fat 180); Fat 20g (Saturated 8g); Cholesterol 55mg; Sodium 380mg; Carbohydrate 43g (Dietary Fiber 1g); Protein 4g. **% Daily Value:** Vitamin A 4%; Vitamin C 0%; Calcium 4%; Iron 10%.

Betty's Tip Calling all cookie lovers! Garnish the top of the torte with mini chocolate sandwich cookies or regular-size chocolate sandwich cookies, cut into 1/2-inch pieces.

Cookies 'n Cream Torte

Chocolate-Mint Swirl Cake

Prep: 20 min * Bake: 50 min * Cool: 1 hr 10 min

16 TO 24 SERVINGS

2 packages (3 ounces each) cream cheese, softened

1/4 cup granulated sugar

1 egg

1/8 teaspoon peppermint extract

3 drops green food color

1 package Betty Crocker SuperMoist devil's food cake mix

1 cup water

1/2 cup butter or margarine, melted

2 eggs

1 1/2 tablespoons semisweet chocolate chips

1 teaspoon shortening

Mint Glaze (below)

Mint Glaze

1 cup powdered sugar

1/4 teaspoon peppermint extract

3 drops green food color

1 tablespoon corn syrup

3 to 4 teaspoons water

1 Heat oven to 350°. Generously grease 12-cup bundt cake pan with shortening; lightly flour.

2 Beat cream cheese in small bowl with electric mixer on high speed until smooth and fluffy. Beat in sugar, 1 egg, the peppermint extract and food color until smooth; set aside.

3 Beat cake mix, water, butter and 2 eggs in large bowl with electric mixer on low speed 30 seconds; beat on medium speed 2 minutes. Pour into pan. Spoon cream cheese mixture over batter.

4 Bake 45 to 50 minutes or until toothpick inserted in center of cake comes out clean. Cool 10 minutes. Turn pan upside down onto wire rack or heatproof plate; remove pan. Cool completely, about 1 hour.

5 Heat chocolate chips and shortening in 1-quart saucepan over low heat, stirring frequently, until chocolate is melted; set aside. Drizzle mint glaze over cake. Immediately spoon melted chocolate over glaze in 1/2-inch-wide ring. Working quickly, pull toothpick through chocolate to make swirls. Refrigerate until serving. Store covered in refrigerator.

Mint Glaze

Mix powdered sugar, peppermint extract, food color, corn syrup and enough of the 3 to 4 teaspoons water to make a thick glaze that can be easily drizzled.

High Altitude (3500 to 6500 feet): Heat oven to 375°. Add 2 tablespoons all-purpose flour to the dry cake mix. Increase water to 1 1/2 cups. Increase 2 eggs to 3. Decrease butter to 1 tablespoon. Beat on low speed 30 seconds, then beat on medium speed 4 minutes.

1 Serving: Calories 285 (Calories from Fat 115); Fat 13g (Saturated 7g); Cholesterol 65mg; Sodium 320mg; Carbohydrate 39g (Dietary Fiber 1g); Protein 4g. **% Daily Value:** Vitamin A 8%; Vitamin C 0%; Calcium 4%; Iron 8%.

Betty's Tip For a special touch, sprinkle with coarsely chopped chocolate mint candies to make this already-incredible cake even more decadent!

Chocolate-Mint Swirl Cake

Café au Lait Cake

Prep: 20 min ✳ Bake: 35 min ✳ Cool: 1 hr 10 min ✳ Chill: 2 hr

12 TO 16 SERVINGS

1 tablespoon instant espresso coffee (dry)

1 1/3 cups water

1 package Betty Crocker SuperMoist devil's food cake mix

1/2 cup vegetable oil

3 eggs

2 teaspoons instant espresso coffee (dry)

1 tablespoon cool water

1 tub Betty Crocker Whipped milk chocolate ready-to-spread frosting or Creamy Chocolate Frosting (page 238)

1 1/2 cups frozen (thawed) whipped topping or Sweetened Whipped Cream (page 243)

Chocolate-covered espresso beans, if desired

1 Heat oven to 350°. Grease bottoms only of 2 round pans, 8 or 9 x 1 1/2 inches, with shortening; lightly flour.

2 Dissolve 1 tablespoon coffee in 1 1/3 cups water. Beat coffee mixture, cake mix, oil and eggs in large bowl with electric mixer on low speed 1 minute, scraping bowl constantly. Pour into pans.

3 Bake 8-inch rounds 30 to 35 minutes, 9-inch rounds 25 to 30 minutes, or until toothpick inserted in center comes out clean. Cool 10 minutes. Run knife around side of pans to loosen cakes; remove from pans to wire rack. Cool completely, about 1 hour.

4 Dissolve 2 teaspoons coffee in 1 tablespoon cool water. Stir 2 teaspoons of the coffee mixture into frosting. Mix whipped topping and remaining coffee mixture in medium bowl; gently stir in 1/4 cup of the frosting mixture.

5 Fill layers with half of the whipped topping mixture (about 3/4 cup) to within 1/4 inch of edge. Frost side and top of cake with frosting. Pipe remaining whipped topping mixture around top of cake. Refrigerate 1 to 2 hours or until chilled. Garnish top of cake with espresso beans. Store covered in refrigerator.

High Altitude (3500 to 6500 feet): Do not use 8-inch rounds. Heat oven to 375°. Dissolve 1 tablespoon coffee in 1 1/2 cups water. Add 2 tablespoons all-purpose flour to dry cake mix. Decrease oil to 1 tablespoon. Beat on low speed 30 seconds, then beat on medium speed 4 minutes. Bake 9-inch rounds 25 to 30 minutes.

1 Serving: Calories 340 (Calories from Fat 155); Fat 17g (Saturated 6g); Cholesterol 55mg; Sodium 340mg; Carbohydrate 44g (Dietary Fiber 1g); Protein 4g. **% Daily Value:** Vitamin A 2%; Vitamin C 0%; Calcium 4%; Iron 10%.

Betty's Tip If the cake is served just after chilling for 1 or 2 hours, the espresso flavor will be mild. The rich coffee flavor develops more fully as the cake continues to chill, and if served the next day, the flavor will be stronger.

Fudgy Chocolate Ring Cake

Prep: 15 min * Bake: 50 min * Cool: 1 hr 15 min * Stand: 5 min

16 SERVINGS

1 can (14 ounces) sweetened condensed milk

1 1/2 cups semisweet chocolate chips

1 package Betty Crocker SuperMoist chocolate fudge cake mix

1/2 cup butter or margarine, melted

2 tablespoons milk

1 teaspoon vanilla

3 eggs

1 Heat oven to 350°. Generously grease 12-cup bundt cake pan with shortening; lightly flour.

2 Heat 1/2 cup of the sweetened condensed milk and 1 cup of the chocolate chips in 1-quart saucepan over medium-low heat, stirring occasionally, until chocolate is melted and mixture is smooth.

3 Mix cake mix, butter, 2 tablespoons milk, the vanilla and eggs in large bowl with spoon until well blended (some dry mix will remain and batter will be thick). Spoon half of the batter into pan; spread evenly. Carefully spoon chocolate mixture in ring over batter (do not touch sides of pan). Carefully spoon remaining batter over chocolate; spread evenly to cover chocolate.

4 Bake 45 to 50 minutes or until toothpick inserted 1 inch from inside edge of pan comes out clean, top of cake feels firm to the touch and cake pulls away slightly from side of pan. Do not underbake. Cool 15 minutes. Turn pan upside down onto heat-proof serving plate; remove pan. Cool cake completely, about 1 hour.

5 Heat remaining sweetened condensed milk and 1/2 cup chocolate chips in 1-quart saucepan over medium-low heat, stirring occasionally, until chocolate is melted and mixture is smooth. Let stand 5 minutes. Pour chocolate mixture over cake, allowing some to drizzle down sides. Store loosely covered at room temperature.

High Altitude (3500 to 6500 feet): Not recommended.

1 Serving: Calories 385 (Calories from Fat 145); Fat 16g (Saturated 9g); Cholesterol 65mg; Sodium 340mg; Carbohydrate 55g (Dietary Fiber 1g); Protein 6g. **% Daily Value:** Vitamin A 8%; Vitamin C 0%; Calcium 14%; Iron 8%.

Peanut Butter-Chocolate Ring Cake: Substitute peanut butter chips for the semisweet chocolate chips.

White Chocolate Ring Cake: Substitute white baking chips for the semisweet chocolate chips.

In 1974, a taste for deep, dark, fudgy heaven helped bridge the generation gap.

Betty's Tip Hidden in the center of this wonderful cake is a layer of dense and fudgy chocolate. Be sure to follow the doneness tests in this recipe, and your cake will turn out moist but not underbaked.

Chocolate Ganache Cake

Prep: 20 min ✳ Bake: 35 min ✳ Cool: 1 hr 10 min ✳ Chill: 1 hr

12 TO 16 SERVINGS

1 package Betty Crocker SuperMoist chocolate fudge cake mix

1 1/3 cups water

1/2 cup vegetable oil

3 eggs

1 tub Betty Crocker Rich & Creamy chocolate ready-to-spread frosting or Creamy Chocolate Frosting (page 238)

1/2 recipe Chocolate Ganache (page 238)

2 bars (1.4 ounces each) chocolate-covered English toffee candy, very coarsely chopped

1 Heat oven to 350°. Generously grease bottoms only of 2 round pans, 8 or 9 x 1 1/2 inches, with shortening.

2 Make cake mix as directed on package, using water, oil and eggs. Pour into pans.

3 Bake 8-inch rounds 30 to 35 minutes, 9-inch rounds 25 to 30 minutes, or until toothpick inserted in center comes out clean. Cool 10 minutes. Run knife around sides of pans to loosen cakes; remove from pans to wire rack. Cool completely, about 1 hour.

4 Fill layers and frost side and top of cake with frosting. Make Chocolate Ganache. Carefully pour ganache onto top center of cake; spread to edge, allowing some to drizzle down side. Garnish top center of cake with candy. Refrigerate about 1 hour or until chocolate is set. Store covered in refrigerator.

High Altitude (3500 to 6500 feet): Do not use 8-inch rounds. Make cake mix following high-altitude directions on package for 9-inch rounds.

1 Serving: Calories 530 (Calories from Fat 250); Fat 28g (Saturated 15g); Cholesterol 65mg; Sodium 360mg; Carbohydrate 67g (Dietary Fiber 3g); Protein 5g. **% Daily Value:** Vitamin A 2%; Vitamin C 0%; Calcium 4%; Iron 6%.

Chocolate-Orange Ganache Cake: Stir 1 tablespoon grated orange peel into the cake batter.

Betty's Tip The Betty Crocker Kitchens developed this most chocolate of chocolate cakes in 2000 to celebrate the millennium—and the addition of Hershey®'s chocolate and cocoa to Betty Crocker dessert mixes.

Chocolate Ganache Cake

Meringue-Swirled Chocolate Cake

Prep: 20 min ✷ Bake: 1 hr 30 min ✷ Cool: 1 hr 10 min

12 SERVINGS

1 package Betty Crocker
SuperMoist chocolate fudge
cake mix

1 1/3 cups water

1/2 cup vegetable oil

3 eggs

3 egg whites

3/4 cup sugar

1 Heat oven to 325°. Generously grease bottom and side of spring-form pan, 9 x 3 inches, with shortening; lightly flour.

2 Make cake mix as directed on package, using water, oil and 3 eggs; set aside. Beat 3 egg whites in medium bowl with electric mixer on high speed until soft peaks form. Beat in sugar, 1 tablespoon at a time; continue beating until stiff and glossy.

3 Spread two-thirds of the meringue up side of pan (do not spread on bottom of pan). Pour cake batter into pan; top with remaining meringue. Cut through meringue on top of cake and cake batter with tip of knife to swirl meringue through batter.

4 Bake about 1 hour 30 minutes or until toothpick inserted in center comes out clean. Cool 10 minutes. Run knife around side of pan to loosen cake; remove side of pan. Cool completely, about 1 hour. Store loosely covered at room temperature.

High Altitude (3500 to 6500 feet): Heat oven to 350°. Use 10-inch springform pan. Add 2 tablespoons all-purpose flour to dry cake mix. Increase water to 1 1/2 cups. Decrease oil to 1 tablespoon. Beat cake mix on low speed 30 seconds, then beat on medium speed 4 minutes. Bake 1 hour 20 minutes to 1 hour 30 minutes.

1 Serving: Calories 380 (Calories from Fat 135); Fat 15g (Saturated 3g); Cholesterol 65mg; Sodium 420mg; Carbohydrate 57g (Dietary Fiber 1g); Protein 5g. **% Daily Value:** Vitamin A 0%; Vitamin C 0%; Calcium 4%; Iron 6%.

Betty's Tip If you don't have a springform pan, you can make this cake in a greased and floured 13 x 9-inch rectangular pan. Bake 40 to 45 minutes or until a toothpick inserted in the center comes out clean.

Meringue-Swirled Chocolate Cake

Mocha Mousse Cake

Prep: 20 min ✳ Bake: 20 min ✳ Cool: 1 hr 10 min ✳ Chill: 2 hr

12 TO 16 SERVINGS

1 package Betty Crocker
SuperMoist chocolate fudge
cake mix

1 1/3 cups water

1/3 cup vegetable oil

1 tablespoon coffee liqueur or
prepared coffee

4 eggs

1 tub Betty Crocker Whipped
chocolate ready-to-spread
frosting or Chocolate Whipped
Cream Topping (page 244)

Mocha Mousse (below)

Mocha Mousse

3/4 cup whipping (heavy)
cream

2 tablespoons sugar

1/3 cup coffee liqueur or
prepared coffee

1 bag (6 ounces) semisweet
chocolate chips (1 cup)

2 teaspoons vanilla

1　Heat oven to 350°. Grease bottoms and sides of 3 round pans, 8 or 9 x 1 1/2 inches, with shortening; lightly flour.

2　Beat cake mix, water, oil, liqueur and eggs in large bowl with electric mixer on low speed 1 minute, scraping bowl constantly. Pour about 1 1/2 cups batter into each pan. (If baking only 2 pans at one time, refrigerate remaining batter until ready to use.)

3　Bake about 20 minutes or until toothpick inserted in center comes out clean. Cool 10 minutes. Run knife around side of pans to loosen cakes; remove from pans to wire rack. Cool completely, about 1 hour.

4　While cake is cooling, make Mocha Mousse. Fill layers with mousse. Frost side and top of cake with frosting. Cover and refrigerate at least 2 hours before serving. Store covered in refrigerator.

Mocha Mousse

Mix 1/4 cup of the whipping cream, the sugar and liqueur in 2-quart saucepan. Cook over medium heat, stirring constantly, until sugar is dissolved and mixture simmers; remove from heat. Stir in chocolate chips with wire whisk until chips are melted. Stir in vanilla. Pour into large bowl; cool about 10 minutes or until room temperature. Beat remaining 1/2 cup whipping cream in chilled medium bowl with electric mixer on high speed just until soft peaks form. Fold whipped cream into chocolate mixture. Cover and refrigerate 30 minutes.

High Altitude (3500 to 6500 feet): For 8- or 9-inch pans, heat oven to 375°. Add 2 tablespoons all-purpose flour to dry cake mix. Decrease oil to 1 tablespoon. Beat on low speed 30 seconds, then beat on medium speed 2 minutes.

1 Serving: Calories 370 (Calories from Fat 170); Fat 19g (Saturated 8g); Cholesterol 85mg; Sodium 350mg; Carbohydrate 47g (Dietary Fiber 2g); Protein 5g. **% Daily Value:** Vitamin A 4%; Vitamin C 0%; Calcium 6%; Iron 10%.

Betty's Tip　If you want to simplify, use a 2.8-ounce package of chocolate or milk chocolate mousse mix instead of making the Mocha Mousse from scratch. For an extra dose of chocolate, sprinkle chopped semisweet chocolate over the top of the frosted cake.

Photo on page 245

Brown Sugar Crunch Torte

Prep: 30 min * Bake: 40 min * Cool: 2 hr

12 TO 16 SERVINGS

1 1/2 cups chopped walnuts

1 1/2 cups vanilla wafer cookie crumbs

1 cup packed brown sugar

1 cup butter or margarine, melted

1 package Betty Crocker SuperMoist German chocolate cake mix

1 1/3 cups water

1/2 cup vegetable oil

3 eggs

1 container (8 ounces) frozen whipped topping, thawed, or 3 cups Sweetened Whipped Cream (page 243)

1 Heat oven to 350°. Grease bottoms only of 2 round pans, 9 x 1 1/2 inches, with shortening.

2 Mix walnuts, cookie crumbs, brown sugar and butter in large bowl. Spread about 3/4 cup walnut mixture in each pan; reserve remaining walnut mixture.

3 Make cake mix as directed on package, using water, oil and eggs. Pour slightly less than 1 1/4 cups batter over walnut mixture in each pan; spread evenly. Refrigerate remaining batter.

4 Bake about 20 minutes or until toothpick inserted in center comes out clean. Immediately remove from pans to wire rack, placing cakes walnut side up. Repeat with remaining walnut mixture and batter to make 4 layers. Cool layers completely, about 1 hour.

5 Fill each layer and top of cake, walnut sides up, with about 3/4 cup whipped topping. Store covered in refrigerator.

High Altitude (3500 to 6500 feet): Make cake mix following high-altitude directions on package for 9-inch rounds. Bake 20 to 25 minutes.

1 Serving: Calories 640 (Calories from Fat 360); Fat 40g (Saturated 14g); Cholesterol 95mg; Sodium 480mg; Carbohydrate 64g (Dietary Fiber 1g); Protein 7g. **% Daily Value:** Vitamin A 12%; Vitamin C 0%; Calcium 8%; Iron 10%.

Betty's Tip For a bakery cake finish, garnish the top of this cake with a decadent mound of chocolate curls (page 183) or shavings.

Photo on page 52

Peanut Butter Silk Cake

Prep: 15 min ✳ Bake: 38 min ✳ Cool: 1 hr 10 min ✳ Chill: 10 min

12 TO 16 SERVINGS

1 package Betty Crocker SuperMoist yellow cake mix

1 1/4 cups water

1/2 cup creamy peanut butter

1/3 cup vegetable oil

3 eggs

1/4 cup butter or margarine

1/4 cup packed brown sugar

1 cup whipping (heavy) cream

1/2 cup creamy peanut butter

1 tub Betty Crocker Rich & Creamy chocolate ready-to-spread frosting or Creamy Chocolate Frosting (page 238)

1 cup chopped peanuts, if desired

1 Heat oven to 350°. Generously grease bottoms only of 2 round pans, 8 or 9 x 1 1/2 inches, with shortening.

2 Make cake mix as directed on package, using water, 1/2 cup peanut butter, the oil and eggs. Pour into pans.

3 Bake 30 to 38 minutes or until toothpick inserted in center comes out clean. Cool 10 minutes. Run knife around side of pans to loosen cakes; remove from pans to wire rack. Cool completely, about 1 hour.

4 Melt butter in 2-quart saucepan over medium heat; stir in brown sugar. Heat to boiling; boil and stir 1 minute. Remove from heat. Refrigerate 10 minutes.

5 Beat whipping cream in chilled medium bowl with electric mixer on high speed until soft peaks form; set aside. Beat 1/2 cup peanut butter and the brown sugar mixture in another medium bowl on medium speed until smooth and creamy. Add whipped cream to peanut butter mixture; beat on medium speed until mixture is smooth and creamy.

6 Split each cake layer horizontally to make 2 layers. Fill each layer with about 2/3 cup peanut butter mixture to within 1/2 inch of edge. Frost side and top of cake with frosting. Press chopped peanuts onto frosting on side of cake. Store covered in refrigerator.

High Altitude (3500 to 6500 feet): Do not use 8-inch rounds. Make cake mix following high-altitude directions on package for 9-inch rounds.

1 Serving: Calories 655 (Calories from Fat 360); Fat 40g (Saturated 18g); Cholesterol 85mg; Sodium 420mg; Carbohydrate 67g (Dietary Fiber 2g); Protein 9g. **% Daily Value:** Vitamin A 8%; Vitamin C 0%; Calcium 12%; Iron 8%.

Betty's Tip If you prefer, decorate the side of this cake with chopped chocolate-covered peanuts or chocolate-coated peanut butter candies instead of the chopped peanuts.

Peanut Butter Silk Cake

Layered Boston Cream Pie

Prep: 20 min * Bake: 35 min * Cool: 1 hr 10 min

12 TO 16 SERVINGS

1 package Betty Crocker
SuperMoist yellow cake mix

1 1/4 cups water

1/3 cup vegetable oil

3 eggs

Easy Chocolate Glaze (page 241)
or Chocolate Glaze (page 241)

Vanilla Filling (below)

Vanilla Filling

1 package (4-serving size) vanilla instant pudding and
pie filling mix

2 cups whipping (heavy) cream

1 Heat oven to 350°. Grease bottoms only of 2 round pans,
8 or 9 x 1 1/2 inches, with shortening. Make cake mix as
directed on package, using water, oil and eggs. Pour into pans.

2 Bake 8-inch rounds 30 to 35 minutes, 9-inch rounds 25 to 30
minutes, or until toothpick inserted in center comes out clean.
Cool 10 minutes. Run knife around side of pans to loosen cakes;
remove from pans to wire rack. Cool completely, about 1 hour.

3 Split each cake layer horizontally to make 2 layers. Fill each layer
with about 2/3 cup Vanilla Filling. Spread Easy Chocolate Glaze
over top of cake, allowing some to drizzle down side. Store
covered in refrigerator.

Vanilla Filling

Beat pudding mix into whipping cream in medium bowl with
wire whisk about 2 minutes or until blended. Let stand about
3 minutes or until set.

High Altitude (3500 to 6500 feet): Do not use 8-inch rounds. Make cake mix
following high-altitude directions on package for 9-inch rounds.

1 Serving: Calories 445 (Calories from Fat 225); Fat 25g (Saturated 12g); Cholesterol 95mg;
Sodium 420mg; Carbohydrate 51g (Dietary Fiber 0g); Protein 4g. **% Daily Value:** Vitamin A 10%;
Vitamin C 0%; Calcium 12%; Iron 4%.

Betty's Tip Despite its name, this dessert is not a pie at all. Boston
Cream Pie is actually a layered golden cake filled with a vanilla custard
and topped with a thick chocolate glaze.

Photo on page 230

Harvey Wallbanger Cake

Prep: 15 min * Bake: 40 min * Cool: 1 hr 10 min

16 TO 24 SERVINGS

1 package Betty Crocker
SuperMoist yellow cake mix

1/2 cup orange juice

1/3 cup vegetable oil

1/4 cup vodka or orange juice

1/4 cup anise-flavored liqueur
or orange juice

3 eggs

Orange Glaze (below)

Orange Glaze

1 cup powdered sugar

1 to 2 tablespoons orange juice

1/4 teaspoon grated orange
peel

1 Heat oven to 350°. Grease 12-cup bundt cake pan with shortening; lightly flour.

2 Beat cake mix, orange juice, oil, vodka, liqueur and eggs in large bowl with electric mixer on low speed 30 seconds, scraping bowl constantly, until moistened. Continue beating on low speed 2 minutes. Pour into pan.

3 Bake 35 to 40 minutes or until toothpick inserted in center of cake comes out clean. Cool 10 minutes. Turn pan upside down onto wire rack or heatproof serving plate; remove pan. Cool cake completely, about 1 hour. Spread Orange Glaze over top of cake, allowing some to drizzle down side. Store loosely covered at room temperature.

Orange Glaze

Mix powdered sugar, 1 tablespoon orange juice and the orange peel. Stir in additional orange juice, 1 teaspoon at a time, until smooth and consistency of thick syrup.

High Altitude (3500 to 6500 feet): Add 1 tablespoon all-purpose flour to dry cake mix. Increase orange juice to 3/4 cup. Decrease oil to 1/4 cup. Bake 40 to 45 minutes.

1 Serving: Calories 230 (Calories from Fat 70); Fat 8g (Saturated 2g); Cholesterol 40mg; Sodium 320mg; Carbohydrate 37g (Dietary Fiber 0g); Protein 2g. **% Daily Value:** Vitamin A 0%; Vitamin C 2%; Calcium 6%; Iron 4%.

Betty's Tip Harvey Wallbanger cake hails from the 1970s. Based on the popular cocktail made of Galliano®, an anise-flavored liqueur, vodka and orange juice, this cake will bring you back to the groovy days of disco.

Piña Colada Cake

Prep: 20 min * Bake: 35 min * Cool: 1 hr 10 min

12 TO 16 SERVINGS

1 can (8 ounces) crushed pineapple in juice, undrained

1 package Betty Crocker SuperMoist yellow cake mix

1 1/4 cups water

1/3 cup vegetable oil

3 eggs

1 teaspoon rum extract

1 package Betty Crocker HomeStyle fluffy white frosting mix

1 teaspoon rum extract

1/4 cup flaked coconut, toasted (page 36)

1 Heat oven to 350°. Grease bottoms and sides of 2 round pans, 8 or 9 x 1 1/2 inches, with shortening; lightly flour.

2 Drain pineapple in colander set over a bowl, pushing pineapple against side and bottom of colander with back of wooden spoon to squeeze out as much juice as possible; reserve juice. Beat cake mix, water, oil, eggs, pineapple and 1 teaspoon rum extract in large bowl with electric mixer on low speed 2 minutes (do not overbeat). Pour into pans.

3 Bake 8-inch rounds 30 to 35 minutes, 9-inch rounds 25 to 30 minutes, or until toothpick inserted in center comes out clean. Cool 10 minutes. Run knife around side of pans to loosen cakes; remove from pans to wire rack. Cool completely, about 1 hour.

4 Add enough water to reserved pineapple juice to measure 1/2 cup; heat to boiling. Make frosting mix as directed on package, using pineapple juice mixture for the boiling water called for in package directions. Beat 1 teaspoon rum extract into frosting with electric mixer on low speed.

5 Fill layers with about 2/3 cup frosting. Frost side and top of cake with remaining frosting. Sprinkle top and side of cake with coconut. Store loosely covered at room temperature.

High Altitude (3500 to 6500 feet): Do not use 8-inch rounds. Add 2 tablespoons all-purpose flour to dry cake mix. Decrease oil to 2 tablespoons. Bake 9-inch rounds 25 to 30 minutes.

1 Serving: Calories 315 (Calories from Fat 100); Fat 11g (Saturated 3g); Cholesterol 55mg; Sodium 300mg; Carbohydrate 51g (Dietary Fiber 0g); Protein 3g. **% Daily Value:** Vitamin A 2%; Vitamin C 2%; Calcium 8%; Iron 4%.

Betty's Tip All the flavors in the popular tropical drink come together in this luscious cake. If you don't have a package of frosting mix, you can substitute the reserved pineapple juice for the milk in the Cream Cheese Frosting on page 234. Then, you'll need to store the frosted cake covered in the refrigerator.

In 1956, who needed marriage counseling? Cake mix solved all sorts of marital stress!

Piña Colada Cake

Lemon-Filled Orange Cake

Prep: 20 min * Bake: 32 min * Cool: 1 hr 10 min * Chill: 1 hr

12 TO 16 SERVINGS

1 package Betty Crocker SuperMoist white cake mix

1 1/4 cups orange juice

1/3 cup vegetable oil

3 egg whites

1 can (15 3/4 ounces) lemon pie filling

1 tub Betty Crocker Whipped fluffy white ready-to-spread frosting or Creamy White Frosting (page 234)

Grated orange peel, if desired

1 Heat oven to 350°. Grease bottoms and sides of 2 round pans, 8 or 9 x 1 1/2 inches, with shortening; lightly flour.

2 Beat cake mix, orange juice, oil and egg whites in large bowl with electric mixer on low speed 30 seconds; beat on medium speed 2 minutes. Pour into pans.

3 Bake 8-inch rounds 27 to 32 minutes, 9-inch rounds 23 to 28 minutes, or until toothpick inserted in center comes out clean. Cool 10 minutes. Run knife around side of pans to loosen cakes; remove from pans to wire rack. Cool completely, about 1 hour.

4 Split each cake layer horizontally to make 2 layers. Fill each layer with generous 1/2 cup pie filling. Frost side and top of cake with frosting. Garnish with orange peel. Refrigerate about 1 hour or until chilled. Store covered in refrigerator.

High Altitude (3500 to 6500 feet): Do not use 8-inch rounds. Bake 9-inch rounds 25 to 30 minutes.

1 Serving: Calories 400 (Calories from Fat 135); Fat 15g (Saturated 5g); Cholesterol 0mg; Sodium 310mg; Carbohydrate 64g (Dietary Fiber 0g); Protein 3g. **% Daily Value:** Vitamin A 0%; Vitamin C 6%; Calcium 4%; Iron 6%.

Betty's Tip Add a touch of easy elegance! Scatter a few fragrant yellow and orange rose petals (just make sure they're pesticide free) on top of the frosted cake. You can also garnish with strips of lemon and orange peel curled together, or for a last-minute embellishment, use small wedges of lemon and orange.

Lemon-Filled Orange Cake

Strawberry Yogurt Cake

Prep: 20 min * Bake: 32 min * Cool: 1 hr 10 min

12 TO 16 SERVINGS

1 package Betty Crocker SuperMoist white cake mix

3/4 cup water

1/3 cup vegetable oil

3 egg whites

1 container (6 ounces) strawberry yogurt (2/3 cup)

1 tub Betty Crocker Whipped vanilla ready-to-spread frosting or Vanilla Buttercream Frosting (page 236)

1 quart (4 cups) strawberries

1 Heat oven to 350°. Generously grease bottoms and sides of 2 round pans, 8 or 9 x 1 1/2 inches, with shortening; lightly flour.

2 Beat cake mix, water, oil, egg whites and yogurt in large bowl with electric mixer on low speed 30 seconds; beat on medium speed 2 minutes. Pour into pans.

3 Bake 8-inch rounds 27 to 32 minutes, 9-inch rounds 23 to 28 minutes, or until toothpick inserted in center comes out clean. Cool 10 minutes. Run knife around side of pans to loosen cakes; remove from pans to wire rack. Cool completely, about 1 hour.

4 Spread 1/3 cup frosting over 1 cake layer to within 1/4 inch of edge. Cut about 10 strawberries into 1/4-inch slices; arrange on frosted layer. Top with second layer. Frost side and top of cake with remaining frosting. Cut remaining strawberries in half; arrange on top of cake. Store loosely covered in refrigerator.

High Altitude (3500 to 6500 feet): Do not use 8-inch rounds.

1 Serving: Calories 390 (Calories from Fat 135); Fat 15g (Saturated 7g); Cholesterol 0mg; Sodium 310mg; Carbohydrate 61g (Dietary Fiber 1g); Protein 4g. **% Daily Value:** Vitamin A 0%; Vitamin C 20%; Calcium 4%; Iron 4%.

Betty's Tip For greater portability, make the cake as directed using a greased and floured rectangular pan, 13 x 9 x 2 inches, and bake 35 to 40 minutes. Cool completely in pan. Spread frosting over top of cake. Garnish with 1 pint (2 cups) of strawberries.

Strawberry Yogurt Cake

Lady Baltimore Cake

Prep: 20 min * Bake: 32 min * Cool: 1 hr 10 min

12 TO 16 SERVINGS

1 package Betty Crocker SuperMoist white cake mix

1 1/4 cups water

1/3 cup vegetable oil

3 egg whites

1 teaspoon almond extract

1/4 cup finely cut-up raisins

1/4 cup finely cut-up figs or dates

1/4 cup finely chopped walnuts

1 tub Betty Crocker Whipped fluffy white ready-to-spread frosting or Creamy White Frosting (page 234)

1 Heat oven to 350°. Grease bottoms only of 2 round pans, 8 or 9 x 1 1/2 inches, with shortening.

2 Make cake mix as directed on package, using water, oil, egg whites and almond extract. Pour into pans.

3 Bake 8-inch rounds 27 to 32 minutes, 9-inch rounds 23 to 28 minutes, or until toothpick inserted in center comes out clean. Cool 10 minutes. Run knife around side of pans to loosen cakes; remove from pans to wire rack. Cool completely, about 1 hour.

4 Stir raisins, figs and walnuts into one-third of the frosting to make filling. Fill layers with half of the filling. Spread remaining filling over top of cake. Frost side of cake with remaining frosting. Store loosely covered at room temperature.

High Altitude (3500 to 6500 feet): Do not use 8-inch rounds. Bake 9-inch rounds 25 to 30 minutes.

1 Serving: Calories 355 (Calories from Fat 110); Fat 12g (Saturated 3g); Cholesterol 0mg; Sodium 330mg; Carbohydrate 59g (Dietary Fiber 1g); Protein 4g. **% Daily Value:** Vitamin A 0%; Vitamin C 0%; Calcium 4%; Iron 4%.

Betty's Tip Described in the 1906 romantic novel *Lady Baltimore* by Owen Wister, this layered white cake quickly became a hit with its filling of raisins, nuts and fruits, and boiled white icing. You're sure to enjoy this easy variation of the original confection, which uses cake mix and fluffy white frosting.

Butter Brickle Cake

Prep: 15 min • Bake: 35 min • Cool: 1 hr 10 min

12 TO 16 SERVINGS

1 package Betty Crocker SuperMoist yellow cake mix

1 package (4-serving size) butterscotch instant pudding and pie filling mix

1 cup milk

1/2 cup butter or margarine, melted

3 eggs

2 cups almond brickle chips

1 tablespoon all-purpose flour

1 1/2 cups whipping (heavy) cream

2 tablespoons packed brown sugar

1 Heat oven to 350°. Generously grease bottoms only of 2 round pans, 9 x 1 1/2 inches, with shortening; lightly flour. (Do not use 8-inch rounds or batter will overflow.)

2 Beat cake mix, pudding mix (dry), milk, butter and eggs in large bowl with electric mixer on low speed 30 seconds; beat on medium speed 2 minutes. Toss 1/2 cup of the brickle chips with flour in small bowl; stir into cake batter (batter will be thick). Spoon evenly into pans.

3 Bake 30 to 35 minutes or until toothpick inserted in center comes out clean. Cool 10 minutes. Run knife around side of pans to loosen cakes; remove from pans to wire rack. Cool completely, about 1 hour.

4 Beat whipping cream and brown sugar in chilled large bowl with electric mixer on high speed until soft peaks form. Spread about 1/2 cup whipped cream mixture over 1 cake layer to within about 1/4 inch of edge; sprinkle with 1/2 cup of the brickle chips. Top with second layer. Frost side and top of cake with remaining whipped cream mixture. Press remaining 1 cup brickle chips into side of cake. Store covered in refrigerator.

High Altitude (3500 to 6500 feet): Heat oven to 375°. When making cake mix, decrease butter to 2 tablespoons and add 1/4 cup all-purpose flour and 1/2 cup water. Bake 32 to 27 minutes.

1 Serving: Calories 600 (Calories from Fat 305); Fat 34g (Saturated 19g); Cholesterol 125mg; Sodium 570mg; Carbohydrate 68g (Dietary Fiber 1g); Protein 6g. **% Daily Value:** Vitamin A 20%; Vitamin C 0%; Calcium 18%; Iron 6%.

Betty's Tip When an article about Butter Brickle Cake ran in the *Chicago Tribune* in March 2001, it must have sparked some memories— the response to the article was tremendous! If you loved Betty Crocker's butter brickle cake mix that was taken off the shelves in 1990, you can recreate the fabulous flavor with just a few easy embellishments to a box of yellow cake mix.

An ice-cream shop favorite turned into a cake mix flavor in the 1960s. Fans scooped this cake mix right up!

Color Vision Cake

Prep: 15 min * Bake: 32 min * Cool: 1 hr 10 min

12 TO 16 SERVINGS

1 package (4-serving size) fruit-flavored gelatin (any flavor)

1 package Betty Crocker SuperMoist white cake mix

1 1/4 cups water

1/3 cup vegetable oil

3 egg whites

Multicolored round candies, if desired

Color Vision Frosting (below)

Color Vision Frosting

Reserved fruit-flavored gelatin (dry)

1/3 cup butter or margarine, melted

3 tablespoons milk

3 1/2 cups powdered sugar

1 Heat oven to 350°. Grease bottoms only of 2 round pans, 8 or 9 x 1 1/2 inches, with shortening; flour lightly. Measure 3 tablespoons of the gelatin (dry); reserve remaining gelatin for the frosting.

2 Make cake mix as directed on package, using water, oil, egg whites and 3 tablespoons dry gelatin. Pour into pans.

3 Bake 8-inch rounds 27 to 32 minutes, 9-inch rounds 23 to 28 minutes, or until toothpick inserted in center comes out clean. Cool 10 minutes. Run knife around side of pans to loosen cakes; remove from pans to wire rack. Cool completely, about 1 hour.

4 Fill layers and frost side and top of cake with Color Vision Frosting. Sprinkle with candies. Store loosely covered at room temperature.

Color Vision Frosting

Beat gelatin, butter and milk in medium bowl with electric mixer on low speed 1 minute, scraping bowl constantly. Gradually beat in powdered sugar until smooth. If necessary, stir in additional milk, 1/2 teaspoon at a time, until spreadable.

High Altitude (3500 to 6500 feet): Do not use 8-inch rounds. Bake 9-inch rounds 25 to 30 minutes.

1 Serving: Calories 455 (Calories from Fat 135); Fat 15g (Saturated 5g); Cholesterol 15mg; Sodium 360mg; Carbohydrate 76g (Dietary Fiber 0g); Protein 4g. **% Daily Value:** Vitamin A 4%; Vitamin C 0%; Calcium 4%; Iron 4%.

Betty's Tip Once you've made this cake, be prepared to make it over and over again because kids love it! With all the flavors of gelatin, you can have a different color and flavor every time you make it! You can also use sugar-free gelatin, if that is what you keep on hand. Reserve 1/2 teaspoon dry sugar-free gelatin for the frosting and use the remaining dry gelatin in the cake.

In 1951, when color movies were the rage, Color Vision Cake brought Technicolor to home kitchens across America.

Color Vision Cake

French Silk Hazelnut Cake

Prep: 20 min   *   Bake: 32 min   *   Cool: 1 hr 10 min

12 TO 16 SERVINGS

1 package Betty Crocker SuperMoist white cake mix

1 1/4 cups water

1/3 cup vegetable oil

3 egg whites

1 1/2 cups finely chopped hazelnuts

1 tub Betty Crocker Rich & Creamy chocolate ready-to-spread frosting or Creamy Chocolate Frosting (page 238)

1   Heat oven to 350°. Grease bottoms only of 2 round pans, 8 or 9 x 1 1/2 inches, with shortening.

2   Make cake mix as directed on package, using water, oil and egg whites. Stir in 1/2 cup of the hazelnuts. Pour into pans.

3   Bake 8-inch rounds 27 to 32 minutes, 9-inch rounds 23 to 28 minutes, or until toothpick inserted in center comes out clean. Cool 10 minutes. Run knife around side of pans to loosen cakes; remove from pans to wire rack. Cool completely, about 1 hour.

4   Fill and frost side and top of cake with frosting. Press remaining 1 cup hazelnuts on side of cake. Store loosely covered at room temperature.

High Altitude (3500 to 6500 feet): Do not use 8-inch rounds. Bake 9-inch rounds 25 to 30 minutes.

1 Serving: Calories 400 (Calories from Fat 250); Fat 28g (Saturated 10g); Cholesterol 0mg; Sodium 310mg; Carbohydrate 59g (Dietary Fiber 2g); Protein 5g. **% Daily Value:** Vitamin A 0%; Vitamin C 0%; Calcium 6%; Iron 8%.

French Silk Pecan Cake: Substitute finely chopped pecans for the hazelnuts.

Betty's Tip   To keep your serving plate clean, line the edge with strips of waxed paper before assembling the cake. Remove the waxed paper after frosting and garnishing the cake.

Neapolitan Cake

Prep: 20 min * Bake: 50 min * Cool: 1 hr 10 min

12 TO 16 SERVINGS

1 package Betty Crocker SuperMoist white cake mix

1 cup water

1/4 cup vegetable oil

3 egg whites

1/4 teaspoon almond extract

12 drops red food color

1/3 cup chocolate-flavored syrup

Easy Chocolate Glaze (page 241) or Chocolate Glaze (page 241)

1 Heat oven to 350°. Grease 12-cup bundt cake pan with shortening; lightly flour.

2 Beat cake mix, water, oil and egg whites in large bowl with electric mixer on low speed 30 seconds; beat on medium speed 2 minutes.

3 Pour about 1 2/3 cups batter into pan. Pour 1 2/3 cups batter into small bowl; stir in almond extract and food color. Carefully pour pink batter over white batter in pan. Stir chocolate syrup into remaining batter. Carefully pour chocolate batter over pink batter.

4 Bake 45 to 50 minutes or until toothpick inserted in center of cake comes out clean. Cool 10 minutes. Turn pan upside down onto wire rack or heatproof serving plate; remove pan. Cool completely, about 1 hour. Drizzle Easy Chocolate Glaze over cake. Store loosely covered at room temperature.

High Altitude (3500 to 6500 feet): No changes.

1 Serving: Calories 295 (Calories from Fat 100); Fat 11g (Saturated 4g); Cholesterol 0mg; Sodium 310mg; Carbohydrate 46g (Dietary Fiber 0g); Protein 3g. **% Daily Value:** Vitamin A 0%; Vitamin C 0%; Calcium 8%; Iron 6%.

Betty's Tip Bundt pans can be a challenge to grease. To make it easier, place a dab of shortening on the outside of a small plastic sandwich bag. Slip the bag on your hand, and rub shortening on the inside of the pan. Repeat with more shortening until every surface is greased.

This triply delicious cake mix recipe had something for everyone. Family togetherness, 1970s style!

Photo on page 52

Lemon Velvet Cream Cake

Prep: 20 min ✳ Bake: 35 min ✳ Cool: 1 hr 10 min

12 TO 16 SERVINGS

1 package Betty Crocker
SuperMoist lemon cake mix

1 1/4 cups water

1/3 cup vegetable oil

3 eggs

Velvet Cream (below)

Grated lemon peel, if desired

Coarse sugar crystals
(decorating sugar), if desired

Velvet Cream

1 package (3 ounces) cream
cheese, softened

1 tablespoon milk

1 tablespoon grated lemon
peel

2 cups whipping (heavy) cream

2/3 cup powdered sugar

1 Heat oven to 350°. Grease bottoms only of 2 round pans,
   8 or 9 x 1 1/2 inches, with shortening.

2 Make cake mix as directed on package, using water, oil and eggs.
   Pour into pans.

3 Bake 8-inch rounds 30 to 35 minutes, 9-inch rounds 25 to 30
   minutes, or until toothpick inserted in center comes out clean.
   Cool 10 minutes. Run knife around side of pans to loosen cakes;
   remove from pans to wire rack. Cool completely, about 1 hour.

4 Split each cake layer horizontally to make 2 layers. Fill each layer
   with 1/2 cup Velvet Cream. Frost side and top with remaining
   Velvet Cream. Garnish with lemon peel. Sprinkle with sugar
   crystals. Store loosely covered in refrigerator.

Velvet Cream

Beat cream cheese, milk and lemon peel in chilled large bowl
with electric mixer on low speed until smooth. Beat in whipping
cream and powdered sugar. Beat on high speed, scraping bowl
occasionally, until stiff peaks form.

High Altitude (3500 to 6500 feet): Do not use 8-inch rounds. Make cake mix following high altitude directions on package for 9-inch rounds.

1 Serving: Calories 440 (Calories from Fat 250); Fat 28g (Saturated 13g); Cholesterol 115mg;
Sodium 300mg; Carbohydrate 43g (Dietary Fiber 0g); Protein 4g. **% Daily Value:** Vitamin A 14%;
Vitamin C 0%; Calcium 12%; Iron 4%.

Chocolate Velvet Cream Cake: Make SuperMoist devil's food cake mix
as directed on package. Make Velvet Cream—except omit lemon peel;
beat in 1/4 cup baking cocoa with the cream cheese and milk.
Garnish with white chocolate curls and raspberries if desired.

Photo on cover.

White Velvet Cream Cake: Make SuperMoist white cake mix as directed on package. Make Velvet Cream—except omit lemon peel; beat in
1 teaspoon vanilla with the cream cheese and milk. Garnish with
fresh berries if desired.

*Wow! As ooey-gooey and luscious
as a cake could be, the recipe
for Velvet Cream Cake took
the prize in 1960.*

Betty's Tip In 1960, Velvet Cream Cake was touted as "Recipe of the
Year." The original version called for a filling made of whipping cream
and Betty Crocker frosting mix. Although the frosting mix has long been
discontinued, the same great flavor can be captured using cream cheese,
powdered sugar and whipping cream.

Fast Frosting Fix-ups

Sometimes simple vanilla or chocolate frosting is just right. But when you're looking for an easy way to jazz up a cake without a lot of fuss, we've got you covered.

Fabulous Flavored Frostings

For chocolate lovers, start with 1 tub Betty Crocker Rich & Creamy or Whipped chocolate ready-to-spread frosting and add your favorite chocolate-enhancing flavors:

Almond-Coconut: 1/4 teaspoon almond extract, 1/4 cup chopped almonds and 1/4 cup toasted flaked coconut

Mocha Chip: 2 teaspoons instant coffee (dry) and 1/2 cup miniature chocolate chips

Peanut Butter Fudge: 1/4 cup peanut butter

Rocky Road: 1/4 cup miniature marshmallows and 1/4 cup chopped walnuts

Turtle Fudge: 1/4 cup caramel topping and 1/4 chopped pecans

Toffee: 1/3 cup almond brickle chips or bits

For vanilla fans, start with 1 tub Betty Crocker Rich & Creamy vanilla or Fluffy white ready-to-spread frosting and add your favorite mix-ins:

Confetti: 1/4 cup candy sprinkles

Maple-Nut: 1/2 teaspoon maple extract and 1/2 cup chopped pecans

Mint Chip: 1/4 teaspoon mint extract, 1/3 cup chocolate chips and 2 or 3 drops green food color

Peanut Brittle: 1/3 cup crushed peanut brittle

Peppermint Crunch: 1/2 teaspoon peppermint extract and 1/3 cup crushed peppermint candy (Add a few drops of red or green food color if desired.)

Terrific Cake Toppers

Looking for some no-fail ways to add pizzazz to your cakes? Just spread on your favorite frosting, and top with:

* Edible flower petals, such as nasturtium, rose, pansy (pesticide free)
* Grated or curled lemon, orange or lime peel
* Shaved or grated chocolate
* Melted white or dark chocolate
* Candy-coated chocolate candies
* Chocolate-covered raisins
* Espresso or jelly beans
* Jelly fruit slices
* Colored sugar, dots and sprinkles
* Cookie crumbs
* Chopped, slivered or sliced nuts
* Toasted or untoasted coconut
* Tinted coconut
* Miniature chocolate chips
* Colored miniature marshmallows

Ultimate Carrot Cake

Prep: 20 min * Bake: 45 min * Cool: 1 hr 10 min

12 TO 16 SERVINGS

1 package Betty Crocker
SuperMoist carrot cake mix

1/2 cup water

1/2 cup vegetable oil

4 eggs

1 can (8 ounces) crushed
pineapple in juice, undrained

1/2 cup chopped nuts

1/2 cup shredded coconut

1/2 cup raisins

1 tub Betty Crocker Rich &
Creamy cream cheese ready-to-
spread frosting or Cream
Cheese Frosting (page 234)

1   Heat oven to 350°. Grease bottoms only of 2 round pans,
8 or 9 x 1 1/2 inches, with shortening; lightly flour.

2   Beat cake mix, water, oil, eggs and pineapple (with juice) in large
bowl with electric mixer on low speed 30 seconds; beat on medium speed 2 minutes. Stir in nuts, coconut and raisins. Pour into
pans.

3   Bake 8-inch rounds 40 to 45 minutes, 9-inch rounds 28 to 32
minutes, or until toothpick inserted in center comes out clean.
Cool 10 minutes. Run knife around side of pans to loosen cakes;
remove from pans to wire rack. Cool completely, about 1 hour.

4   Fill layers and frost side and top of cake with frosting. Store
covered in refrigerator.

High Altitude (3500 to 6500 feet): Do not use 8-inch rounds. Heat oven to 375°.
Add 1/3 cup all-purpose flour to dry cake mix. Decrease oil to 1/3 cup.

1 Serving: Calories 470 (Calories from Fat 290); Fat 32g (Saturated 11g); Cholesterol 100mg;
Sodium 400mg; Carbohydrate 40g (Dietary Fiber 1g); Protein 6g. **% Daily Value:** Vitamin A 10%;
Vitamin C 2%; Calcium 2%; Iron 4%.

Betty's Tip   This popular cake has remained a favorite since the 1960s.
For even more homemade flavor and taste, you can add extra carrots to
the recipe. Omit the water and add 3/4 cup finely shredded carrots.
Decrease the bake time for 8-inch rounds to about 35 minutes (bake
time for 9-inch rounds remains the same).

Photo on page 235

Chocolate Angel Cake
with Raspberry-Orange Sauce

Prep: 20 min ✳ Bake: 47 min ✳ Cool: 2 hr

12 SERVINGS

2 tablespoons baking cocoa

1 package Betty Crocker 1-step white angel food cake mix

1 1/4 cups cold water

Raspberry-Orange Sauce (below)

1 container (8 ounces) frozen whipped topping, thawed, or 3 cups Sweetened Whipped Cream (page 243)

Raspberry-Orange Sauce

1 package (10 ounces) frozen raspberries in light syrup, thawed

1/4 cup sugar

2 tablespoons cornstarch

2 tablespoons orange juice

Tender, fluffy and light! In the 1950s, angel food cake was a challenge to make. But Betty made it easy to bring heaven right to the table!

1 Move oven rack to lowest position (remove other racks). Heat oven to 350°.

2 Stir cocoa into cake mix. Beat cake mix and cold water in extra-large glass or metal bowl with electric mixer on low speed 30 seconds; beat on medium speed 1 minute. Pour into ungreased angel food cake (tube) pan, 10 x 4 inches. (Do not use bundt cake pan or 9 x 3 1/2-inch angel food pan or batter will overflow.)

3 Bake 37 to 47 minutes or until top is dark golden brown and cracks feel very dry and not sticky. Do not underbake. Immediately turn pan upside down onto glass bottle until cake is completely cool, about 2 hours.

4 While cake is cooling, make Raspberry-Orange Sauce.

5 Run knife around edges of cake; remove from pan. Split cake horizontally to make 3 layers. Spread 1 cup whipped topping and slightly less than 1/2 cup sauce over 1 cake layer (sauce may not completely cover layer). Repeat with second layer. Top with remaining layer. Spread remaining sauce over top of cake. Drop remaining whipped topping in dollops on top of sauce. Store covered in refrigerator.

Raspberry-Orange Sauce

Drain raspberries, reserving liquid. Add enough water to raspberry liquid to measure 2/3 cup. Mix sugar and cornstarch in 1-quart saucepan; stir in liquid mixture. Heat over medium heat, stirring constantly, until mixture thickens and boils; boil and stir 1 minute. Stir in orange juice and raspberries. Cool completely, about 30 minutes.

High Altitude (3500 to 6500 feet): Heat oven to 325°. Add 1/3 cup cornstarch to the cocoa and dry cake mix. Increase water to 1 1/3 cups. Beat on low speed 30 seconds, then beat on medium speed 3 minutes. Bake 53 to 58 minutes.

1 Serving: Calories 220 (Calories from Fat 20); Fat 2g (Saturated 2g); Cholesterol 0mg; Sodium 260mg; Carbohydrate 48g (Dietary Fiber 1g); Protein 4g. **% Daily Value:** Vitamin A 2%; Vitamin C 8%; Calcium 2%; Iron 4%.

Betty's Tip For the sauce, be sure to mix the sugar and cornstarch together before the liquid is added to prevent the cornstarch from getting lumpy. If you have any leftover sauce, it also makes a great topping for chocolate cake or ice cream!

Strawberry-Rhubarb Angel Torte

Prep: 25 min * Bake: 47 min * Cool: 2 hr

12 SERVINGS

1 package Betty Crocker 1-step
white angel food cake mix

1 1/4 cups cold water

2 teaspoons grated
orange peel

Strawberry-Rhubarb Filling
(below)

1 container (15 ounces)
ricotta cheese

1/4 cup powdered sugar

1 container (8 ounces) frozen
whipped topping, thawed, or
3 cups Sweetened Whipped
Cream (page 243)

1/2 cup sliced strawberries

Strawberry-Rhubarb Filling

2 cups sliced fresh rhubarb

1/2 cup granulated sugar

2 tablespoons orange juice

1 1/2 cups sliced strawberries

4 drops red food color, if
desired

1 Move oven rack to lowest position (remove other racks). Heat
oven to 350°.

2 Beat cake mix, cold water and orange peel in extra-large glass
or metal bowl with electric mixer on low speed 30 seconds; beat
on medium speed 1 minute. Pour into ungreased angel food
cake (tube) pan, 10 x 4 inches. (Do not use bundt cake pan
or 9 x 3 1/2-inch angel food pan or batter will overflow.)

3 Bake 37 to 47 minutes or until top is dark golden brown
and cracks feel very dry and not sticky. Do not underbake.
Immediately turn pan upside down onto glass bottle until
cake is completely cool, about 2 hours.

4 While cake is cooling, make Strawberry-Rhubarb Filling. Beat
ricotta cheese and powdered sugar in large bowl with electric
mixer on medium speed until fluffy. Fold in whipped topping.

5 Run knife around edges of cake; remove from pan. Split cake
horizontally to make 3 layers. Fill layers with filling. Frost side
and top of cake with ricotta mixture. Arrange strawberries over
top of cake. Store covered in refrigerator.

Strawberry-Rhubarb Filling

Mix rhubarb, sugar and orange juice in 2-quart saucepan. Cook
over medium heat 10 minutes, stirring occasionally. Cool 15 minutes. Stir in strawberries. Add food color if deeper red color is
desired. Refrigerate about 1 hour.

High Altitude (3500 to 6500 feet): Heat oven to 325°. Add 1/3 cup cornstarch to dry
cake mix. Increase water to 1 1/3 cups. Beat on low speed 30 seconds, then beat on
medium speed 3 minutes. Bake 53 to 58 minutes.

1 Serving: Calories 315 (Calories from Fat 45); Fat 5g (Saturated 4g); Cholesterol 15mg; Sodium
445mg; Carbohydrate 60g (Dietary Fiber 1g); Protein 9g. **% Daily Value:** Vitamin A 4%; Vitamin C
30%; Calcium 18%; Iron 2%.

Betty's Tip In the chilly months of winter, frozen rhubarb that has
been thawed and well drained makes a great substitution for the
fresh rhubarb.

Strawberry-Rhubarb Angel Torte

Key Lime–Coconut Angel Cake

Prep: 25 min • Bake: 47 min • Cool: 2 hr

12 SERVINGS

1 package Betty Crocker 1-step white angel food cake mix

1 1/4 cups cold water

1 can (14 ounces) sweetened condensed milk

1/3 cup Key lime or regular lime juice

1 teaspoon grated lime peel

1 container (8 ounces) frozen whipped topping, thawed, or 3 cups Sweetened Whipped Cream (page 243)

1 cup flaked coconut

1 Move oven rack to lowest position (remove other racks). Heat oven to 350°.

2 Beat cake mix and cold water in extra-large glass or metal bowl with electric mixer on low speed 30 seconds; beat on medium speed 1 minute. Pour into ungreased angel food cake (tube) pan, 10 x 4 inches. (Do not use bundt cake pan or 9 x 3 1/2-inch angel food pan or batter will overflow.)

3 Bake 37 to 47 minutes or until top is dark golden brown and cracks feel very dry and not sticky. Do not underbake. Immediately turn pan upside down onto glass bottle until cake is completely cool, about 2 hours.

4 Beat condensed milk, lime juice and lime peel in large bowl with wire whisk until smooth and thickened. Fold in whipped topping

5 Run knife around edges of cake; remove from pan. Split cake horizontally to make 3 layers. Fill each layer with about 2 cups lime mixture. Frost top and side of cake with remaining lime mixture. Sprinkle with coconut. Store covered in refrigerator.

High Altitude (3500 to 6500 feet): Make cake mix following high-altitude directions on package for angel food pan.

1 Serving: Calories 370 (Calories from Fat 60); Fat 7g (Saturated 5g); Cholesterol 15mg; Sodium 450mg; Carbohydrate 60g (Dietary Fiber 1g); Protein 7g. **% Daily Value:** Vitamin A 2%; Vitamin C 8%; Calcium 12%; Iron 4%.

Betty's Tip A flexible metal or plastic spatula and a light touch work wonders when frosting this delicate angel food cake. For splitting the cake, an electric knife cuts the cake into clean, even layers.

Key Lime–Coconut Angel Cake

3
Special
Celebrations

Classic White Wedding Cake (page 94) with Vanilla Buttercream Frosting (page 236) and Petits Fours (page 97)

All-Time FAVORITE

Classic White Wedding Cake

Prep: 4 hr * Bake: 2 hr 10 min * Cool: 2 hr 30 min

ABOUT 115 SERVINGS

5 packages Betty Crocker SuperMoist white cake mix

6 1/4 cups water

1 2/3 cups vegetable oil

15 egg whites

6 tubs Betty Crocker Rich & Creamy vanilla ready-to-spread frosting or 6 recipes Vanilla Buttercream Frosting (page 236) or Creamy White Frosting (page 234)

1 Heat oven to 350°. Grease bottom only of round pan, 10 x 2 inches, with shortening. Make 1 cake mix as directed on package, using 1 1/4 cups water, 1/3 cup oil and 3 egg whites. Pour 3 1/4 cups batter into pan. Reserve remaining batter covered in refrigerator. Bake 25 to 30 minutes or until toothpick inserted in center comes out clean. Cool 15 minutes. Run knife around side of pan to loosen cake; remove from pan to wire rack. Cool completely, about 1 hour.

2 Grease bottom only of 1 round pan, 6 x 2 inches, and 1 round pan, 14 x 2 inches, with shortening. Make 2 cake mixes as directed on package, using 2 1/2 cups water, 2/3 cup oil and 6 egg whites. Pour 1 cup batter into 6-inch pan and 6 cups batter into 14-inch pan. Reserve remaining batter covered in refrigerator. Bake 6-inch layer 28 to 33 minutes, 14-inch layer 25 to 30 minutes, or until toothpick inserted in center comes out clean. Cool 15 minutes. Run knife around sides of pans to loosen cakes; remove from pans to wire rack. Cool completely, about 1 hour.

Basic white, the classically elegant dessert... flavor co-ordinated by Betty Crocker.

From 1968 to today, cake mix was always stylish, no matter what else was in fashion!

❋ Wedding Cake Serving Yields ❋

Each serving measures 2 x 1 inch from a 2-layer tier 3 inches high.

Layer	Round	Square
6 inches	10	18
7 inches	15	—
8 inches	22	32
9 inches	28	40
10 inches	35	50
12 inches	50	72
14 inches	70	98
16 inches	100	128
18 x 12-inch rectangle	—	108

How to Cut a Round Tiered Wedding Cake

Use a thin, sharp or serrated knife. Insert knife into cake, keeping point down and handle up. Slice, pulling knife toward you. If frosting sticks, dip knife in hot water or wipe with damp paper towel after cutting each slice.

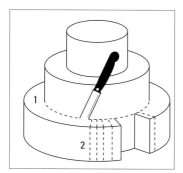

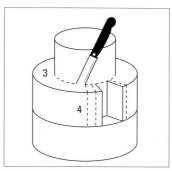

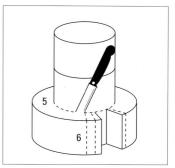

Cut vertically through bottom layer at edge of second layer as indicated by dotted line 1; then cut into wedges as indicated by dotted line 2.

Follow same procedure with middle layer by cutting vertically through second layer at edge of top layer as indicated by dotted line 3; then cut into wedges as indicated by dotted line 4.

Return to bottom layer and cut along dotted line 5; then cut into wedges as indicated by dotted line 6. Separate remaining layers (traditionally the top layer is frozen for the couple's first anniversary); cut as desired.

3 Make remaining 2 cake mixes as directed on package, using remaining 2 1/2 cups water, 2/3 cup oil and 6 egg whites. Repeat above process for baking one each 10 x 2-inch, 6 x 2-inch and 14 x 2-inch layer, using cake mix batter and reserved batter (stir before using). Each tier of wedding cake will consist of 2 layers, making a total of 6 layers. Tops of layers should be flat for ease in stacking; slice off rounded tops if necessary.

4 Place one 14-inch cake layer on large round plate, mirror or aluminum-foil covered cardboard, 16 inches in diameter. Frost top of cake layer with 1 cup frosting; top with remaining 14-inch layer. Frost side and top with 3 cups frosting.

5 Cover 10-inch cardboard circle with aluminum foil; place on first tier. Place one 10-inch cake layer on cardboard. Frost top of cake layer with 2/3 cup frosting; top with remaining 10-inch layer. Frost side and top with 2 cups frosting.

6 Cover 6-inch cardboard circle with aluminum foil; place on second tier. Place one 6-inch cake layer on cardboard. Frost top of cake layer with 1/3 cup frosting; top with remaining 6-inch layer. Frost side and top with 1 cup frosting. Decorate as desired (see page 96). Store loosely covered at room temperatue.

Decorating the Cake

Place 2 cups frosting in decorating bag with star tip. Pipe shell border around top edge and base of each tier. Decorate as desired using remaining frosting (see page 232 for All "Dec'd" Out). Top with fresh flowers if desired.

High Altitude (3500 to 6500 feet): Bake 10-inch rounds 30 to 35 minutes, 6-inch rounds 28 to 33 minutes and 14-inch rounds 30 to 35 minutes.

1 Serving: Calories 210 (Calories from Fat 70); Fat 8g (Saturated 3g); Cholesterol 0mg; Sodium 160mg; Carbohydrate 32g (Dietary Fiber 0g); Protein 2g. **% Daily Value:** Vitamin A 0%; Vitamin C 0%; Calcium 2%; Iron 2%.

Betty's Tip The photo of this elegant cake may inspire you to make the frosting from scratch, but if you want to keep it simple, you can use ready-to-spread frosting. To save even more time, measure ingredients ahead. Bake the cake layers the day before they are to be assembled, and store loosely covered at room temperature; or bake them earlier and freeze.

Photo on page 92

✳ Baking Different Sizes ✳

Layers other than sizes baked for Classic White Wedding Cake can be made. One package white cake mix makes about 4 1/2 cups batter.

Pan Size	Amount of Batter	Baking Time
6-inch round	1 cup	28 to 33 minutes
7-inch round	1 1/2 cups	28 to 33 minutes
8-inch round	2 cups	28 to 33 minutes
9-inch round	2 1/2 cups	28 to 33 minutes
10-inch round	3 1/4 cups	25 to 30 minutes
12-inch round	4 1/2 cups	25 to 30 minutes
14-inch round	6 cups	25 to 30 minutes
16-inch round	8 cups	25 to 30 minutes
18-inch half round	5 cups	25 to 30 minutes
15 x 11 x 2-inch sheet	6 1/2 cups	25 to 30 minutes
18 x 12 x 2-inch sheet	9 cups	25 to 30 minutes

Petits Fours

Prep: 30 min ✳ Bake: 30 min; Cool: 40 min ✳ Stand: 15 min

ABOUT 54 PIECES

1 package Betty Crocker
SuperMoist white cake mix

1 1/4 cups water

1/3 cup vegetable oil

3 egg whites

Shiny Almond Glaze (below)

2 cups powdered sugar

2 to 3 tablespoons water

Shiny Almond Glaze

8 cups powdered sugar

1/2 cup water

1/2 cup corn syrup

2 teaspoons almond extract

1 Heat oven to 350°. Grease bottom and sides of jelly roll pan, 15 1/2 x 10 1/2 x 1 inch, with shortening. Make cake mix as directed on package, using 1 1/4 cups water, the oil and egg whites. Pour into pan.

2 Bake 25 to 30 minutes or until toothpick inserted in center comes out clean. Cool 10 minutes. Run knife around sides of pan to loosen cake. Cool completely, about 30 minutes.

3 Cut cake into 1 1/2-inch squares, rounds, diamonds or hearts. Place several cakes on a wire rack set over a baking pan, without crowding. Pour enough Shiny Almond Glaze over cakes to cover top and sides. When most of extra glaze has dripped off, move rack off pan and allow cakes to stand on rack at least 15 minutes for glaze to set up. Scrape up extra glaze and reheat until luke-warm and pourable. Repeat with remaining cakes and glaze.

4 Mix powdered sugar and just enough of the 2 to 3 tablespoons water to make a frosting that holds its shape. Place frosting in decorating bag with round writing tip. Decorate as desired. Store loosely covered at room temperature.

Shiny Almond Glaze

Mix all ingredients in top of double boiler until smooth. Heat just until lukewarm; remove from heat. Let glaze remain over hot water to prevent thickening. If necessary, add hot water, a few drops at a time, for desired consistency.

High Altitude (3500 to 6500 feet): No changes.

1 Serving: Calories 150 (Calories from Fat 20); Fat 2g (Saturated 1g); Cholesterol 0mg; Sodium 70mg; Carbohydrate 32g (Dietary Fiber 0g); Protein 1g. **% Daily Value:** Vitamin A 0%; Vitamin C 0%; Calcium 0%; Iron 2%.

Betty's Tip Use your imagination when decorating these miniature cakes. Small candies, tinted frosting, colored sugars and edible flowers all make lovely adornments.

Variety is the spice of life! Here's a great idea from 1959 that makes multiplicity from a mix.

Photo on page 93

Baby Bib Shower Cake

Prep: 30 min * Bake: 32 min * Cool: 1 hr 10 min

12 TO 16 SERVINGS

1 package Betty Crocker SuperMoist white cake mix

1 1/4 cups water

1/3 cup vegetable oil

3 egg whites

2 tubs Betty Crocker Rich & Creamy vanilla ready-to-spread frosting or 2 recipes Vanilla Buttercream Frosting (page 236)

2 drops blue food color

2 drops red food color

Green and yellow food colors, if desired

Pastel candy mints

1 Heat oven to 350°. Grease bottoms only of 2 round pans, 8 or 9 x 1 1/2 inches, with shortening. Make cake mix as directed on package, using water, oil and egg whites. Pour into pans.

2 Bake 8-inch rounds 27 to 32 minutes, 9-inch rounds 23 to 28 minutes, or until toothpick inserted in center comes out clean. Cool 10 minutes. Run knife around side of pans to loosen cakes; remove from pans to wire rack. Cool completely, about 1 hour.

3 Fill layers and frost side and top of cake with 1 tub frosting. Make horizontal lines on side of cake with decorating comb or tines of fork if desired.

4 Place 1/2 cup frosting in decorating bag with star tip. Pipe zigzag border around outer top edge of cake.

5 Tint 1/4 cup of the remaining frosting with blue food color and place in decorating bag with writing tip. Pipe outer border of bib with blue frosting. Pipe inner opening of bib about 3 inches in diameter; join circles with tie at top. Tint 1/4 cup of the remaining frosting with red food color. Write desired message in bib opening with pink frosting. Tint remaining frosting with green, yellow or desired food color. Pipe stars on bib with small star tip. Arrange mints around base of cake. Store loosely covered at room temperature.

High Altitude (3500 to 6500 feet): Do not use 8-inch rounds. Bake 9-inch rounds 25 to 30 minutes.

1 Serving: Calories 555 (Calories from Fat 190); Fat 21g (Saturated 12g); Cholesterol 5mg; Sodium 310mg; Carbohydrate 89g (Dietary Fiber 0g); Protein 3g. **% Daily Value:** Vitamin A 0%; Vitamin C 0%; Calcium 8%; Iron 4%.

Betty's Tip Writing tips come in many sizes and can be used to write messages and make dots, beads and outlines. Popular writing tips include numbers 1 through 4 (small), 5 through 12 (medium), and 1A and 2A (large). We found that a number 5 writing tip works great for writing and making a bow on this cake.

Baby Bib Shower Cake

Let's Celebrate Cake

Prep: 25 min * Stand: 8 hr * Bake: 32 min * Cool: 1 hr 10 min

12 TO 16 SERVINGS

Streamers (below)

1 package Betty Crocker SuperMoist white cake mix

1 1/4 cups water

1/3 cup vegetable oil

3 egg whites

1 tub Betty Crocker Rich & Creamy vanilla ready-to-spread frosting or Vanilla Buttercream Frosting (page 236)

Assorted sugar sequins and colored sugars

3 drops yellow food color

Party Blowers (below)

Streamers

1 roll chewy fruit snack (from 5-ounce package) in desired color

Party Blowers

3 candy sticks (5 inches long)

1 roll chewy fruit snack (from 5-ounce package) in desired color

Reserved frosting

1   Make Streamers. Heat oven to 350°. Grease bottoms only of 2 round pans, 8 or 9 x 1 1/2 inches, with shortening. Make cake mix as directed on package, using water, oil and egg whites. Pour into pans.

2   Bake 8-inch rounds 27 to 32 minutes, 9-inch rounds 23 to 28 minutes, or until toothpick inserted in center comes out clean. Cool 10 minutes. Run knife around side of pans to loosen cakes; remove from pans to wire rack. Cool completely, about 1 hour.

3   Reserve 1/4 cup frosting for Party Blowers. Fill layers and frost side and top of cake with remaining frosting. Press sugar sequins and colored sugars into frosting on side and along outer edge of top of cake.

4   Tint reserved frosting with food color. Make Party Blowers. Place Party Blowers on top of cake with candy sticks toward center of cake. Unwrap streamers from spoon handles. Reshape into desired curl and place between Party Blowers and around base of cake. Store loosely covered at room temperature.

Streamers

Unroll fruit snack roll and cut lengthwise into 1/4-inch strips with a knife and a straightedge. Roll each strip in a spiral around handle of wooden spoon. Store at room temperature at least 8 hours to set curl to make streamers.

Party Blowers

To make each Party Blower, break candy stick in half. Cut a 4-inch piece from fruit snack roll. Place small amount of frosting 1/4 inch from broken end of 1 candy stick half. Wrap narrow end of piece of fruit roll over frosting. Pipe 2 rows of frosting stars over seam with decorating bag and star tip. Curl the end of the fruit roll to about 1 1/2 inches from star rows and secure with small amount of frosting if needed.

High Altitude (3500 to 6500 feet): Do not use 8-inch rounds. Make cake mix following high-altitude directions on package.

1 Serving: Calories 400 (Calories from Fat 145); Fat 16g (Saturated 7g); Cholesterol 0mg; Sodium 310mg; Carbohydrate 61g (Dietary Fiber 0g); Protein 3g. **% Daily Value:** Vitamin A 0%; Vitamin C 0%; Calcium 8%; Iron 4%.

Betty's Tip Chewy fruit snack rolls make great decorations like these streamers. You can also tie them into bows and ribbons for other cakes.

Let's Celebrate Cake

Rainbow Angel Birthday Cake

Prep: 15 min * Bake: 47 min * Cool: 2 hr

12 SERVINGS

1 package Betty Crocker 1-step white angel food cake mix

1 1/4 cups cold water

1 teaspoon grated lemon or orange peel

6 to 8 drops red food color

6 to 8 drops yellow food color

6 to 8 drops green food color

Easy Vanilla Glaze (page 242) or Vanilla Glaze (page 242)

Candy confetti sprinkles

1/2 tub Betty Crocker Rich & Creamy vanilla ready-to-spread frosting or 1/2 recipe Vanilla Buttercream Frosting (page 236)

12 to 15 square candy fruit chews

1. Move oven rack to lowest position (remove other racks). Heat oven to 350°. Beat cake mix, water and lemon peel in extra-large glass or metal bowl on low speed 30 seconds; beat on medium speed 1 minute.

2. Divide batter evenly among 3 bowls. Gently stir 1 food color into each of the batters. Pour red batter into ungreased angel food cake (tube) pan, 10 x 4 inches. (Do not use bundt cake pan or 9 x 3 1/2-inch angel food pan, or batter will overflow.) Spoon yellow batter over red batter. Spoon green batter over top.

3. Bake 37 to 47 minutes or until top is dark golden brown and cracks feel very dry and not sticky. Do not underbake. Immediately turn pan upside down onto glass bottle until cake is completely cool, about 2 hours. Run knife around edges of cake; remove from pan.

4. Drizzle Easy Vanilla Glaze over cake. Sprinkle with confetti. Place frosting in decorating bag with writing tip. Pipe a ribbon and bow on each candy square to look like a wrapped package. Arrange packages on top of cake. Store loosely covered at room temperature.

High Altitude (3500 to 6500 feet): Make cake mix following high-altitude directions on package for angel food pan.

1 Serving: Calories 215 (Calories from Fat 25); Fat 3g (Saturated 3g); Cholesterol 0mg; Sodium 250mg; Carbohydrate 55g (Dietary Fiber 0g); Protein 3g. **% Daily Value:** Vitamin A 0%; Vitamin C 0%; Calcium 0%; Iron 2%.

Betty's Tip This colorful cake is perfect for lots of occasions, including birthday parties, baby or bridal showers and Mother's Day. To save on last-minute preparations, make the packages the day before. Loosely cover and store at room temperature until you're ready to decorate the cake.

The perfect day—your birthday, circa 1950. Presents, balloons, your best friends and the yummiest cake imaginable.

Rainbow Angel Birthday Cake

Frosted Cupcake Cones

Prep: 20 min   ∗   Bake: 25 min per pan   ∗   Cool: 1 hr

30 TO 36 CUPCAKE CONES

1 package Betty Crocker
SuperMoist cake mix
(any flavor)

Water, oil and eggs called for
on cake mix package

30 to 36 flat-bottom ice-cream
cones

1 tub Betty Crocker Whipped
frosting (any flavor), Vanilla
Buttercream Frosting (page 236)
or Creamy Chocolate Frosting
(page 238)

Assorted candies, cookies,
miniature chocolate chips
or colored candy sprinkles,
if desired

1 Heat oven to 350°. Make cake mix as directed on package, using water, oil and eggs. Fill each cone about half full of batter. Stand cones in muffin pan.

2 Bake 20 to 25 minutes or until toothpick carefully inserted in center comes out clean. Cool completely, about 1 hour. Frost with frosting and decorate with assorted candies. Store loosely covered at room temperature.

High Altitude (3500 to 6500 feet): Make cake mix following high-altitude directions on package. Bake at 350° for 20 to 25 minutes.

1 Cupcake: Calories 160 (Calories from Fat 55); Fat 6g (Saturated 2g); Cholesterol 20mg; Sodium 140mg; Carbohydrate 25g (Dietary Fiber 0g); Protein 2g. **% Daily Value:** Vitamin A 0%; Vitamin C 0%; Calcium 0%; Iron 2%.

Betty's Tip These fun cupcakes are perfect for any kid's birthday party. Create some exciting "creatures" on the top using small cookies for bodies, mini candy-coated chocolate candies for eyes and small pieces of licorice for legs and antennae.

Frosted Cupcake Cones

Kids' Birthday Bash

No child's (or adult's, for that matter) birthday party is complete without the final touch—the cake! With cake mix, it's easy for everyone—the cake baker included—to celebrate and have a great time.

Birthday Countdown

Here are some tips to make your cake and party fun and stress free:

* **Keep it kid-friendly:** Consider the ages and individual tastes of the kids you'll be serving, and keep the menu simple for them and easy for you.

* **Set up ahead:** Do as much of the food preparation, game planning and decorating as you can ahead of time.

* **Bake before:** The day before the party, bake and frost the cake so you don't have to worry about it at the last minute.

* **Make it mini:** Instead of making one big cake, make cupcakes and get the kids involved in decorating their very own mini-cake.

* **Super-scoop it:** Cake and ice cream are a kid's favorite pair! Here's a handy do-ahead trick for serving ice cream. Up to 2 weeks before the party, line a muffin pan with paper liners. Scoop the ice cream into the muffin pan, then cover and freeze until ready to serve.

* **Set up a sundae bar:** Along with the cake, offer a make-your-own sundae bar. Set out different flavors of ice cream along with assorted toppings or sauces, candies, crushed cookies and whipped cream.

* **Supply some no-yawn crayons:** For when the troops get restless, keep a box of crayons or markers and a pad of paper nearby. Let the party-goers color and decorate their own place mats or name cards.

* **Prepare for spills:** Manage the party mess by putting a plastic drop cloth under the table to catch all of the inevitable fallen crumbs, drips and spills. Also, be sure to keep a sponge handy for quick and easy wipe-ups.

✳ Kids' Picks ✳

Looking for cake recipes with real kid appeal? Here are some of our favorites:

Cherry-Chocolate Chip Cake (page 44)

Color Vision Cake (page 80)

Frosted Cupcake Cones (page 104)

Train Cake (page 114)

Sand Castle Cake (page 118)

Lollipop Cookies (page 212)

Butterfly Cake

Prep: 20 min • Bake: 35 min • Cool: 1 hr 10 min

**2 CAKES
(6 TO 8 SERVINGS EACH)**

1 package Betty Crocker
SuperMoist cake mix
(any flavor)

Water, oil and eggs called for
on cake mix package

2 tubs Betty Crocker Whipped
fluffy white ready-to-spread
frosting or 2 recipes Creamy
White Frosting (page 234)

Colored sugars, decorating gel

Assorted candies, such as jelly
beans (cut in half), pastel mints,
miniature jawbreakers and
cherry rock candy

1 roll chewy fruit snack (from
5-ounce package) in desired color

Betty's Tip If you need only
one Butterfly Cake, wrap and
freeze one of the layers for
another use. The cake can be
kept frozen up to 4 months.

1 Heat oven to 350°. Grease bottoms only of 2 round pans, 8 or
9 x 1 1/2 inches, with shortening. Make cake mix as directed
on package, using water, oil and eggs. Pour into pans. Bake cake
as directed on package. Cool 10 minutes. Run knife around side
of pans to loosen cakes; remove from pans to wire rack. Cool
completely, about 1 hour.

2 Cut each cake layer as shown in diagram. Freeze pieces uncovered
about 1 hour for easier frosting if desired. For each cake,
cover large flat tray or piece of cardboard with plastic wrap or
aluminum foil. Arrange cake pieces on tray to form butterfly
as shown in diagram. Frost cake with 1 tub frosting, attaching
pieces with small amount of frosting. Repeat with second cake
layer and remaining tub frosting.

3 Sprinkle colored sugars over butterflies. Outline wings and bodies
with decorating gel. Decorate wings with assorted candies as
desired. Roll fruit snack into antennae. Store loosely covered at
room temperature.

High Altitude (3500 to 6500 feet): Do not use 8-inch rounds. Make cake mix
following high-altitude directions on package for 9-inch rounds.

1 Serving: Calories 500 (Calories from Fat 170); Fat 19g (Saturated 10g); Cholesterol 55mg;
Sodium 290mg; Carbohydrate 79g (Dietary Fiber 0g); Protein 3g. **% Daily Value:** Vitamin A 2%;
Vitamin C 0%; Calcium 8%; Iron 4%.

Cutting and Assembling Butterfly Cake

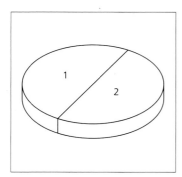

Cut cake layer in half.

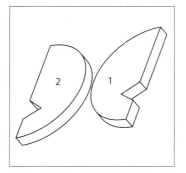

Cut notch on cut sides, slightly
below center. Arrange pieces
on tray to form wings.

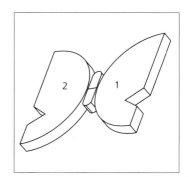

Trim 2 notched pieces and use
to form body.

Computer Cake

Prep: 30 min • Bake: about 30 min • Cool: 1 hr 10 min

24 TO 32 SERVINGS

2 packages Betty Crocker
SuperMoist cake mix
(any flavor)

Water, oil and eggs called for
on cake mix package

2 tubs Betty Crocker Rich &
Creamy vanilla ready-to-spread
frosting or 2 recipes Vanilla
Buttercream Frosting (page 236)

7 drops blue food color

Licorice candies in desired color

Pastel mint candies

Betty's Tip If you don't care
for mints, you can use jelly
beans or almonds to form keys
on the keyboard.

1 Heat oven to 350°. Grease bottoms only of 2 rectangular pans,
13 x 9 x 2 inches, with shortening. Make cake mixes as directed on
package, using water, oil and eggs. Pour half the batter into each
pan. Bake cakes as directed on package for 13 x 9-inch rectangle.
Cool 10 minutes. Run knife around sides of pans to loosen cakes;
remove from pans to wire rack. Cool completely, about 1 hour.

2 Leave 1 cake layer whole for screen. Cut second cake layer as
shown in diagram. Freeze cake pieces about 1 hour for easier
frosting if desired. Reserve 3/4 cup frosting. Cover large flat tray
or piece of cardboard with plastic wrap or aluminum foil. Arrange
cake pieces on tray to form computer as shown in diagram. Frost
cake, attaching pieces with small amount of frosting.

3 Drop 1 drop food color about 3 inches in from each corner of the
screen area. Blend into frosting with spatula to within 1 inch
of edges to make screen. Outline with licorice. Arrange mint
candies on keyboard. Trim mouse to desired shape. Frost with
1/2 cup reserved frosting. Outline mouse keys with licorice.

4 Place mouse next to keyboard. Tint remaining frosting with
3 drops blue food color. Place frosting in decorating bag with
writing tip. Pipe desired message on screen. Pipe cord from
mouse to keyboard. Store loosely covered at room temperature.

High Altitude (3500 to 6500 feet): Make cake mix following high-altitude
directions on package for 13 x 9-inch rectangle.

1 Serving: Calories 435 (Calories from Fat 155); Fat 17g (Saturated 8g); Cholesterol 55mg; Sodium
340mg; Carbohydrate 66g (Dietary Fiber 0g); Protein 4g. **% Daily Value:** Vitamin A 2%; Vitamin C
0%; Calcium 4%; Iron 8%.

Cutting and Assembling Computer Cake

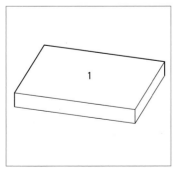

Leave first layer whole for
screen.

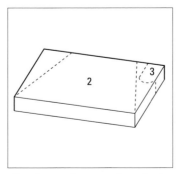

Cut diagonal pieces from both
sides of second cake layer to
form keyboard; cut mouse.

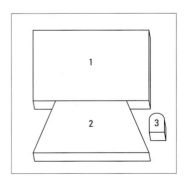

Arrange uncut cake layer above
cut cake. Place mouse next to
keyboard.

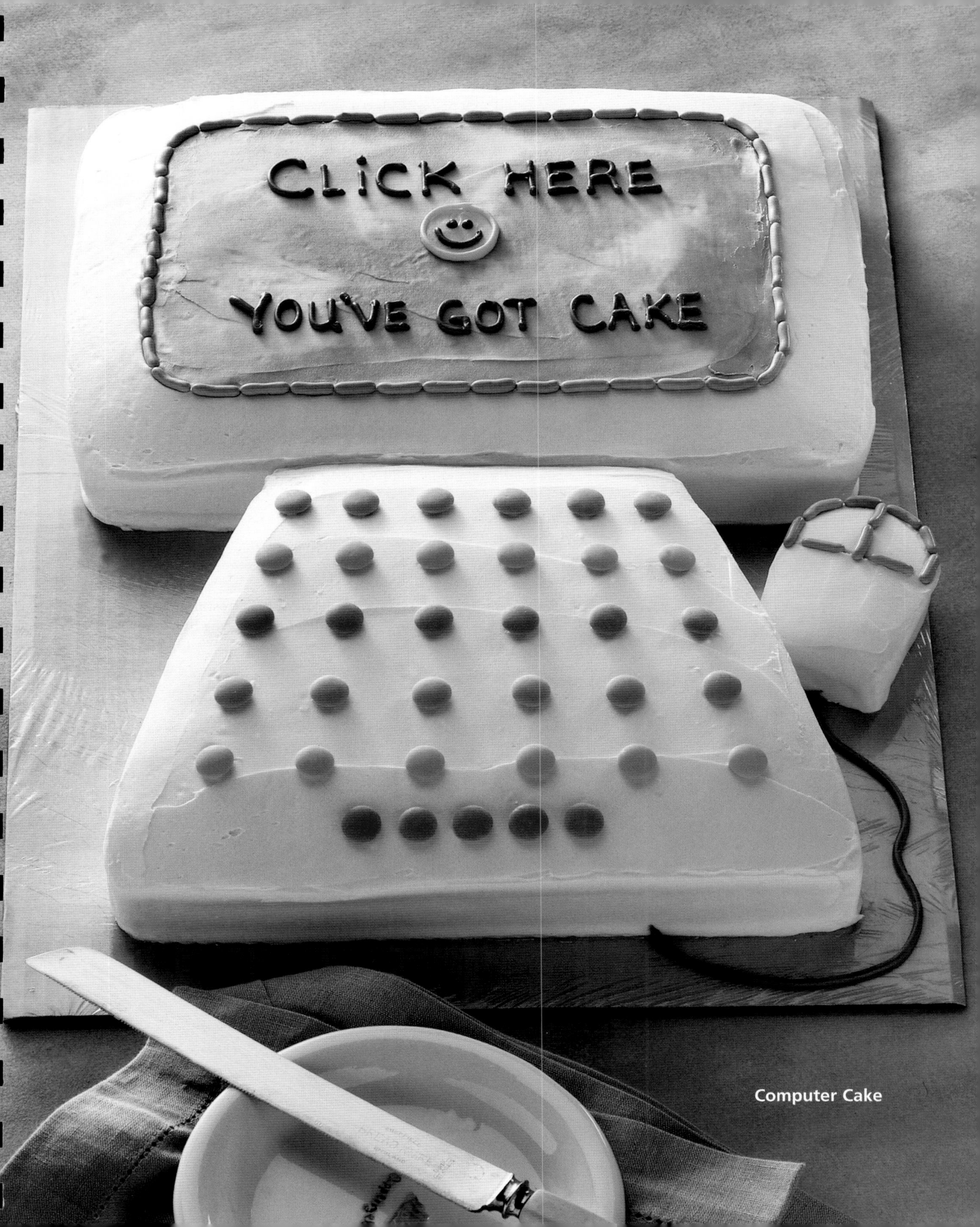

CLICK HERE
☺
YOU'VE GOT CAKE

Computer Cake

Mini Cupcake Mortarboards

Prep: 30 min · Bake: 20 min per pan · Cool: 30 min

60 CUPCAKES

1 package Betty Crocker
SuperMoist cake mix
(any flavor)

Water, oil and eggs called for
on cake mix package

1 package (4.5 ounces) chewy
fruit snack in 3-foot rolls (any
flavor) or shoestring licorice

1 tub Betty Crocker Rich &
Creamy vanilla ready-to-spread
frosting or Vanilla Buttercream
Frosting (page 236)

60 square shortbread cookies
(from two 10-ounce packages)

60 candy-coated chocolate or
fruit-flavored candies

1 Heat oven to 350°. Line 24 mini muffin cups, 1 3/4 x 1 inch,
with mini paper baking cups. Make cake mix as directed on
package, using water, oil and eggs. Fill cups 2/3 full (about
1 rounded tablespoon each). Refrigerate remaining batter.

2 Bake 15 to 20 minutes or until toothpick inserted in center of
cupcake comes out clean. Remove from pan to wire rack. Cool
completely, about 30 minutes. Repeat with remaining batter.
(Leave paper baking cups on cupcakes so mortarboards are
quicker and easier to make and more portable for serving.)

3 To make tassels, cut sixty 2 1/2-inch lengths from fruit snack
rolls. Cut each length into several strips up to 1/2 inch from
one end. Roll uncut end between fingertips to make fringes on
ends of tassels. Or cut several pieces of shoestring licorice
into 2 1/2-inch lengths.

4 Frost bottoms of cookies. Place 1 candy on center of bottom of
each cookie. Turn cupcakes upside down so bottom side is up.
For each mortarboard, place small dollop of frosting on bottom
of cupcake; top with cookie. Press uncut end of fruit snack or
3 or 4 pieces of licorice into frosted cookie next to candy.
Store loosely covered.

High Altitude (3500 to 6500 feet): Make cake mix following high-altitude
directions on package for cupcakes. Fill cups 1/2 full.

1 Cupcake: Calories 140 (Calories from Fat 55); Fat 6g (Saturated 2g); Cholesterol 15mg; Sodium
110mg; Carbohydrate 20g (Dietary Fiber 0g); Protein 1g. **% Daily Value:** Vitamin A 0%; Vitamin C
0%; Calcium 0%; Iron 2%.

Betty's Tip Share these cupcakes with family and friends of your
graduate, using paper baking cups that match school or class colors.
You can even tint the frosting with food color to match the baking cups.

Mini Cupcake Mortarboards

Housewarming Cake

Prep: 25 min   •   Bake: about 30 min   •   Cool: 1 hr

12 TO 16 SERVINGS

1 package Betty Crocker
SuperMoist cake mix
(any flavor)

Water, oil and eggs called for
on cake mix package

1 tub Betty Crocker Rich &
Creamy vanilla ready-to-spread
frosting or Vanilla Buttercream
Frosting (page 236)

Black shoestring licorice

Assorted candies and cookies

5 drops food color (any color)

Decorating gel

1   Heat oven to 350°. Grease bottom only of rectangular pan, 13 x 9 x 2 inches, with shortening; lightly flour. Make cake mix as directed on package, using water, oil and eggs. Pour into pan.

2   Bake cake as directed on package for 13 x 9-inch rectangle. Cool 10 minutes. Run knife around side of pan to loosen cake; remove from pan to wire rack. Cool completely, about 1 hour.

3   Cover large flat tray or piece of cardboard with plastic wrap or aluminum foil. Place cake on tray. Reserve 2 tablespoons frosting. Frost side and top of cake with remaining frosting. Draw outline of door and make bricks with a toothpick or knife.

4   Press shoestring licorice into frosting to outline door frame. Decorate with candies and cookies as desired. Tint reserved frosting with food color. Place in decorating bag with round writing tip. Pipe on house number and mailbox. Write new neighbor's name with decorating gel. Store loosely covered at room temperature.

High Altitude (3500 to 6500 feet): Make cake mix following high-altitude directions on package for 13 x 9-inch rectangle.

1 Serving: Calories 420 (Calories from Fat 115); Fat 13g (Saturated 6g); Cholesterol 45mg; Sodium 260mg; Carbohydrate 52g (Dietary Fiber 0g); Protein 3g. **% Daily Value:** Vitamin A 2%; Vitamin C 0%; Calcium 2%; Iron 2%.

Betty's Tip   Greeting your new neighbors? Why not bake this cake for them as a welcome to the neighborhood? You'll make new friends instantly. Write your new neighbor's name on the house with decorating gel.

Sailboat Cake

Prep: 20 min ✳ Bake: about 30 min ✳ Cool: 1 hr 10 min

12 TO 16 SERVINGS

1 package Betty Crocker
SuperMoist cake mix
(any flavor)

Water, oil and eggs called for
on cake mix package

1 tub Betty Crocker Whipped
fluffy white ready-to-spread
frosting or Creamy White
Frosting (page 234)

1 tablespoon baking cocoa

Betty's Tip Add portholes to
the hull of your sailboat with
colored ring-shaped candies.

1 Heat oven to 350°. Grease bottom only of rectangular pan,
   13 x 9 x 2 inches, with shortening. Make cake mix as directed on
   package, using water, oil and eggs. Pour into pan. Bake cake as
   directed on package for 13 x 9-inch rectangle. Cool 10 minutes.
   Run knife around side of pan to loosen cake; remove from pan to
   wire rack. Cool completely, about 1 hour.

2 Cut cake as shown in diagram. Freeze pieces uncovered about
   1 hour for easier frosting if desired. Reserve 1 cup frosting.
   Cover large flat tray or piece of cardboard with plastic wrap or
   aluminum foil. Arrange cake pieces on tray to form sailboat as
   shown in diagram, leaving space between sails for mast. Frost
   sails with remaining frosting.

3 Gently fold cocoa into reserved frosting until blended. Frost hull
   of sailboat with cocoa frosting. Roll up aluminum foil for mast;
   place between sails. Store loosely covered at room temperature.

High Altitude (3500 to 6500 feet): Make cake mix following high-altitude
directions on package for 13 x 9-inch rectangle.

1 Serving: Calories 370 (Calories from Fat 135); Fat 15g (Saturated 6g); Cholesterol 55mg; Sodium
290mg; Carbohydrate 56g (Dietary Fiber 0g); Protein 3g. **% Daily Value:** Vitamin A 2%; Vitamin C
0%; Calcium 8%; Iron 4%.

Cutting and Assembling Sailboat Cake

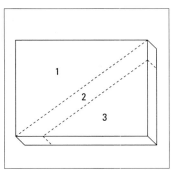

Cut cake diagonally into
3 pieces.

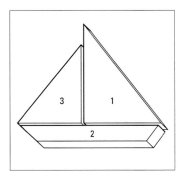

Arrange pieces to form sailboat,
leaving space between sails
for mast.

Train Cake

Prep: 45 min * Bake: 40 min * Cool: 1 hr 10 min

12 TO 16 SERVINGS

1 package Betty Crocker
SuperMoist chocolate fudge
cake mix

1 1/3 cups water

1/2 cup vegetable oil

3 eggs

1 tub Betty Crocker Rich &
Creamy chocolate ready-to-
spread frosting or Creamy
Chocolate Frosting (page 238)

1 flat-bottom ice-cream cone

8 rainbow-colored vanilla
wafer cookies

Black licorice twists

Assorted candies, cookies,
crackers, cereal and popcorn,
if desired

1 tub Betty Crocker Rich &
Creamy vanilla ready-to-spread
frosting or Vanilla Buttercream
Frosting (page 236)

Food colors, if desired

1 Heat oven to 350°. Grease bottoms and sides of 2 loaf pans,
9 x 5 x 3 inches, with shortening. Make cake mix as directed
on package, using water, oil and eggs. Pour batter into pans.

2 Bake 35 to 40 minutes or until toothpick inserted in center
comes out clean. Cool 10 minutes. Run knife around sides of
pans to loosen cakes; remove from pans to wire rack. Cool
completely, about 1 hour.

3 Cut first cake as shown in diagram to make engine, being careful
not to cut all the way through piece 1 when removing piece 2.
Cut second cake into 4 equal pieces to make cars as shown in
diagram. Trim pieces 3 and 5 flat on top if desired. Freeze pieces
uncovered about 1 hour for easier frosting if desired.

4 Cover large flat rectangular tray or piece of cardboard with plastic
wrap or aluminum foil. Place piece 1 on tray for engine, stacking
piece 2 on top for engine house as shown in diagram. Frost
with chocolate frosting. Place ice-cream cone on front of engine
house. Place wafer cookies on side of engine for wheels. Cut
licorice twists into pieces; place on front of engine for cow-catcher.
Decorate with candies.

5 Place pieces 3, 4 and 5 on tray for cars. Frost with vanilla frosting
(tinted with food colors if desired). Decorate with candies.

6 Place piece 6 on tray for caboose. Trim to make shorter and
rounded on top if desired. Frost with vanilla frosting (tinted with
food colors if desired). Decorate with candies. Connect cars
together with pieces of licorice twists if desired. Store loosely
covered at room temperature.

High Altitude (3500 to 6500 feet): Heat oven to 375°. Add 2 tablespoons
all-purpose flour to dry cake mix. Increase water to 1 1/2 cups. Decrease oil to
1 tablespoon. Beat cake mix on low speed 30 seconds, then beat on medium
speed 4 minutes. Bake 40 to 45 minutes.

1 Serving: Calories 560 (Calories from Fat 215); Fat 24g (Saturated 14g); Cholesterol 55mg; Sodium
340mg; Carbohydrate 87g (Dietary Fiber 2g); Protein 4g. **% Daily Value:** Vitamin A 2%; Vitamin C
0%; Calcium 6%; Iron 8%.

Betty's Tip Instead of baking the cake in two large loaves, you can use
one 9-inch loaf pan and four miniature loaf pans, 4 1/2 x 2 3/4 x 1 1/4
inches each. Pour 1/2 cup batter into each mini loaf pan. Pour remaining
batter into 9-inch loaf pan. Bake mini loaf pans 20 to 25 minutes; 9-inch
loaf 35 to 40 minutes.

Cutting and Assembling Train Cake

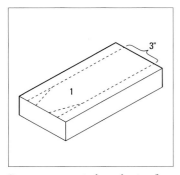

Cut narrow strip lengthwise from each side of one loaf. Trim front corners on the diagonal.

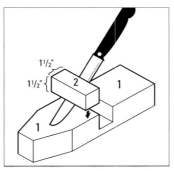

Being careful not to cut all the way through piece 1, remove a section from piece 1 that is 1 1/2 inches wide and 1 1/2 inches thick. Place piece 2 on top of piece 1 for engine house.

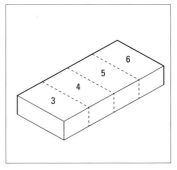

Cut second loaf crosswise into fourths.

Train Cake

Ballet Slippers Cake

Prep: 30 min * Bake: 33 min * Cool: 1 hr 10 min

12 TO 16 SERVINGS

1 package Betty Crocker
SuperMoist white cake mix

1 1/4 cups water

1/3 cup vegetable oil

3 egg whites

2 tubs Betty Crocker Rich &
Creamy vanilla ready-to-spread
frosting or 2 recipes Vanilla
Buttercream Frosting (page 236)

3 drops red food color

Betty's Tip To give the frosting a fabric-like appearance,
carefully cover frosting with a
paper towel and gently pat;
remove towel. It's easier to do
this before piping the beaded
border and bow. For an extra-
special touch, look for paper
towels with an imprinted
design, such as circles or swirls.
For ballet laces, attach wide,
pink ribbon to sides of slippers.

1 Heat oven to 350°. Grease bottom only of rectangular pan,
   13 x 9 x 2 inches, with shortening. Make cake mix as directed
   on package, using water, oil and egg whites. Pour into pan.

2 Bake 28 to 33 minutes or until toothpick inserted in center comes out
   clean. Cool 10 minutes. Run knife around sides of pan to loosen cake;
   remove from pan to wire rack. Cool completely, about 1 hour.

3 Cut cake as shown in diagram. Freeze pieces uncovered about
   1 hour for easier frosting if desired. Reserve 1 cup frosting.
   Tint remaining frosting with food color; reserve 1/2 cup.

4 Cover large flat tray or piece of cardboard with plastic wrap or aluminum foil. Arrange cake pieces on tray as shown in diagram. Trim
   pieces to form slippers. Frost sides of both slippers with pink frosting. Frost top of each slipper about 3 inches from the edge for the
   toes, tapering to about 1 inch around the outside edge for the rest
   of the slipper. Frost the center oval with reserved white frosting.

5 Place reserved 1/2 cup pink frosting in decorating bag with writing
   tip. Pipe a small beaded border where pink frosting edge meets
   white edge. Pipe a small bow at each toe with pink or white frosting.
   Store loosely covered at room temperature.

High Altitude (3500 to 6500 feet): Make cake mix following high-altitude directions
on package for 13 x 9-inch rectangle.

1 Serving: Calories 555 (Calories from Fat 190); Fat 21g (Saturated 12g); Cholesterol 5mg; Sodium
310mg; Carbohydrate 89g (Dietary Fiber 0g); Protein 3g. **% Daily Value:** Vitamin A 0%; Vitamin C
0%; Calcium 8%; Iron 4%.

Cutting and Assembling Ballet Slippers Cake

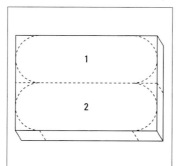

Cut cake lengthwise in half.
Trim corners to round.

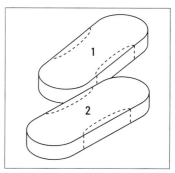

Arrange cake pieces on tray.
Trim pieces to form slippers.

Ballet Slippers Cake

Sand Castle Cake

Prep: 30 min * Bake: about 30 min * Cool: 1 hr 10 min

12 TO 16 SERVINGS

1 package Betty Crocker SuperMoist cake mix (any flavor)

Water, oil and eggs called for on cake mix package

1 cup packed brown sugar

1/2 cup granulated sugar

1/2 cup graham cracker crumbs

3 tubs Betty Crocker Rich & Creamy vanilla ready-to-spread frosting or 3 recipes Vanilla Buttercream Frosting (page 236)

2 sugar-style ice-cream cones with pointed ends

20 miniature butter cookies (from 10-ounce package)

28 small gumdrops

14 flat round candies

1 graham cracker square

1 bar (1.65 ounces) milk chocolate candy

Gummy fish candies or sugar-coated fish candies, if desired

1 Heat oven to 350°. Grease bottom only of rectangular pan, 13 x 9 x 2 inches, with shortening. Make cake mix as directed on package, using water, oil and eggs. Bake cake as directed on package. Cool 10 minutes. Run knife around sides of pan to loosen cake; remove from pan to wire rack. Cool completely, about 1 hour.

2 Mix brown sugar, granulated sugar and cracker crumbs in medium bowl; cover and set aside. Cut cake as shown in diagram. Freeze pieces uncovered about 1 hour for easier frosting if desired.

3 Cover large flat tray or piece of cardboard with blue plastic wrap, blue foil or aluminum foil. Arrange cake pieces on tray as shown in diagram. Frost cake, attaching pieces with small amount of frosting. Sprinkle entire cake with about 1 cup brown sugar mixture to coat.

4 Spread outside of ice-cream cones with thin layer of frosting. (Place cones over fingers to frost.) Roll cones in brown sugar mixture to coat; place upside down on top of towers. Arrange cookies around base of cones. Arrange gumdrops along top edges of castle. Press flat candies into side of castle.

5 Break graham cracker in half. Place one half in center of lower portion of castle to form door. Break off two pieces of candy bar. Place one piece on each side of graham cracker to resemble opened doors. Reserve remaining candy bar for the drawbridge.

6 Spread remaining frosting on covered tray in front of castle. Sprinkle with remaining brown sugar mixture to create a beach, leaving space between the castle and the sand for a moat. Place drawbridge across, and arrange fish in moat. Store loosely covered at room temperature.

High Altitude (3500 to 6500 feet): Make cake mix following high-altitude directions on package for 13 x 9-inch rectangle.

1 Serving: Calories 660 (Calories from Fat 225); Fat 25g (Saturated 14g); Cholesterol 55mg; Sodium 370mg; Carbohydrate 106g (Dietary Fiber 2g); Protein 4g. **% Daily Value:** Vitamin A 2%; Vitamin C 0%; Calcium 4%; Iron 6%.

Betty's Tip Make flags for your castle with chewy fruit snack rolls. Cut fruit snack into triangle shapes, and wrap around toothpicks. Insert 1 flag in tip of each cone (cut off tip of cone if necessary). If blue plastic wrap or foil is unavailable, create the moat using canned blue decorating frosting or a tube of decorating gel.

Cutting and Assembling Sand Castle Cake

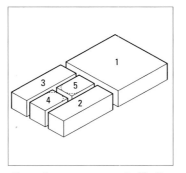

Cut cake crosswise in half. Cut 1 half into 3 equal pieces. Cut center piece in half to make 2 small squares. Trim squares, using a sharp knife, to round the cut edges. (These pieces will be the tower bases.)

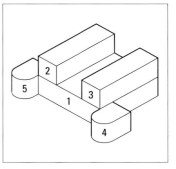

Place piece 1 on center of tray. Place pieces 2 and 3 on top of piece 1. Place pieces 4 and 5 at front corners of cake so they extend beyond front edge.

Sand Castle Cake

Fish Cake

Prep: 25 min * Bake: 35 min * Cool: 1 hr 10 min

12 TO 16 SERVINGS

1 package Betty Crocker SuperMoist lemon cake mix

1 1/4 cups water

1/3 cup vegetable oil

3 eggs

1 tub Betty Crocker Rich & Creamy lemon ready-to-spread frosting or Lemon Buttercream Frosting (page 236)

Blue, red and yellow food color

1 round mint candy

Betty's Tip Anglers and tropical fish lovers will be hooked on this cake! For a fun presentation, cover the board with blue plastic wrap and decorate with green decorating gel or frosting for seaweed. Add sea creatures and shells as desired.

1 Heat oven to 350°. Grease bottom only of rectangular pan, 13 x 9 x 2 inches, with shortening. Make cake mix as directed on package, using water, oil and eggs. Pour into pan.

2 Bake 30 to 35 minutes or until toothpick inserted in center comes out clean. Cool 10 minutes. Run knife around side of pan to loosen cake; remove from pan to wire rack. Cool completely, about 1 hour.

3 Cut cake as shown in diagram. Freeze pieces uncovered about 1 hour for easier frosting if desired. Cover large flat tray or piece of cardboard with plastic wrap or aluminum foil. Arrange cake pieces on tray to form fish as shown in diagram. Frost cake with frosting, attaching pieces with small amount of frosting.

4 To make purple color, mix 5 drops blue food color and 5 drops red food color in small bowl. Drop purple color along top of fish. Drop 6 drops blue along center and 6 drops yellow along bottom. Starting from top edge of fish, blend colors into frosting with small spatula or spoon, working purple down into blue and blue down into yellow. Use back of spoon to form scales. Define lips with edge of spatula. Mark tail and fins with fork. Use candy for eye. Store loosely covered at room temperature.

High Altitude (3500 to 6500 feet): Make cake mix following high-altitude directions on package for 13 x 9-inch rectangle.

1 Serving: Calories 410 (Calories from Fat 145); Fat 16g (Saturated 7g); Cholesterol 55mg; Sodium 290mg; Carbohydrate 63g (Dietary Fiber 0g); Protein 3g. **% Daily Value:** Vitamin A 2%; Vitamin C 0%; Calcium 8%; Iron 4%.

. . . .

Cutting and Assembling Fish Cake

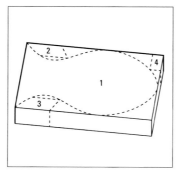

Cut cake to form body, fins and mouth of fish.

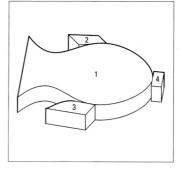

Arrange pieces on tray to form fish.

. . . .

Fish Cake

4
Heavenly
Holidays

Gingerbread Cake Cottage (page 140) with Caramel Frosting (page 240) and Spiced Pumpkin Praline Roll (page 136)

Chocolate Sweetheart Cake

Prep: 15 min * Bake: 35 min * Cool: 1 hr 10 min

12 TO 16 SERVINGS

1 package Betty Crocker SuperMoist devil's food cake mix

1 1/3 cups water

1/2 cup vegetable oil

3 eggs

1 tub Betty Crocker Whipped chocolate ready-to-spread frosting or Creamy Chocolate Frosting (page 238)

Betty's Tip Surprise your valentine with this sweetheart cake. For a truly special presentation, garnish with fresh small strawberries or raspberries and curls of white chocolate. Or for real chocolate lovers, press miniature chocolate chips onto the side of the frosted cake.

1 Heat oven to 350°. Grease bottom only of 1 round pan, 8 x 1 1/2 inches, and 1 square pan, 8 x 8 x 2 inches, with shortening. Make cake mix as directed on package, using water, oil and eggs. Pour into pans.

2 Bake 30 to 35 minutes or until toothpick inserted in center comes out clean. Cool 10 minutes. Run knife around sides of pans to loosen cakes; remove from pans to wire rack. Cool completely, about 1 hour.

3 Cut round layer in half as shown in diagram. Freeze uncovered about 1 hour for easier frosting if desired. Arrange pieces on serving platter to form heart as shown in diagram. Frost cake with frosting, attaching pieces with small amount of frosting. Store loosely covered at room temperature.

High Altitude (3500 to 6500 feet): Heat oven to 375°. Make cake mix following high-altitude directions on package. Bake 33 to 38 minutes.

1 Serving: Calories 395 (Calories from Fat 180); Fat 20g (Saturated 8g); Cholesterol 55mg; Sodium 340mg; Carbohydrate 52g (Dietary Fiber 2g); Protein 4g. **% Daily Value:** Vitamin A 2%; Vitamin C 0%; Calcium 4%; Iron 10%.

Cutting and Assembling Chocolate Sweetheart Cake

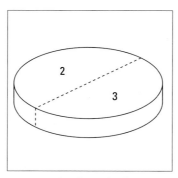

Cut round cake in half.

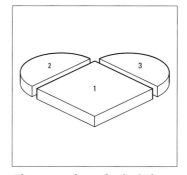

Place cut edges of cake halves against sides of square cake to form heart.

Chocolate Sweetheart Cake

Easter Bunny Cake

Prep: 30 min * Bake: 30 min * Cool: 1 hr 10 min

8 SERVINGS

1 package Betty Crocker
SuperMoist carrot cake mix

1 cup water

1/2 cup vegetable oil

3 eggs

1 tub Betty Crocker Whipped
cream cheese or white ready-
to-spread frosting or Whipped
Cream Cheese Frosting
(page 236)

1 cup flaked or shredded
coconut

Pink construction paper

Jelly beans or small gumdrops

Betty's Tip Surround your bunny
cake with green grass. To make
grass, shake 1 cup coconut and 3
drops green food color in tightly
covered jar until evenly tinted.

1 Heat oven to 350°. Grease bottoms only of 2 round pans, 8 or
9 x 1 1/2 inches, with shortening. Make cake mix as directed
on package, using water, oil and eggs. Pour into pans.

2 Bake 8-inch rounds 25 to 30 minutes, 9-inch rounds 22 to 27
minutes, or until toothpick inserted in center comes out clean.
Cool 10 minutes. Run knife around side of pans to loosen cakes;
remove from pans to wire rack. Cool completely, about 1 hour.

3 Reserve 1 cake layer for another use or to make a second bunny.
Cut 1 cake layer in half as shown in diagram. Freeze pieces uncovered about 1 hour for easier frosting if desired. Cover large flat
tray or piece of cardboard with aluminum foil. Put halves together
with frosting to form body. Place rounded side up on tray.

4 Cut out a piece about one-third of the way up one edge of body
to form tail as shown in diagram. Attach tail with toothpick.
Frost bunny with remaining frosting, rounding out head and body.
Sprinkle with coconut. Cut ears from construction paper; press
into head. Use jelly beans for eyes and nose. Store loosely
covered at room temperature.

High Altitude (3500 to 6500 feet): Do not use 8-inch rounds. Make cake mix following high-altitude directions on package for 9-inch rounds.

1 Serving: Calories 330 (Calories from Fat 145); Fat 15g (Saturated 5g); Cholesterol 45mg; Sodium
270mg; Carbohydrate 43g (Dietary Fiber 0g); Protein 3g. **% Daily Value:** Vitamin A 4%; Vitamin C
0%; Calcium 6%; Iron 4%.

Cutting and Assembling Easter Bunny Cake

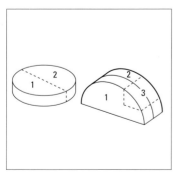

Cut cake layer in half. Put
halves together to form body.
Cut out piece to form tail.

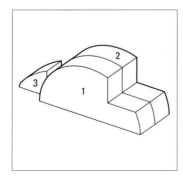

Attach tail with toothpick.

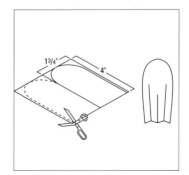

Cut 4 x 1 3/4-inch ears from
pink construction paper.
Fold as shown.

Easter Bunny Cake

Easter Basket Cake

Prep: 30 min * Bake: 35 min * Cool: 1 hr 10 min

12 TO 16 SERVINGS

1 package Betty Crocker SuperMoist yellow cake mix

1 1/4 cups water

1/3 cup vegetable oil

3 eggs

1 tub Betty Crocker Rich & Creamy chocolate ready-to-spread frosting or Creamy Chocolate Frosting (page 238)

1 cup shredded coconut

3 or 4 drops green food color

Candy Easter eggs or jelly beans

1 Heat oven to 350°. Grease bottoms only of 2 round pans, 8 or 9 x 1 1/2 inches, with shortening. Make cake mix as directed on package, using water, oil and eggs. Pour into pans.

2 Bake 8-inch rounds 30 to 35 minutes, 9-inch rounds 25 to 30 minutes, or until toothpick inserted in center comes out clean. Cool 10 minutes. Run knife around side of pans to loosen cakes; remove from pans to wire rack. Cool completely, about 1 hour.

3 Fill layers and frost side of cake with frosting. Spread thin layer of frosting on top of cake. Make a basket-weave pattern in frosting on side of cake by drawing inch-long horizontal and vertical lines with tines of fork.

4 Shake coconut and food color in tightly covered jar until coconut is evenly tinted; sprinkle over top of cake, leaving a 1-inch border around outside edge. Place candy eggs on coconut. Store loosely covered at room temperature.

High Altitude (3500 to 6500 feet): Do not use 8-inch rounds. Make cake mix following high-altitude directions on package for 9-inch rounds.

1 Serving: Calories 465 (Calories from Fat 205); Fat 23g (Saturated 12g); Cholesterol 55mg; Sodium 340mg; Carbohydrate 62g (Dietary Fiber 1g); Protein 4g. **% Daily Value:** Vitamin A 2%; Vitamin C 0%; Calcium 6%; Iron 6%.

Betty's Tip Make decorating the cake a little easier by leaving a smooth finish on the frosting instead of the basket-weave pattern. Your results will be equally delicious.

What better way to announce "Springtime's here!" in 1957 than with a fluffy coconut-frosted cake?

May Day Baskets

Prep: 20 min * Bake: 23 min per pan * Cool: 40 min

24 CUPCAKES

1 package Betty Crocker SuperMoist yellow cake mix

1 1/4 cups water

1/3 cup vegetable oil

3 eggs

1 tub Betty Crocker Rich & Creamy ready-to-spread frosting (any flavor) or Vanilla Buttercream Frosting (page 236)

Shoestring licorice

Assorted small candies or jelly beans

1 Heat oven to 350°. Grease bottoms only of 24 medium muffin cups, 2 1/2 x 1 1/4 inches, with shortening, or line with paper baking cups. Make cake mix as directed on package, using water, oil and eggs. Fill cups 2/3 full.

2 Bake 18 to 23 minutes or until toothpick inserted in center comes out clean. Cool 10 minutes. Remove from pan to wire rack. Cool completely, about 30 minutes.

3 Spread frosting over tops of cupcakes. Make handles with licorice. Decorate with candies. Store loosely covered at room temperature.

High Altitude (3500 to 6500 feet): Make cake mix following high-altitude directions on package for cupcakes. Makes 30 cupcakes.

1 Cupcake: Calories 240 (Calories from Fat 80); Fat 9g (Saturated 4g); Cholesterol 25mg; Sodium 170mg; Carbohydrate 38g (Dietary Fiber 0g); Protein 2g. **% Daily Value:** Vitamin A 2%; Vitamin C 0%; Calcium 2%; Iron 2%.

Betty's Tip It's easy to make these baskets look springtime special. Tint the frosting with a few drops of food color. Pick out fun foil or decorated muffin cup liners at your supermarket or paper supply store.

Photo on page 231

Flag Day Cake

Prep: 15 min * Bake: 35 min * Cool: 1 hr 10 min

15 SERVINGS

1 package Betty Crocker
SuperMoist yellow cake mix

1 1/4 cups water

1/3 cup vegetable oil

3 eggs

1 tub Betty Crocker Rich &
Creamy or Whipped vanilla
ready-to-spread frosting or
Vanilla Buttercream Frosting
(page 236)

1/3 cup blueberries

1 pint (2 cups) strawberries,
stems removed and
strawberries cut in half

1 Heat oven to 350°. Grease bottom only of rectangular pan,
13 x 9 x 2 inches, with shortening. Make cake mix as directed
on package, using water, oil and eggs. Pour into pan.

2 Bake 30 to 35 minutes or until toothpick inserted in center
comes out clean. Cool 10 minutes. Run knife around sides of
pan to loosen cake; remove from pan to wire rack. Cool completely, about 1 hour.

3 Frost top and sides of cake with frosting. For flag design, arrange
blueberries on upper left corner of frosted cake to create stars;
arrange strawberries in rows over frosted cake to create stripes.
Serve immediately. Store covered in refrigerator.

High Altitude (3500 to 6500 feet): Make cake mix following high-altitude
directions on package for 13 x 9-inch rectangle.

1 Serving: Calories 425 (Calories from Fat 155); Fat 17g (Saturated 7g); Cholesterol 55mg; Sodium
320mg; Carbohydrate 65g (Dietary Fiber 1g); Protein 4g. **% Daily Value:** Vitamin A 2%; Vitamin C
4%; Calcium 6%; Iron 4%.

Betty's Tip This patriotic cake is so simple and so versatile! Feel free
to use any flavor of cake mix in this recipe—just follow the package
directions. To make this cake easy to take, you can frost and decorate
it right in the pan.

Flag Day Cake

Halloween Black Cat Cake

Prep: 20 min • Bake: 35 min • Cool: 1 hr 10 min

12 TO 16 SERVINGS

1 package Betty Crocker SuperMoist devil's food cake mix

1 1/3 cups water

1/2 cup vegetable oil

3 eggs

1 1/2 tubs Betty Crocker Rich & Creamy chocolate ready-to-spread frosting or Creamy Chocolate Frosting (page 238)

2 large yellow gumdrops

1 small black gumdrop

Black shoestring licorice

Betty's Tip Can't find black shoestring licorice? Use black decorating gel instead; you can find it near the cake and frosting items in your supermarket.

1 Heat oven to 350°. Grease bottoms only of 2 round pans, 8 or 9 x 1 1/2 inches, with shortening. Make cake mix as directed on package, using water, oil and eggs. Pour into pans.

2 Bake 8-inch rounds 30 to 35 minutes, 9-inch rounds 25 to 30 minutes, or until toothpick inserted in center comes out clean. Cool 10 minutes. Run knife around side of pans to loosen cakes; remove from pans to wire rack. Cool completely, about 1 hour.

3 Leave 1 cake layer whole for body. Cut second cake layer as shown in diagram. Freeze pieces uncovered about 1 hour for easier frosting if desired. Cover large flat tray or piece of cardboard with aluminum foil. Arrange uncut layer and the pieces on tray to form cat as shown in diagram. Frost cake with frosting, attaching pieces with small amount of frosting. Cut slice off bottom of each yellow gumdrop; use slices for eyes. Use black gumdrop for nose and shoestring licorice for whiskers, lines on eyes and to outline paws. Store loosely covered at room temperature.

High Altitude (3500 to 6500 feet): Do not use 8-inch rounds. Make cake mix following high-altitude directions on package for 9-inch rounds.

1 Serving: Calories 460 (Calories from Fat 205); Fat 23g (Saturated 11g); Cholesterol 55mg; Sodium 340mg; Carbohydrate 63g (Dietary Fiber 2g); Protein 4g. **% Daily Value:** Vitamin A 2%; Vitamin C 0%; Calcium 4%; Iron 10%.

Photo on page 239

Cutting and Assembling Halloween Black Cat Cake

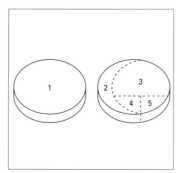

Leave first cake layer whole for body. Cut second layer to form head, ears and tail of cat.

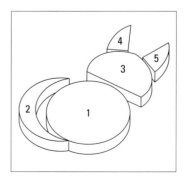

Arrange cake pieces around uncut layer to form cat.

Spiderweb Cupcakes

Prep: 20 min * Bake: 23 min per pan * Cool: 40 min

24 CUPCAKES

1 package Betty Crocker SuperMoist devil's food cake mix

1 1/3 cups water

1/2 cup vegetable oil

3 eggs

1 tub Betty Crocker Rich & Creamy vanilla ready-to-spread frosting or Vanilla Buttercream Frosting (page 236)

3 drops red food color

4 or 5 drops yellow food color

1 tube black or white decorating gel

48 large black gumdrops

1 Heat oven to 350°. Grease bottoms only of 24 medium muffin cups, 2 1/2 x 1 1/4 inches, with shortening, or line with paper baking cups. Make cake mix as directed on package, using water, oil and eggs. Fill cups 2/3 full.

2 Bake 18 to 23 minutes or until toothpick inserted in center comes out clean. Cool 10 minutes. Remove from pan to wire rack. Cool completely, about 30 minutes.

3 Tint frosting with red and yellow food colors to make orange frosting. Spread frosting over tops of cupcakes.

4 Squeeze circles of decorating gel on each cupcake; pull knife through gel from center outward to make web. To make each spider, roll out 1 gumdrop and cut out 8 strips for legs; place another gumdrop on top. Place spider on cupcake. Store loosely covered at room temperature.

High Altitude (3500 to 6500 feet): Make cake mix following high-altitude directions on package for cupcakes. Makes 30 cupcakes.

1 Cupcake: Calories 265 (Calories from Fat 70); Fat 8g (Saturated 3g); Cholesterol 15mg; Sodium 130mg; Carbohydrate 47g (Dietary Fiber 0g); Protein 1g. **% Daily Value:** Vitamin A 0%; Vitamin C 0%; Calcium 2%; Iron 10%.

Holly Wreath Cupcakes: Use green-tinted frosting instead of orange. Squeeze circles of red decorating gel on each cupcake to make wreath, and decorate with small, red, cinnamon candy "berries."

Betty's Tip Get the kids to help! Kids can make spider legs without cutting gumdrops by pinching and gently rolling gumdrops back and forth between their fingertips into long thin strips. The more they roll them, the stickier the gumdrops will become. Have the kids dip rolled gumdrops in sugar as needed to make them less sticky.

Photo on page 135

In 1953, there were a lot more treats than tricks with a box of cake mix and Mom's special touch.

Jack-o'-Lantern Cake

Prep: 30 min • Bake: 1 hr 15 min per cake • Cool: 1 hr 15 min per cake

24 SERVINGS

2 packages Betty Crocker SuperMoist devil's food, yellow or white cake mix

Water, oil and eggs called for on cake mix packages

2 tubs Betty Crocker Rich & Creamy vanilla ready-to-spread frosting or 2 recipes Vanilla Buttercream Frosting (page 236)

9 drops yellow food color

6 drops red food color

1 green flat-bottom ice-cream cone

10 to 12 large black gumdrops

2 small green gumdrops

2 green chewy fruit snack rolls (from 5-ounce package)

1 Heat oven to 325°. Grease bottom and side of 2-quart round casserole with shortening; lightly flour. Make 1 cake mix as directed on package, using water, oil and eggs. Pour batter into casserole.

2 Bake about 1 hour 15 minutes or until toothpick inserted in center comes out clean. Cool 15 minutes. Remove cake from casserole; place rounded side up on wire rack. Cool completely, about 1 hour. Repeat with remaining cake mix.

3 Tint frosting with yellow and red food colors to make orange frosting. Place 1 cake, rounded side down, on large round serving plate. Spread 2/3 cup frosting on flat side, almost to edge. Place remaining cake, rounded side up, on frosted cake to make pumpkin. Frost with remaining frosting.

4 Make vertical lines over cake with knife to shape pumpkin. Trim cone to desired height for stem; place upside down on cake. Roll black gumdrops between sheets of waxed paper to 1/4-inch thickness. Cut out eyes, eyebrows, nose and mouth, and arrange on pumpkin for face. Cut green gumdrops in half, and place on eyes. Cut out vines and leaves from fruit snack rolls. Arrange on pumpkin. Store loosely covered at room temperature.

High Altitude (3500 to 6500 feet): For devil's food: Heat oven to 350°. Make each cake mix with 1 1/2 cups water, 2 tablespoons all-purpose flour, 1 tablespoon oil and 3 eggs; beat on low speed 30 seconds, then on medium speed 4 minutes. For yellow: Make each cake mix with 1 1/2 cups water, 1 tablespoon all-purpose flour, 2 tablespoons oil and 3 eggs. For white: no changes.

1 Serving: Calories 400 (Calories from Fat 135); Fat 15g (Saturated 7g); Cholesterol 55mg; Sodium 340mg; Carbohydrate 62g (Dietary Fiber 0g); Protein 4g. **% Daily Value:** Vitamin A 1%; Vitamin C 0%; Calcium 4%; Iron 8%.

Betty's Tip Make a face with chewy fruit snack rolls instead of the gumdrops. Choose any color or flavor you like.

Jack-o'-Lantern Cake and Spiderweb Cupcakes (page 133)

Spiced Pumpkin Praline Roll

Prep: 25 min * Bake: 12 min * Cool: 30 min

10 SERVINGS

3 eggs

3/4 cup canned pumpkin (not pumpkin pie mix)

1/4 package Betty Crocker SuperMoist yellow cake mix (1 cup)

1 1/2 teaspoons ground cinnamon

1/2 teaspoon ground nutmeg

1/8 teaspoon ground cloves

Powdered sugar

1/2 package (8-ounce size) cream cheese, softened

1/2 cup packed brown sugar

1 cup whipping (heavy) cream

1/4 cup chopped pecans, toasted (page 36)

1 Heat oven to 375°. Line jelly roll pan, 15 1/2 x 10 1/2 x 1 inch, with aluminum foil or waxed paper; grease foil or waxed paper with shortening.

2 Beat eggs in medium bowl with electric mixer on high speed about 2 minutes or until very thick and lemon colored. Beat in pumpkin until well mixed. Gradually beat in cake mix, cinnamon, nutmeg and cloves on low speed; continue beating 1 minute. Pour into pan, spreading to corners.

3 Bake 8 to 12 minutes or until cake springs back when touched lightly in center. Immediately loosen cake from edges of pan and turn upside down onto towel generously sprinkled with powdered sugar. Remove pan; carefully remove foil. While hot, carefully roll cake and towel from narrow end. Cool on wire rack at least 30 minutes.

4 Beat cream cheese and brown sugar in medium bowl with electric mixer on high speed until smooth. Gradually add whipping cream; beat until stiff. Stir in 2 tablespoons of the pecans.

5 Unroll cake and remove towel. Spread half of the cream cheese mixture over cake; roll up. Spread remaining cream cheese mixture over outside of cake. Sprinkle with remaining 2 tablespoons pecans. Store covered in refrigerator.

High Altitude (3500 to 6500 feet): No changes.

1 Serving: Calories 255 (Calories from Fat 145); Fat 16g (Saturated 8g); Cholesterol 100mg; Sodium 65mg; Carbohydrate 25g (Dietary Fiber 1g); Protein 4g. **% Daily Value:** Vitamin A 90%; Vitamin C 0%; Calcium 6%; Iron 6%.

Betty's Tip You can use the remaining cake mix (about 2 3/4 cups) for cupcakes. To make the cupcakes, add 2 eggs, 3/4 cup water and 3 tablespoons vegetable oil to the cake mix. Mix and bake as directed on the package. Frost with Cream Cheese Frosting (page 234), and decorate with mini candy pumpkins.

Photo on page 122

Heavenly Holiday Baking

Get in the spirit of the holidays early this year by baking ahead! Use cake mix to create a unique cake or dessert to serve family and friends, or to make a lasting-impression gift for the special people in your life.

Dazzling Decorations

Holiday Quilt Cake: Spread the top of a 13 x 9-inch baked cake with white frosting. Pipe on lines with red or green frosting, dividing the cake into 24 squares. To make a quilt pattern, decorate every other square with green and red candies or sugars.

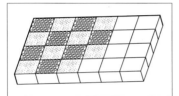

Holly Berry Cake: Spread the top and side of a layered cake or the top of a 13 x 9-inch baked cake with white frosting. Cut green jelly fruit slices into holly leaf shapes, and place on cake. Decorate with round red candies for berries.

Poinsettia Cake: Spread the top and side of a layered cake or top of a 13 x 9-inch baked cake with white or pink frosting. Cut as many fresh strawberries as you would like into 5 wedges each. For each poinsettia, arrange 5 strawberry wedges (outer side of strawberry facing up and pointed ends facing outward) to look like flower petals on top of cake; tuck 3 fresh mint leaves under strawberry wedges for each poinsettia to look like leaves.

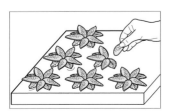

Wrap It Up!

Layer cakes and bundt cakes: Buy white cake boxes from a local bakery, or give the cake in a cake server purchased at discount or housewares stores. You can freeze the cake right in the cake server. Or place the cake on an attractive serving plate, wrap the cake and plate with clear cellophane and tie with a colorful ribbon on top.

Cake loaves: Bake cakes in loaf pans; remove from the pans and cool, then place back in loaf pans. Wrap loaves, pan and all, in colored cellophane. Or wrap loaves first in plastic wrap and next in a holiday dish towel. For a more special gift, place the wrapped cake in a basket along with a jar of your favorite jam or jelly.

Bars and cookies: Cool bars and cookies completely, then cut and transfer to a pretty paper plate or tray and wrap in cellophane. Or place the treats in decorated boxes, lined holiday tins or baskets.

✳ Happy Holidays ✳

Here are some great cakes to add to your holiday gift-giving list:

Spiced Pumpkin Praline Roll (page 136)

Candy Cane Cake (page 144)

Old-Fashioned Gingerbread (page 147)

Best-Ever Fruitcake Loaves (page 148)

Cranberry-Orange Pound Cake (page 156)

Pumpkin Bread (page 168)

Snowman Cake

Prep: 30 min * Bake: 32 min * Cool: 1 hr 10 min

12 TO 16 SERVINGS

1 package Betty Crocker
SuperMoist white cake mix

1 1/4 cups water

1/3 cup vegetable oil

3 egg whites

2 candy canes, unwrapped

2 flat-bottom ice-cream cones

Vanilla-flavored candy coating
(almond bark), melted

1 tub Betty Crocker Rich &
Creamy vanilla ready-to-spread
frosting or Vanilla Buttercream
Frosting (page 236)

1 package (7 ounces) flaked or
shredded coconut

5 large black gumdrops

1 large orange gumdrop

7 small black gumdrops

2 pretzel rods

1 Heat oven to 350°. Grease bottoms only of 2 round pans, 8 or
9 x 1 1/2 inches, with shortening. Make cake mix as directed on
package, using water, oil and egg whites. Pour into pans.

2 Bake 8-inch rounds 27 to 32 minutes, 9-inch rounds 23 to 28
minutes, or until toothpick inserted in center comes out clean.
Cool 10 minutes. Run knife around side of pans to loosen cakes;
remove from pans to wire rack. Cool completely, about 1 hour.

3 Cover large flat tray or piece of cardboard with aluminum foil.
Attach candy cane to open end of each cone, using melted candy
coating, to make ice skates; let stand until set. Arrange cake
rounds with sides touching on tray. Frost top and sides of cake
with frosting. Sprinkle with coconut, pressing gently so it stays
on frosting.

4 Use large black gumdrops for eyes and buttons, large orange
gumdrop for nose and small black gumdrops for mouth. Arrange
pretzel rods for arms and cones for feet with ice skates. Store
loosely covered at room temperature.

High Altitude (3500 to 6500 feet): Do not use 8-inch rounds. Make cake mix
following high-altitude directions on package for 9-inch rounds.

1 Serving: Calories 360 (Calories from Fat 110); Fat 12g (Saturated 7g); Cholesterol 25mg; Sodium
230mg; Carbohydrate 62g (Dietary Fiber 1g); Protein 2g. **% Daily Value:** Vitamin A 0%; Vitamin C
0%; Calcium 2%; Iron 4%.

Betty's Tip Outfit your snowman with earmuffs and a scarf. For earmuffs, place a creme-filled chocolate sandwich cookie on each side of
snowman's head, and connect them across the top of the head with
black shoestring licorice. For the scarf, any flavor of chewy fruit snack
roll will work.

Snowman Cake

Gingerbread Cake Cottage

Prep: 1 hr * Bake: 35 min * Cool: 1 hr 10 min * Freeze: 1 hr * Stand: 1 hr

12 TO 16 SERVINGS

1 package Betty Crocker SuperMoist yellow cake mix

1 1/4 cups water

1/3 cup vegetable oil

3 eggs

2 recipes Caramel Frosting (page 240)

1 tub Betty Crocker Rich & Creamy vanilla ready-to-spread frosting or Creamy White Frosting (page 234)

2 red or green peppermint candy sticks (5 inches each)

2 chocolate sugar wafer cookies (4 1/2 inches each)

5 small green gumdrops

2 sticks striped gum (any flavor)

5 red cinnamon candies

4 strawberry or vanilla sugar wafer cookies (4 1/2 inches each)

Cotton candy, if desired

Multicolored round candies, if desired

Round holiday candies, if desired

1 Heat oven to 350°. Grease bottom only of rectangular pan, 13 x 9 x 2 inches, with shortening; lightly flour. Make cake mix as directed on package, using water, oil and eggs. Pour into pan.

2 Bake 30 to 35 minutes or until toothpick inserted in center comes out clean. Cool 10 minutes. Run knife around sides of pan to loosen cake; remove from pan to wire rack. Cool completely, about 1 hour.

3 Cover large flat tray or piece of cardboard with aluminum foil. Cut cake into 3 pieces as shown in diagram. Make Caramel Frosting; remove 1 1/2 cups. Cover remaining frosting and reserve. Place piece 1 on tray; frost top with Caramel Frosting. Frost top of piece 2; top with piece 3. Stand pieces 2 and 3 upright on piece 1 as shown in diagram to form cottage. Trim corners and base so pieces fit smoothly. (Roof point will be slightly off center.) Freeze cake about 1 hour or until firm.

4 Remove cake from freezer. Frost exterior of house with reserved Caramel Frosting. Smooth frosting on front, sides and back of house with slightly dampened large spatula. Use the edge of a small spatula to press lines on front of cottage to look like bricks or logs.

5 Place about 1/3 cup vanilla frosting at a time in decorating bag with writing tip. Break one candy stick in half. Pipe a strip of frosting down the length of each candy stick half. Press one half to each vertical front edge of house. Attach remaining candy stick along top roof line. Let stand about 30 minutes or until set.

6 Pipe small amount of vanilla frosting on back of chocolate wafer cookies. Place on front of house to make door. Cut each gumdrop in half. Pipe small amount of vanilla frosting on back of each piece and arrange in a circle above door to make wreath. Pipe on frosting for outlines of window panes and door frame. Cut each stick of gum in half to make shutters; attach to window. Attach red cinnamon candies for door handles and berries on wreath.

7 Cut strawberry wafer cookies to make chimney pieces. The inside piece should be 1 1/2 inches long, the outside piece 2 1/2 inches long. For the front and back sides, cut 2 pieces each 2 1/2 inches long, then cut end of each piece at an angle to fit slant of roof. Pipe vanilla frosting on inside vertical edges of 2 slanted chimney pieces. Press side pieces of chimney into frosting to form box. Hold a few minutes until set; let dry. Pipe frosting on bottom edges of chimney; place on roof. Fill chimney with cotton candy to make smoke.

8 Pipe any remaining vanilla frosting along roof lines and around base of chimney a with writing tip to create snowdrifts. Decorate edges of roof lines with multicolored round candies. Attach round holiday candies at base of house. Let stand about 30 minutes or until set. Store loosely covered at room temperature.

High Altitude (3500 to 6500 feet): Make cake mix following high-altitude directions on package for 13 x 9-inch rectangle.

1 Serving: Calories 725 (Calories from Fat 250); Fat 28g (Saturated 18g); Cholesterol 55mg; Sodium 310mg; Carbohydrate 115g (Dietary Fiber 0g); Protein 3g. **% Daily Value:** Vitamin A 2%; Vitamin C 0%; Calcium 12%; Iron 8%.

Betty's Tip For a true "gingerbread" color cottage, make and decorate with the Caramel Frosting. If you prefer a darker color, use 2 tubs Betty Crocker Rich & Creamy milk chocolate or chocolate ready-to-spread frosting instead.

Photo on page 122

Cutting and Assembling Gingerbread Cake Cottage

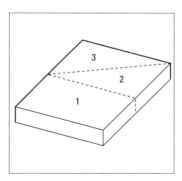

Cut cake crosswise in half; cut one half on the diagonal into two triangles.

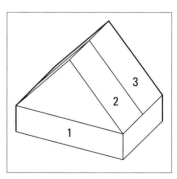

Place piece 1 on tray; frost top. Frost top of piece 2; top with piece 3. Stand pieces 2 and 3 upright on piece 1 to form cottage.

Rudolph Cupcakes

Prep: 20 min * Bake: 20 min per pan * Cool: 30 min

24 CUPCAKES

1 package Betty Crocker SuperMoist cake mix (any flavor)

Water, oil and eggs called for on cake mix package

1 tub Betty Crocker Rich & Creamy chocolate ready-to-spread frosting or Creamy Chocolate Frosting (page 238)

Chocolate sprinkles

24 large pretzel twists

24 miniature marshmallows

12 candied whole cherries

24 red cinnamon candies

1 Heat oven to 350°. Bake and cool cake mix as directed on package for cupcakes, using water, oil and eggs.

2 Spread frosting over tops of cupcakes. Sprinkle with chocolate shot.

3 For each cupcake, break pretzel twist in half; arrange on cupcake for reindeer antlers. Cut marshmallow in half; arrange on cupcake for eyes. Cut cherries in half; arrange on cupcake for nose. Place red cinnamon candy below cherry for mouth. Store loosely covered at room temperature.

High Altitude (3500 to 6500 feet): Make cake mix following high-altitude directions on package for cupcakes. Makes 30 cupcakes.

1 Cupcake: Calories 230 (Calories from Fat 70); Fat 8g (Saturated 4g); Cholesterol 15mg; Sodium 400mg; Carbohydrate 38g (Dietary Fiber 1g); Protein 3g. **% Daily Value:** Vitamin A 0%; Vitamin C 0%; Calcium 2%; Iron 6%.

Betty's Tip Save time during the holidays! Freeze the unfrosted cupcakes in an airtight freezer container for up to 4 months. Decorate the frozen cupcakes; they'll thaw while you're decorating.

Rudolph Cupcakes

Candy Cane Cake

Prep: 15 min * Bake: 50 min * Cool: 1 hr 10 min

16 TO 24 SERVINGS

1 package Betty Crocker SuperMoist white cake mix

1 1/4 cups water

1/3 cup vegetable oil

3 egg whites

1/2 teaspoon red food color

1/2 teaspoon peppermint extract

Easy Vanilla Glaze (page 242) or Vanilla Glaze (page 242)

1 Heat oven to 350°. Generously grease 12-cup bundt cake pan with shortening; lightly flour. Make cake mix as directed on package, using water, oil and egg whites. Pour about 2 cups batter into pan. Pour about 3/4 cup batter into small bowl; stir in food color and peppermint extract. Carefully pour pink batter over white batter in pan. Carefully pour remaining white batter over pink batter.

2 Bake 45 to 50 minutes or until toothpick inserted in center comes out clean. Cool 10 minutes. Turn pan upside down onto wire rack or heatproof serving plate; remove pan. Cool completely, about 1 hour.

3 Spread Easy Vanilla Glaze over cake, allowing some to drizzle down side. Store loosely covered at room temperature.

High Altitude (3500 to 6500 feet): No changes.

1 Serving: Calories 275 (Calories from Fat 80); Fat 9g (Saturated 2g); Cholesterol 0mg; Sodium 310mg; Carbohydrate 45g (Dietary Fiber 0g); Protein 3g. **% Daily Value:** Vitamin A 0%; Vitamin C 0%; Calcium 4%; Iron 4%.

Betty's Tip Sprinkle the top of this festive cake with crushed candy canes or crushed hard peppermint candies. To easily crush peppermint candies, place them in a resealable plastic freezer bag, seal the bag and pound with a rolling pin or meat mallet to crush.

Candy Cane Cake

Holiday Eggnog Cake

Prep: 15 min * Bake: 35 min * Cool: 1 hr 10 min

12 TO 16 SERVINGS

1 package Betty Crocker
SuperMoist yellow cake mix

1 cup eggnog

1/2 cup butter or margarine,
softened

2 teaspoons ground nutmeg

2 tablespoons light rum or
1 teaspoon rum extract plus
2 tablespoons water

3 eggs

Eggnog Fluff (below)

Additional ground nutmeg or
cinnamon, if desired

Eggnog Fluff

1 1/2 cups whipping (heavy)
cream

1/2 cup powdered sugar

1 tablespoon rum or
1/2 teaspoon rum extract

1 Heat oven to 350°. Grease bottoms only of 2 round pans,
   9 x 1 1/2 inches, with shortening. (Do not use 8-inch rounds
   or batter will overflow.)

2 Beat cake mix, eggnog, butter, 2 teaspoons nutmeg, the rum and
   eggs in large bowl with electric mixer on low speed 30 seconds;
   beat on medium speed 2 minutes. Pour into pans.

3 Bake 30 to 35 minutes or until toothpick inserted in center
   comes out clean. Cool 10 minutes. Run knife around side of
   pans to loosen cakes; remove from pans to wire rack. Cool
   completely, about 1 hour.

4 Fill layers and frost cake with Eggnog Fluff. Sprinkle lightly with
   additional nutmeg. Store covered in refrigerator.

Eggnog Fluff

Beat all ingredients in chilled medium bowl with electric mixer
on high speed until soft peaks form.

High Altitude (3500 to 6500 feet): Do not use 8-inch rounds. Grease and flour pans.
Heat oven to 375°. Decrease butter to 2 tablespoons. Add 1/2 cup water and 1/4
cup all-purpose flour. Bake 9-inch rounds 25 to 30 minutes.

1 Serving: Calories 385 (Calories from Fat 200); Fat 22g (Saturated 12g); Cholesterol 120mg;
Sodium 360mg; Carbohydrate 43g (Dietary Fiber 0g); Protein 4g. **% Daily Value:** Vitamin A 14%;
Vitamin C 0%; Calcium 12%; Iron 4%.

Betty's Tip This cake is easy to make and take at holiday time. Bake
the cake in a 13 x 9 x 2-inch rectangular pan for 30 to 35 minutes or
until a toothpick inserted in the center comes out clean. Cool, then frost
with Eggnog Fluff.

*In 1954, a little bit of love
was wrapped up with every
gift you baked.*

Old-Fashioned Gingerbread

Prep: 10 min • Bake: 35 min • Cool: 1 hr 10 min

16 SERVINGS

1 package Betty Crocker
SuperMoist carrot cake mix

2/3 cup water

1/3 cup molasses

1/3 cup butter or margarine,
softened

1 teaspoon ground ginger

1/2 teaspoon ground allspice

1/4 teaspoon ground cloves

3 eggs

Powdered sugar, if desired

2 cups frozen (thawed)
whipped topping or
Sweetened Whipped Cream
(page 243), if desired

1 Heat oven to 350°. Grease 12-cup bundt cake pan with shortening; lightly sugar.

2 Beat cake mix, water, molasses, butter, ginger, allspice, cloves and eggs in large bowl with electric mixer on low speed 30 seconds; beat on medium speed 2 minutes. Pour into pan.

3 Bake 30 to 35 minutes or until toothpick inserted in center comes out clean. Cool 10 minutes. Turn pan upside down onto wire rack or heatproof serving plate; remove pan. Cool completely, about 1 hour. Sprinkle with powdered sugar. Serve with whipped topping. Store cake loosely covered at room temperature.

High Altitude (3500 to 6500 feet): Heat oven to 375°. Increase water to 3/4 cup and add 1/4 cup all-purpose flour with the cake mix. Bake 40 to 45 minutes.

1 Serving: Calories 200 (Calories from Fat 65); Fat 7g (Saturated 3g); Cholesterol 40mg; Sodium 250mg; Carbohydrate 31g (Dietary Fiber 0g); Protein 3g. **% Daily Value:** Vitamin A 4%; Vitamin C 0%; Calcium 6%; Iron 6%.

Betty's Tip Grease and sugar the pan? That's right. Dusting the pan with sugar instead of flour gives this cake a sparkly, sweet and delicate crust.

Best-Ever Fruitcake Loaves

Prep: 20 min * Bake: 1 hr 10 min * Cool: 2 hr 30 min * Chill: 24 hr

2 LOAVES, 16 SLICES EACH

1 cup dried cherries

1 cup chopped dried apricots

1 cup chopped dates

1 cup dried cranberries

1 cup chopped dried mixed fruit

1 can (10 ounces) deluxe mixed nuts (2 cups)

1/2 cup all-purpose flour

1 package Betty Crocker SuperMoist white cake mix

1/2 cup butter or margarine, melted

1/4 cup brandy or 2 teaspoons brandy extract plus 1/4 cup water

1 package (4-serving size) vanilla instant pudding and pie filling mix

3 eggs

1/4 cup light corn syrup

2 tablespoons brandy or 1 teaspoon brandy extract plus 2 tablespoons water

Pecan halves, if desired

Candied cherries, if desired

1 Heat oven to 300°. Generously grease 2 loaf pans, 9 x 5 x 3 inches, with shortening; lightly flour.

2 Toss dried cherries, apricots, dates, cranberries, mixed fruit, nuts and flour in very large bowl. Beat cake mix, butter, 1/4 cup brandy, the pudding mix (dry) and eggs in large bowl with electric mixture on medium speed 1 minute (batter may climb beaters slightly). Spoon batter over fruit and nut mixture; mix well (batter will be very stiff). Press batter evenly into pans.

3 Bake 1 hour to 1 hour 10 minutes or until toothpick inserted in cake comes out almost clean and loaves are golden brown. Cool 30 minutes on wire rack.

4 Remove loaves from pans to wire rack. Mix corn syrup and 2 tablespoons brandy in small bowl; brush on warm loaves. Garnish with pecan halves and candied cherries. Cool completely, about 2 hours. Store tightly wrapped in refrigerator at least 24 hours before slicing. Store any remaining fruitcake tightly wrapped in refrigerator.

High Altitude (3500 to 6500 feet): Heat oven to 325°. Decrease butter to 1/4 cup; increase 1/4 cup brandy to 1/3 cup. Bake 1 hour 10 minutes to 1 hour 20 minutes.

1 Slice: Calories 240 (Calories from Fat 90); Fat 10g (Saturated 4g); Cholesterol 25mg; Sodium 240mg; Carbohydrate 37g (Dietary Fiber 2g); Protein 3g. **% Daily Value:** Vitamin A 10%; Vitamin C 0%; Calcium 4%; Iron 4%.

Betty's Tip You'll find it easiest to cut these dense and fruity loaves into slices if you use a thin-bladed serrated knife.

New Year's Eve Champagne Cake

Prep: 15 min ✳ Bake: 50 min ✳ Cool: 1 hr 10 min

16 TO 24 SERVINGS

1 package Betty Crocker
SuperMoist white cake mix

1 1/3 cups champagne or
nonalcoholic sparkling white
grape juice

4 eggs

1 package (4-serving size)
vanilla pudding and pie filling
mix (instant or regular)

Champagne Glaze (below)

Glitter sugars or coarse sugar
crystals (decorating sugar),
if desired

Champagne Glaze

1 cup powdered sugar

1 tablespoon champagne or
nonalcoholic sparkling white
grape juice

1 Heat oven to 350°. Grease 12-cup bundt cake pan with shortening; lightly flour. Beat cake mix, champagne, eggs and pudding mix (dry) in large bowl with electric mixer on low speed 30 seconds; beat on medium speed 2 minutes. Pour into pan.

2 Bake 45 to 50 minutes or until toothpick inserted in center comes out clean. Cool 10 minutes. Turn pan upside down onto wire rack or heatproof serving plate; remove pan. Cool completely, about 1 hour.

3 Drizzle Champagne Glaze over cake. Sprinkle with glitter sugars. Store loosely covered at room temperature.

Champagne Glaze

Stir ingredients until smooth and thin enough to drizzle.

High Altitude (3500 to 6500 feet): Stir champagne to remove most of the bubbles before adding to cake mixture.

1 Serving: Calories 215 (Calories from Fat 35); Fat 4g (Saturated 1g); Cholesterol 55mg; Sodium 320mg; Carbohydrate 42g (Dietary Fiber 0g); Protein 3g. **% Daily Value:** Vitamin A 2%; Vitamin C 0%; Calcium 6%; Iron 4%.

Betty's Tip For this recipe, it doesn't matter if you use instant or regular pudding and pie filling mix. Either one will work just fine.

*"Every bite of cake tastes rich, moist and grandmother-good!"
No wonder the holidays were so bright and beautiful in 1957.*

5
Come for
Brunch

Almond-Raspberry Coffee Cake (page 162) and Lemon Citrus Muffins (page 170)

Lemon–Poppy Seed Brunch Cake

Prep: 10 min * Bake: 40 min * Cool: 1 hour 10 min

16 TO 24 SERVINGS

1 package Betty Crocker
SuperMoist lemon cake mix

1 1/4 cups water

1/3 cup vegetable oil

3 eggs

2 tablespoons poppy seed

Lemon Glaze (below)

Grated lemon peel, if desired

Lemon Glaze

1 cup powdered sugar

1 to 2 tablespoons lemon juice

1/4 teaspoon grated lemon
peel

1 Heat oven to 350°. Grease 12-cup bundt cake pan with
shortening; lightly flour.

2 Make cake mix as directed on package, using water, oil and eggs.
Stir poppy seed into batter. Pour into pan.

3 Bake 35 to 40 minutes or until toothpick inserted in center
comes out clean. Cool 10 minutes. Turn pan upside down onto
wire rack or heatproof serving plate; remove pan. Cool cake
completely, about 1 hour.

4 Spread Lemon Glaze over top of cake, allowing some to drizzle
down side. Garnish with lemon peel. Store loosely covered at
room temperature.

Lemon Glaze

Mix powdered sugar, 1 tablespoon lemon juice and the lemon
peel. Stir in additional lemon juice, 1 teaspoon at a time, until
smooth and consistency of thick syrup.

High Altitude (3500 to 6500 feet): Add 1 tablespoon all-purpose flour to dry cake
mix. Increase water to 1 1/2 cups; decrease oil to 2 tablespoons. Bake 40 to
45 minutes.

1 Serving: Calories 275 (Calories from Fat 115); Fat 13g (Saturated 4g); Cholesterol 40mg; Sodium
220mg; Carbohydrate 37g (Dietary Fiber 0g); Protein 2g. **% Daily Value:** Vitamin A 0%; Vitamin C
0%; Calcium 8%; Iron 2%.

Betty's Tip **Poppy seed can become rancid if stored for long periods
of time in your cupboard. Put it in your freezer, and it will keep
indefinitely.**

Bake Sale Basics

Want to turn your love of baking into something profitable and have a lot of fun? Try a bake sale! Bake sales have been a tasty way to raise money for generations of Americans. To make the most of your baking and selling efforts, follow these tips for sure success.

Planning Is Everything

* Hold a bake sale around a holiday—Christmas, Valentine's Day or Halloween are good ones. When people are in a festive mood, they tend to buy more.

* Display foods with seasonal items or props. Let someone who has an eye for "propping" arrange the table.

* Plan ahead and advertise. Use radio or a neighborhood newspaper, or go high-tech and promote by e-mail.

Make Baked Items Irresistible

* Keep a sample plate with tiny pieces of cookies, bars or cake ready for sampling. Have small cups of water or coffee available so tasters will have a beverage to go with the samples.

* Instead of offering a plate of plain cupcakes, bars or cookies, dress them up! Who can resist holiday cupcakes at a December bake sale?

* Bake quick bread mixes in regular or mini loaf pans. Frost, then decorate with foot-long chewy fruit snack rolls to look like a ribbon on a gift package.

Variety Adds Spice—and Success

* Include everything from decadent chocolate treats to items for special diets.

* Offer a variety of sizes: single servings to large cakes, loaves, muffins and bars.

* Have a variety of prices; keep prices simple and divisible by 25 cents.

The Experts Advise

* Schedule a bake day to prepare for the event; school and church kitchens are ideal.

* Have recipes printed and available to take home.

* Make your bake sale a tradition people will come to expect every year.

* Bake while the sale is in progress—caramel rolls, muffins or other aromatic baked goods make it impossible for people to walk away.

* Furnish bags large enough for customers to carry more than one item home.

✶ Blue Ribbon Winners ✶

At your next sale, bring along some of these best-sellers:

Chocolate Turtle Cake (page 18)

Hummingbird Cake (page 49)

Fudgy Chocolate Ring Cake (page 61)

Lemon-Poppy Seed Brunch Cake (page 152)

Honey-Walnut Breakfast Loaves (page 166)

Chocolate-Caramel-Oatmeal Bars (page 223)

Cream Cheese Coffee Cake with Fruit Salsa

Prep: 15 min   •   Bake: 40 min   •   Cool: 1 hr 10 min

16 TO 24 SERVINGS

1 package Betty Crocker SuperMoist yellow cake mix

1 cup milk

1 package (3 ounces) cream cheese, softened

1 teaspoon vanilla

3 eggs

Fruit Salsa (below)

Powdered sugar, if desired

Fruit Salsa

2 medium kiwifruit, peeled and cut into large chunks (1 1/3 cups)

2 medium oranges, separated into sections and chopped (1 cup)

1 cup sliced strawberries

2 tablespoons lime juice

4 teaspoons sugar

1/2 teaspoon ground ginger or 1 teaspoon finely chopped gingerroot, if desired

1. Heat oven to 350°. Generously grease 12-cup bundt cake pan with shortening; lightly flour.

2. Beat cake mix, milk, cream cheese, vanilla and eggs in medium bowl with electric mixer on low speed 1 minute, scraping bowl constantly. Beat 2 minutes longer. Pour into pan.

3. Bake 35 to 40 minutes or until toothpick inserted in center comes out clean. Cool 10 minutes. Turn pan upside down onto wire rack or heatproof serving plate; remove pan. Cool completely, about 1 hour.

4. Make Fruit Salsa. Place cake on serving plate; sprinkle with powdered sugar. Serve with Fruit Salsa. Store cake loosely covered at room temperature.

Fruit Salsa

Mix all ingredients in large bowl. Cover and refrigerate about 1 hour or until chilled.

High Altitude (3500 to 6500 feet): Heat oven to 375°. Increase milk to 1 1/4 cups. Beat on low speed 1 minute, then beat 3 minutes longer.

1 Serving: Calories 190 (Calories from Fat 55); Fat 6g (Saturated 3g); Cholesterol 35mg; Sodium 240mg; Carbohydrate 32g (Dietary Fiber 1g); Protein 3g. **% Daily Value:** Vitamin A 4%; Vitamin C 20%; Calcium 10%; Iron 4%.

Lemon-Cream Cheese Coffee Cake: Substitute 1 package SuperMoist lemon cake mix for the yellow cake mix. Omit vanilla; increase the first beat time to 2 minutes.

Betty's Tip   **Leftover cake? Make a Cream Cheese Cake Trifle:** Cut the cake into large cubes, and place them in a large glass or plastic bowl. Sprinkle with a little orange-flavored liqueur or orange juice, cover with plastic wrap and refrigerate about 2 hours. Layer cake, whipped cream and fresh fruit in goblets. Cover and refrigerate at least 1 hour before serving.

Cream Cheese Coffee Cake with Fruit Salsa

Cranberry-Orange Pound Cake

Prep: 25 min * Bake: 1 hr 10 min * Cool: 1 hr 10 min

16 TO 24 SERVINGS

1 package Betty Crocker
SuperMoist yellow cake mix

1 package (4-serving size)
vanilla instant pudding and
pie filling mix

1 cup water

1/2 cup butter or margarine,
melted

1 teaspoon grated orange peel

4 eggs

1 1/2 cups fresh or frozen
cranberries, chopped (do not
thaw frozen cranberries)

Orange Butter Sauce (below)

Orange Butter Sauce

1 cup sugar

1 tablespoon all-purpose flour

1/2 cup orange juice

1/2 cup butter or margarine,
cut into 8 pieces

1 Heat oven to 350°. Grease 12-cup bundt cake pan with shortening; lightly flour.

2 Beat cake mix, pudding mix (dry), water, butter, orange peel and eggs in large bowl with electric mixer on low speed 30 seconds; beat on medium speed 2 minutes. Fold in cranberries. Spread in pan.

3 Bake 1 hour 5 minutes to 1 hour 10 minutes or until toothpick inserted in center comes out clean. Cool 10 minutes. Turn pan upside down onto wire rack or heatproof serving plate; remove pan. Cool completely, about 1 hour. Serve with Orange Butter Sauce. Store cake loosely covered at room temperature.

Orange Butter Sauce

Mix sugar and flour in 1-quart saucepan. Stir in orange juice. Add butter. Cook over medium heat about 4 minutes, stirring constantly, until thickened and bubbly. Serve warm.

High Altitude (3500 to 6500 feet): For Orange Butter Sauce, increase flour to 2 tablespoons. Cook over medium heat until butter is melted, then cook 4 minutes longer.

1 Serving: Calories 335 (Calories from Fat 135); Fat 15g (Saturated 6g); Cholesterol 70mg; Sodium 420mg; Carbohydrate 47g (Dietary Fiber 0g); Protein 3g. **% Daily Value:** Vitamin A 12%; Vitamin C 2%; Calcium 8%; Iron 4%.

Betty's Tip Pound cake freezes beautifully! Wrap the unfrosted cake tightly and label. Freeze up to 3 or 4 months. To thaw, loosen the wrap and thaw at room temperature 2 to 3 hours.

Strawberry-Rhubarb Custard Coffee Cake

Prep: 15 min ✳ Bake: 1 hr 15 min ✳ Cool: 30 min ✳ Chill: 1 hr

15 SERVINGS

1 package Betty Crocker
SuperMoist yellow cake mix

1 cup water

1/3 cup vegetable oil

3 eggs

2 cups sliced fresh or frozen
(thawed and well drained)
rhubarb

2 cups sliced strawberries

1 cup sugar

2 cups whipping (heavy) cream

1 Heat oven to 350°. Grease bottom and sides of rectangular pan,
13 x 9 x 2 inches, with shortening; lightly flour.

2 Make cake mix as directed on package, using water, oil and eggs.
Pour into pan. Top with rhubarb and strawberries; sprinkle with
sugar. Pour whipping cream over top of mixture.

3 Bake 1 hour to 1 hour 15 minutes or until toothpick inserted
in center comes out clean. Cool 30 minutes on wire rack.
Refrigerate 1 hour. Serve slightly warm or cool. Store covered
in refrigerator.

High Altitude (3500 to 6500 feet): Make cake mix following high-altitude
directions on package for 13 x 9 x 2-inch rectangle. Bake 1 hour 5 minutes to
1 hour 20 minutes.

1 Serving: Calories 345 (Calories from Fat 160); Fat 18g (Saturated 8g); Cholesterol 75mg; Sodium
240mg; Carbohydrate 44g (Dietary Fiber 1g); Protein 3g. **% Daily Value:** Vitamin A 8%; Vitamin C
10%; Calcium 12%; Iron 14%.

Betty's Tip If using thawed frozen rhubarb, be sure to drain it on
paper towels and pat dry with more paper towels, so the custard layer
doesn't get too runny.

Honey Bun Cake

Prep: 15 min * Bake: 45 min * Cool: 1 hr

15 SERVINGS

1 package Betty Crocker
SuperMoist yellow cake mix

2/3 cup vegetable oil

4 eggs

1 container (8 ounces) sour
cream

1 cup packed brown sugar

1/3 cup chopped pecans

2 teaspoons ground cinnamon

Easy Vanilla Glaze (page 242)
or Vanilla Glaze (page 242)

1 Heat oven to 350°. Grease bottom and sides of rectangular pan, 13 x 9 x 2 inches, with shortening; lightly flour.

2 Beat cake mix, oil, eggs and sour cream in large bowl with electric mixer on low speed 30 seconds; beat on medium speed 2 minutes. Spread half of the batter in pan. Mix brown sugar, pecans and cinnamon; sprinkle over batter in pan. Carefully spread remaining batter evenly over pecan mixture.

3 Bake about 45 minutes or until deep golden brown. Prick surface of warm cake several times with fork. Drizzle Easy Vanilla Glaze over cake. Run knife around side of pan to loosen cake. Cool completely, about 1 hour. Store loosely covered at room temperature.

High Altitude (3500 to 6500 feet): Decrease oil to 1/3 cup.

1 Serving: Calories 380 (Calories from Fat 160); Fat 18g (Saturated 4g); Cholesterol 65mg; Sodium 240mg; Carbohydrate 51g (Dietary Fiber 0g); Protein 3g. **% Daily Value:** Vitamin A 2%; Vitamin C 0%; Calcium 10%; Iron 4%.

Mocha Coffee Cake: Stir 1 to 2 tablespoons instant coffee (dry) into cake batter until dissolved.

Betty's Tip What could be better for breakfast or brunch than this rich coffee cake that looks and tastes like a giant sticky bun? If you like, use chopped walnuts or almonds instead of the pecans.

Honey Bun Cake

Fruit Swirl Coffee Cake

Prep: 10 min * Bake: 25 min * Cool: 30 min

18 SERVINGS

1 package Betty Crocker
SuperMoist white cake mix

1/2 cup sour cream

1/3 cup butter or margarine,
softened

1 teaspoon vanilla

2 eggs

1 can (21 ounces) pie filling
(any flavor)

Easy Vanilla Glaze (page 242)
or Vanilla Glaze (page 242)

1 Heat oven to 350°. Grease bottom and sides of jelly roll pan,
   15 1/2 x 10 1/2 x 1 inch, with shortening; lightly flour.

2 Stir cake mix, sour cream, butter, vanilla and eggs in large bowl,
   using large spoon, until soft dough forms; reserve 1 cup dough.
   Spread remaining dough in pan. Spread pie filling over dough in
   pan. Drop reserved dough by slightly less than 1 tablespoonfuls
   onto pie filling.

3 Bake about 25 minutes or until toothpick inserted near center
   comes out clean. Drizzle Easy Vanilla Glaze over warm coffee
   cake. Cool 30 minutes. Serve warm or cool. Store covered
   in refrigerator.

High Altitude (3500 to 6500 feet): Heat oven to 375°. Bake 25 to 30 minutes.

1 Serving: Calories 315 (Calories from Fat 80); Fat 9g (Saturated 5g); Cholesterol 35mg; Sodium
210mg; Carbohydrate 56g (Dietary Fiber 0g); Protein 2g. **% Daily Value:** Vitamin A 4%; Vitamin C
0%; Calcium 6%; Iron 2%.

Lemon Swirl Coffee Cake: Substitute 1 cup lemon curd for the can
of pie filling.

Betty's Tip Leftovers of this classic coffee cake will taste as good as
the day you baked it. To reheat coffee cake, wrap in aluminum foil and
heat in a 350° oven for 10 to 15 minutes.

Fruit Swirl Coffee Cake

Almond-Raspberry Coffee Cake

Prep: 15 min * Bake: 45 min * Cool: 15 min

16 SERVINGS

1 package Betty Crocker
SuperMoist white cake mix

1/4 cup sour cream

1 teaspoon almond extract

2 eggs

1 package (8 ounces) cream
cheese, softened

1/4 cup sugar

1/2 cup raspberry preserves

1/2 cup sliced almonds

1 Heat oven to 350°. Grease springform pan, 10 x 3 inches, with
   shortening; lightly flour.

2 Mix cake mix, sour cream, almond extract and 1 egg in large bowl
   with electric mixer on low speed until crumbly. Reserve 1/2 cup
   crumb mixture. Press remaining crumb mixture in bottom and
   1 inch up sides of pan. (Lightly coat fingers with flour when
   pressing crumb mixture in pan to keep from sticking.) Bake 15
   to 20 minutes or until light golden brown.

3 Beat cream cheese, sugar and remaining egg in small bowl with
   electric mixer on low speed until smooth and creamy. Pour over
   baked crust. Drop teaspoonfuls of preserves evenly over cream
   cheese mixture; do not swirl. Mix reserved crumb mixture and
   almonds; sprinkle over preserves.

4 Bake 20 to 25 minutes or until filling is set and crust is golden
   brown. Cool 15 minutes on wire rack. Run knife around side of
   pan to loosen cake; remove side of pan. Serve slightly warm or
   cool. Store covered in refrigerator.

High Altitude (3500 to 6500 feet): Increase first bake time to 18 to 23 minutes;
increase second bake time to 28 to 33 minutes.

1 Serving: Calories 260 (Calories from Fat 100); Fat 11g (Saturated 5g); Cholesterol 45mg; Sodium
270mg; Carbohydrate 36g (Dietary Fiber 0g); Protein 4g. **% Daily Value:** Vitamin A 4%; Vitamin C
0%; Calcium 8%; Iron 4%.

Betty's Tip Don't worry if you don't have a springform pan. You can
also make this elegant coffee cake in a 9-inch square baking pan; just
increase second bake time to 25 to 30 minutes. Cut coffee cake into
squares and serve straight from the pan. Garnish with fresh raspberries
and mint leaves for an extra-special touch.

Photo on page 150

Cinnamon-Apple Crumble

Prep: 10 min * Bake: 50 min

15 SERVINGS

1 package Betty Crocker SuperMoist white cake mix

1 cup quick-cooking or old-fashioned oats

1/3 cup butter or margarine, softened

1 teaspoon ground cinnamon

1 tablespoon water

1 egg

1 can (21 ounces) apple pie filling

1 tablespoon lemon juice

1 cup chopped nuts

2 cups half-and-half, if desired

1 Heat oven to 350°. Grease bottom and sides of rectangular pan, 13 x 9 x 2 inches, with shortening.

2 Beat cake mix, 1/2 cup of the oats, the butter, cinnamon, water and egg in large bowl with electric mixer on low speed until crumbly. Reserve 1 cup crumb mixture.

3 Press remaining crumb mixture in pan. Bake 12 to 15 minutes or until edges are light golden brown.

4 Mix pie filling and lemon juice in medium bowl, breaking up any large slices of apple; spoon evenly over baked crust. Mix reserved crumb mixture, the nuts and remaining 1/2 cup oats in small bowl; sprinkle evenly over apple filling. Bake 30 to 35 minutes or until golden brown. Serve warm or cool.

5 To serve, place in individual bowls. Pour about 2 tablespoons half-and-half over each serving. Store covered in refrigerator.

High Altitude (3500 to 6500 feet): Heat oven to 375°.

1 Serving: Calories 290 (Calories from Fat 115); Fat 13g (Saturated 4g); Cholesterol 25mg; Sodium 260mg; Carbohydrate 42g (Dietary Fiber 2g); Protein 42g. **% Daily Value:** Vitamin A 4%; Vitamin C 0%; Calcium 6%; Iron 6%.

Betty's Tip If they don't devour the whole thing the day you serve it, this comfy crumble tastes just as good the next day. Reheat any leftovers at 350° for 15 to 20 minutes or until warm. Individual servings can be reheated in the microwave on High for 10 to 15 seconds.

Coconut-Topped Oatmeal Cake

Prep: 15 min * Bake: 40 min * Broil: 3 min

15 SERVINGS

1 package Betty Crocker
SuperMoist carrot cake mix

1/2 cup quick-cooking oats

1 1/4 cups water

1/3 cup vegetable oil

4 eggs

Coconut Topping (below)

Coconut Topping

1 cup flaked coconut

2/3 cup packed brown sugar

1/2 cup chopped pecans

6 tablespoons butter or margarine, softened

1/4 cup milk

1 Heat oven to 350°. Grease bottom and sides of rectangular pan,
   13 x 9 x 2 inches, with shortening; lightly flour.

2 Beat cake mix, oats, water, oil and eggs in large bowl with
   electric mixer on low speed 30 seconds; beat on medium speed
   2 minutes. Pour into pan.

3 Bake 35 to 40 minutes or until toothpick inserted in center
   comes out clean. While cake is baking, make Coconut Topping.
   Spread topping over hot cake.

4 Set oven control to broil. Broil cake with top 3 to 5 inches from
   heat 2 to 3 minutes or until topping bubbles and is golden brown
   (watch carefully because topping burns easily). Serve warm.
   Store covered in refrigerator.

Coconut Topping

Mix all ingredients.

High Altitude Directions (3500 to 6500 feet): Heat oven to 375°. Decrease oil to 1/4
cup; add 2 tablespoons all-purpose flour. Beat on low speed 30 seconds; beat on
medium speed 3 minutes.

1 Serving: Calories 345 (Calories from Fat 160); Fat 18g (Saturated 7g); Cholesterol 70mg; Sodium
290mg; Carbohydrate 43g (Dietary Fiber 1g); Protein 4g. **% Daily Value:** Vitamin A 4%; Vitamin C
0%; Calcium 8%; Iron 6%.

Betty's Tip This coco-nutty cake reheats in a snap. Just cover with
aluminum foil and heat in a 350° oven about 10 minutes.

*Why wait until late to have
cake? As this 1959 ad shows,
you can have cake for breakfast
and dessert!*

Banana Bread

Prep: 10 min ✳ Bake: 1 hr ✳ Cool: 1 hr 10 min

2 LOAVES, 16 SLICES EACH

1 package Betty Crocker
SuperMoist yellow cake mix

1 cup mashed very ripe
bananas (about 2 medium)*

1/2 cup buttermilk

1/3 cup vegetable oil

3 eggs

1 cup chopped nuts, if desired

*Do not use frozen bananas.
Frozen bananas contain too
much moisture and may cause
a gummy layer to form at the
bottom of the loaves.*

1 Heat oven to 350°. Grease 2 loaf pans, 8 1/2 x 4 1/2 x 2 1/2 or
9 x 5 x 3 inches, with shortening; lightly flour.

2 Beat cake mix, bananas, buttermilk, oil and eggs in large bowl
with electric mixer on low speed 30 seconds; beat on medium
speed 2 minutes. Pour into pans. Sprinkle each loaf with
1/2 cup nuts.

3 Bake 8-inch loaves 50 to 60 minutes, 9-inch loaves 40 to 45 minutes, or until toothpick inserted in center comes out clean. Cool
10 minutes. Remove from pans to wire rack. Cool completely,
about 1 hour. Wrap tightly and store at room temperature up to
4 days, or refrigerate up to 10 days.

High Altitude (3500 to 6500 feet): Heat oven to 375°. Add 2 tablespoons
all-purpose flour to dry cake mix. Bake 8-inch loaves 48 to 58 minutes,
9-inch loaves 38 to 48 minutes.

1 Slice: Calories 100 (Calories from Fat 35); Fat 4g (Saturated 3g); Cholesterol 20mg; Sodium
110mg; Carbohydrate 15g (Dietary Fiber 0g); Protein 1g. **% Daily Value:** Vitamin A 0%; Vitamin C
0%; Calcium 4%; Iron 2%.

Betty's Tip If you don't have any buttermilk, use 1 1/2 teaspoons
lemon juice or white vinegar and enough milk to measure 1/2 cup.
Let the mixture rest a few minutes before using.

Honey-Walnut Breakfast Loaves

Prep: 10 min * Bake: 1 hr * Cool: 1 hr 10 min

2 LOAVES, 8 SLICES EACH

1 package Betty Crocker SuperMoist yellow or butter recipe yellow cake mix

1 cup water

1/2 cup chopped walnuts or pecans

1/3 cup butter or margarine, softened

1/4 cup honey

3 eggs

Easy Vanilla Glaze (page 242) or Vanilla Glaze (page 242)

Additional chopped walnuts or pecans, if desired

1 Heat oven to 350°. Grease bottom and sides of 2 loaf pans, 8 1/2 x 4 1/2 x 2 1/2 or 9 x 5 x 3 inches, with shortening; lightly flour.

2 Beat cake mix, water, 1/2 cup walnuts, the butter, honey and eggs in large bowl with electric mixer on low speed 30 seconds; beat on medium speed 2 minutes. Pour into pans.

3 Bake 8-inch loaves 50 to 60 minutes, 9-inch loaves 40 to 45 minutes, or until toothpick inserted in center comes out clean. Cool 10 minutes. Run knife around sides of pans to loosen loaves; remove from pans. Cool completely, about 1 hour.

4 Spread Easy Vanilla Glaze over tops of loaves, allowing some to drizzle down sides. Sprinkle with additional walnuts. Store loosely covered at room temperature.

High Altitude (3500 to 6500 feet): Decrease butter to 3 tablespoons; increase water to 1 1/4 cups. Add 1/4 cup all-purpose flour.

1 Serving: Calories 285 (Calories from Fat 110); Fat 12g (Saturated 5g); Cholesterol 50mg; Sodium 240mg; Carbohydrate 42g (Dietary Fiber 0g); Protein 2g. **% Daily Value:** Vitamin A 4%; Vitamin C 0%; Calcium 6%; Iron 4%.

Betty's Tip These homey breakfast loaves make a great gift. Wrap cooled and frosted loaves in clear or colored plastic wrap, and tie with a colorful bow. Add a reminder that the cakes are at their best if eaten within 2 or 3 days or frozen until ready to serve.

Honey-Walnut Breakfast Loaves

Pumpkin Bread

Prep: 10 min * Bake: 1 hr * Cool: 1 hr 10 min

2 LOAVES, 16 SLICES EACH

1 package Betty Crocker
SuperMoist yellow cake mix

1/3 cup vegetable oil

2 teaspoons ground cinnamon

1/2 teaspoon ground ginger

1/4 teaspoon ground cloves

1/4 teaspoon ground nutmeg

1 can (15 ounces) pumpkin
(not pumpkin pie mix)

3 eggs

1 cup currants or raisins,
if desired

1 Heat oven to 350°. Grease bottom and sides of 2 loaf pans, 8 1/2 x 4 1/2 x 2 1/2 or 9 x 5 x 3 inches, with shortening; lightly flour.

2 Beat cake mix, oil, cinnamon, ginger, cloves, nutmeg, pumpkin and eggs in large bowl with electric mixer on low speed 30 seconds; beat on medium speed 2 minutes. Stir in currants. Pour into pans.

3 Bake 8-inch loaves 50 to 60 minutes, 9-inch loaves 40 to 45 minutes, or until toothpick inserted in center comes out clean. Cool 10 minutes. Remove from pans to wire rack. Cool completely, about 1 hour. Wrap tightly and store at room temperature up to 4 days, or refrigerate up to 10 days.

High Altitude (3500 to 6500 feet): Heat oven to 375°. Add 2 tablespoons all-purpose flour to dry cake mix. Bake 8-inch loaves 48 to 58 minutes, 9-inch loaves 40 to 45 minutes.

1 Slice: Calories 95 (Calories from Fat 35); Fat 4g (Saturated 1g); Cholesterol 20mg; Sodium 110mg; Carbohydrate 14g (Dietary Fiber 0g); Protein 1g. **% Daily Value:** Vitamin A 42%; Vitamin C 0%; Calcium 4%; Iron 2%.

Betty's Tip Turn this breakfast bread into a divine dessert. Frost tops of loaves with 1 tub Betty Crocker Rich & Creamy cream cheese ready-to-spread frosting or Cream Cheese Frosting (page 234). Sprinkle with chopped nuts.

A 1958 morning just made for loafing.

Blueberry–Cream Cheese Muffins

Prep: 10 min ✳ Bake: 20 min per pan

24 MUFFINS

1 package Betty Crocker SuperMoist white cake mix

1 cup milk

1/3 cup vegetable oil

1 package (3 ounces) cream cheese, softened

3 egg whites

1 1/2 cups fresh blueberries

2 tablespoons white coarse sugar crystals (decorating sugar) or granulated sugar

1 Heat oven to 375°. Grease bottoms only of 24 medium muffin cups, 2 1/2 x 1 1/4 inches, with shortening, or line with paper baking cups.

2 Beat cake mix, milk, oil, cream cheese and egg whites in large bowl with electric mixer on low speed 30 seconds; beat on medium speed 2 minutes. Gently stir in blueberries. Divide batter evenly among muffin cups. Sprinkle with sugar crystals.

3 Bake 15 to 20 minutes or until toothpick inserted in center comes out clean. Serve warm or cool. Store tightly covered at room temperature.

High Altitude (3500 to 6500 feet): Use paper baking cups. Bake 17 to 20 minutes. Makes 30 muffins.

1 Muffin: Calories 140 (Calories from Fat 55); Fat 6g (Saturated 2g); Cholesterol 5mg; Sodium 170mg; Carbohydrate 20g (Dietary Fiber 0g); Protein 2g. **% Daily Value:** Vitamin A 2%; Vitamin C 0%; Calcium 4%; Iron 2%.

Betty's Tip Bake and freeze these muffins for an anytime treat. Place cooled muffins in a resealable plastic freezer bag and freeze up to 3 months. Thaw overnight at room temperature, or reheat in the microwave on high about 30 seconds.

Lemon Citrus Muffins

Prep: 10 min * Bake: 20 min per pan

24 MUFFINS

1 package Betty Crocker SuperMoist lemon cake mix

1/2 cup vegetable oil

4 eggs

1 can (11 ounces) mandarin orange segments, undrained

2 tablespoons white coarse sugar crystals (decorating sugar) or granulated sugar

1 Heat oven to 375°. Grease bottoms only of 24 medium muffin cups, 2 1/2 x 1 1/4 inches, with shortening, or line with paper baking cups.

2 Beat cake mix, oil, eggs and orange segments (with juice) in large bowl with electric mixer on low speed 2 minutes. Divide batter evenly among muffin cups. Sprinkle with sugar crystals.

3 Bake 15 to 20 minutes or until toothpick inserted in center comes out clean. Serve warm or cool. Store uncovered at room temperature.

High Altitude (3500 to 6500 feet): Use paper baking cups. Add 2 tablespoons all-purpose flour to dry cake mix. Makes 30 muffins.

1 Muffin: Calories 150 (Calories from Fat 65); Fat 7g (Saturated 2g); Cholesterol 35mg; Sodium 150mg; Carbohydrate 20g (Dietary Fiber 0g); Protein 2g. **% Daily Value:** Vitamin A 2%; Vitamin C 2%; Calcium 4%; Iron 2%.

Betty's Tip Take the guesswork out of filling muffin cups: use a spring-handled ice-cream scoop! The different sizes are identified by number; we recommend a No. 20 or 24.

Photo on page 151

Chocolate Chunk Muffins

Prep: 10 min * Bake: 20 min per pan

24 MUFFINS

1 package Betty Crocker SuperMoist chocolate fudge cake mix

1/2 cup chocolate milk

1/3 cup butter or margarine, melted

1 container (8 ounces) sour cream

3 eggs

1 tablespoon all-purpose flour

1 2/3 cups semisweet chocolate chunks or large semisweet chocolate chips

Powdered sugar, if desired

1 Heat oven to 375°. Line 24 medium muffin cups, 2 1/2 x 1 1/4 inches, with paper baking cups.

2 Beat cake mix, milk, butter, sour cream and eggs in large bowl with electric mixer on low speed 1 minute, scraping bowl constantly. Toss flour and chocolate in medium bowl; fold into batter. Divide batter evenly among muffin cups.

3 Bake 15 to 20 minutes or until toothpick inserted in center comes out clean. Sprinkle with powdered sugar. Serve warm or cool. Store tightly covered at room temperature.

High Altitude (3500 to 6500 feet): Add 2 tablespoons all-purpose flour to dry cake mix.

1 Muffin: Calories 200 (Calories from Fat 90); Fat 10g (Saturated 6g); Cholesterol 40mg; Sodium 190mg; Carbohydrate 26g (Dietary Fiber 1g); Protein 3g. **% Daily Value:** Vitamin A 4%; Vitamin C 0%; Calcium 4%; Iron 6%.

White Chocolate Chip Muffins: Substitute white baking chips for the semisweet chocolate chunks.

Betty's Tip Our testing showed that paper liners work best in this recipe. When baked in greased muffin cups, these rich and chocolatey cupcakes stuck to the bottom of the cups.

In 1983, you and Betty Crocker baked someone happy with a double dose of chocolate indulgence!

Carrot Scones

Prep: 15 min * Bake: 25 min * Cool: 10 min

12 SCONES

2 packages (3 ounces each)
cream cheese, softened

1 package Betty Crocker
SuperMoist carrot cake mix

1/3 cup half-and-half

1 egg

1/2 cup chopped walnuts

1/2 cup raisins

1/4 cup Easy Vanilla Glaze
(page 242) or 1/2 recipe Vanilla
Glaze (page 242)

1 Heat oven to 400°. Cut cream cheese into cake mix in large
bowl, using fork, until mixture looks like fine crumbs. Stir in
half-and-half, egg, walnuts and raisins until soft dough forms.
Place on well-floured surface. Knead 6 times.

2 Divide dough in half; shape each half into a ball. Press each ball
into 3/4-inch-thick circle (about 6 1/2 inches in diameter). Cut
each circle into 6 wedges with lightly floured knife. Place wedges
1 inch apart on ungreased cookie sheet.

3 Bake 20 to 25 minutes or until edges just begin to brown.
Remove from cookie sheet. Cool 10 minutes. Drizzle Easy
Vanilla Glaze over scones. Serve warm. Store covered at room
temperature.

High Altitude (3500 to 6500 feet): No changes.

1 Scone: Calories 330 (Calories from Fat 115); Fat 13g (Saturated 5g); Cholesterol 35mg; Sodium
360mg; Carbohydrate 50g (Dietary Fiber 1g); Protein 4g. **% Daily Value:** Vitamin A 4%; Vitamin C
0%; Calcium 12%; Iron 6%.

Betty's Tip Not into raisins? Go ahead and replace them with your
favorite dried fruit. Snip dried apricots and other large dried fruits into
smaller pieces before adding to the batter.

Carrot Scones

6
Scrumptious
Desserts

Strawberry Trifle (page 193) and Fresh Fruit Tart (page 189)

Cherry-Chocolate Baked Alaska Cake

Prep: 30 min * Bake: 35 min * Cool: 1 hr 10 min * Freeze: 6 hr

10 SERVINGS

1 package Betty Crocker
SuperMoist devil's food
cake mix

1 1/3 cups water

1/2 cup vegetable oil

3 eggs

4 cups cherry ice cream,
slightly softened

2/3 cup sugar

2 tablespoons baking cocoa

3 egg whites

1/2 teaspoon cream of tartar

1 Heat oven to 350°. Grease bottom and sides of 2 round pans,
   9 x 1 1/2 inches, with shortening. Make cake mix as directed
   on package, using water, oil and 3 eggs. Pour into pans.

2 Bake 25 to 30 minutes or until toothpick inserted in center
   comes out clean. Cool 10 minutes. Run knife around side of
   pans to loosen cakes; remove from pans to wire rack. Cool
   completely, about 1 hour. Reserve 1 layer for another use.
   Freeze remaining layer about 2 hours or until firm.

3 Cover cookie sheet with aluminum foil. Cut frozen cake layer
   horizontally to make 2 layers. Fill layers with 2 cups of the ice
   cream. Spread remaining ice cream over top of cake. Freeze
   about 4 hours or until firm.

4 Heat oven to 450°. Mix sugar and cocoa. Beat 3 egg whites and
   cream of tartar in medium bowl with electric mixer on high
   speed until foamy. Beat in sugar mixture, 1 tablespoon at a time,
   until stiff and glossy.

5 Spread meringue over top and side of cake, sealing completely.
   Bake about 5 minutes or until firm to the touch. Serve immediately, or return to freezer about 2 hours and serve frozen.

High Altitude (3500 to 6500 feet): Make cake mix following high-altitude
directions on package for 9-inch rounds.

1 Serving: Calories 380 (Calories from Fat 80); Fat 9g (Saturated 7g); Cholesterol 85mg; Sodium
460mg; Carbohydrate 69g (Dietary Fiber 1g); Protein 7g. **% Daily Value:** Vitamin A 6%; Vitamin C
0%; Calcium 12%; Iron 10%.

Betty's Tip This is the perfect do-ahead dessert. You can make it
ahead, then cover and freeze for up to two weeks. Or make and fill the
cakes ahead and prepare the meringue at the last minute to impress
your guests.

Cherry-Chocolate Baked Alaska Cake

Ice-Cream Sandwiches

Prep: 30 min * Bake: 8 min * Cool: 30 min * Freeze: 24 hr

16 SANDWICHES

1 package Betty Crocker
SuperMoist devil's food
cake mix

1/2 cup shortening

1/4 cup butter or margarine,
softened

1 teaspoon vanilla

1 egg

1 half-gallon brick vanilla
ice cream

1 Heat oven to 375°. Mix about half of the cake mix, the shortening, butter, vanilla and egg in large bowl with spoon until smooth.
Stir in remaining cake mix until dough forms.

2 Divide dough into 4 equal parts. Roll each part into rectangle,
10 x 6 inches, on lightly floured surface. Cut into rectangles,
3 x 2 1/2 inches. Place on ungreased cookie sheet.

3 Bake 6 to 8 minutes or until edges are set (cookies will be
slightly puffed). Prick surfaces of cookies lightly with fork.
Cool 1 minute; remove from cookie sheet to wire rack. Cool
completely, about 30 minutes.

4 Remove ice cream from carton and place on cutting board. Cut
ice cream lengthwise into 8 slices, each 1/2 inch thick. Cut each
slice in half to form about a 3 1/2 x 2 3/4-inch rectangle. Place
each ice-cream rectangle between 2 cooled cookies. Wrap in
aluminum foil or plastic wrap; freeze at least 24 hours but no
longer than 1 month.

High Altitude (3500 to 6500 feet): No changes.

1 Serving: Calories 350 (Calories from Fat 170); Fat 19g (Saturated 9g); Cholesterol 50mg; Sodium
320mg; Carbohydrate 42g (Dietary Fiber 1g); Protein 4g. **% Daily Value:** Vitamin A 4%; Vitamin C
0%; Calcium 12%; Iron 8%.

Betty's Tip Kids of all ages will love this heavenly taste treat! Take
your pick of frosty ice-cream flavors. Mint chocolate, cookies and cream
or chocolate chip cookie dough are super ice-cream sandwich stuffers.

*In 1974, kids found a sensational
way to sandwich in the fun with
cake and ice cream.*

Marble Cheesecake

Prep: 15 min * Bake: 35 min * Cool: 30 min * Chill: 4 hr 30 min

15 SERVINGS

1 package Betty Crocker SuperMoist devil's food cake mix

3 tablespoons butter or margarine, melted

3 eggs

1/3 cup sugar

1 package (8 ounces) cream cheese, softened

3/4 teaspoon vanilla

1 container (8 ounces) sour cream

3/4 cup whipping (heavy) cream

1 Heat oven to 350°. Grease bottom and sides of rectangular pan, 13 x 9 x 2 inches, with shortening

2 Reserve 1 cup dry cake mix for filling. Beat remaining cake mix, the butter and 1 egg in large bowl with electric mixer on low speed just until dough forms. Press in pan.

3 Beat sugar, cream cheese and vanilla in large bowl with electric mixer on medium speed until smooth. Beat in remaining 2 eggs, the sour cream and 1/2 cup of the whipping cream on low speed until smooth; reserve 1 cup cream cheese mixture. Pour remaining cream cheese mixture over crust.

4 Beat reserved cake mix, reserved cream cheese mixture and remaining 1/4 cup whipping cream in medium bowl on low speed until smooth. Drop chocolate cream cheese mixture by spoonfuls over cream cheese mixture in pan. Swirl chocolate cream cheese mixture through cream cheese mixture with knife for marbled design. Tap bottom of pan sharply on counter to level cream cheese mixtures.

5 Bake 30 to 35 minutes or until sharp knife inserted 1 inch from edge comes out clean. Cool 30 minutes on wire rack. Refrigerate 30 minutes. Run knife around sides of pan to loosen cheesecake. Refrigerate at least 4 hours until chilled. Store covered in refrigerator.

High Altitude (3500 to 6500 feet): Bake 38 to 43 minutes.

1 Serving: Calories 310 (Calories from Fat 155); Fat 17g (Saturated 10g); Cholesterol 90mg; Sodium 340mg; Carbohydrate 34g (Dietary Fiber 0g); Protein 5g. **% Daily Value:** Vitamin A 12%; Vitamin C 0%; Calcium 6%; Iron 8%.

Betty's Tip Since the chocolate cream cheese mixture is denser than the plain cream cheese mixture, it leaves ridges and hills on top of the batter. Tapping the pan sharply on the counter helps to level the batter and keeps the cheesecake from cracking.

Chocolate-Berry Cheesecake

Prep: 15 min * Bake: 45 min * Chill: 2 hr

15 SERVINGS

1 package Betty Crocker SuperMoist chocolate fudge cake mix

1/2 cup butter or margarine, softened

2 packages (8 ounces each) cream cheese, softened

1 container (6 ounces) raspberry yogurt (2/3 cup)

1 tub Betty Crocker Rich & Creamy chocolate ready-to-spread frosting or Creamy Chocolate Frosting (page 238)

3 eggs

1 1/2 cups sliced strawberries

1/2 cup blueberries

1 can (21 ounces) strawberry pie filling

1 Heat oven to 325°. Grease bottom only of rectangular pan, 13 x 9 x 2 inches, with shortening.

2 Beat cake mix and butter in large bowl with electric mixer on low speed until crumbly; reserve 1 cup. Press remaining crumbly mixture, using floured fingers, in bottom of pan.

3 Beat cream cheese, yogurt and frosting in same bowl on medium speed until smooth. Beat in eggs until blended. Pour into pan. Sprinkle with reserved crumbly mixture.

4 Bake about 45 minutes or until center is set and dry to the touch. Refrigerate at least 2 hours until chilled. Just before serving, stir strawberries and blueberries into pie filling. Top each serving with berry mixture. Store covered in refrigerator.

High Altitude (3500 to 6500 feet): Heat oven to 350°.

1 Serving: Calories 485 (Calories from Fat 245); Fat 27g (Saturated 18g); Cholesterol 90mg; Sodium 410mg; Carbohydrate 58g (Dietary Fiber 3g); Protein 6g. **% Daily Value:** Vitamin A 14%; Vitamin C 16%; Calcium 8%; Iron 8%.

Betty's Tip To quickly soften cream cheese, use your microwave. Remove foil wrapper and place cream cheese in a microwavable bowl. Microwave uncovered on Medium (50%) 1 minute to 1 minute 30 seconds for an 8-ounce package of cream cheese.

Chocolate-Berry Cheesecake

Cherry Cheesecake

Prep: 15 min * Bake: 40 min * Cool: 1 hr * Chill: 8 hr

24 SERVINGS

1 package Betty Crocker
SuperMoist yellow cake mix

1/2 cup butter or margarine,
softened

1/2 cup finely chopped slivered
almonds

1 egg

3 packages (8 ounces each)
cream cheese, softened

3 eggs

1 1/4 cups sugar

1 tablespoon vanilla

1 1/2 cups sour cream

1/3 cup sugar

2 teaspoons vanilla

2 cans (21 ounces each)
cherry pie filling

1 Heat oven to 350°. Grease jelly roll pan, 15 1/2 x 10 1/2 x 1 inch,
   with shortening.

2 Beat cake mix, butter, almonds and 1 egg in large bowl with
   electric mixer on low speed until crumbly. Press lightly in pan.
   Bake 10 to 12 minutes or until light brown; cool while continuing
   with recipe.

3 Beat cream cheese, 3 eggs, 1 1/4 cups sugar and 1 tablespoon
   vanilla in large bowl on low speed until smooth and fluffy. Spread
   over cake mixture. Bake 25 to 28 minutes or until center is set
   when lightly touched.

4 Mix sour cream, 1/3 cup sugar and 2 teaspoons vanilla until
   smooth; spread over cheesecake. Cool at room temperature
   1 hour. Spread pie filling over sour cream mixture. Cover and
   refrigerate at least 8 hours but no longer than 24 hours. Store
   covered in refrigerator.

High Altitude (3500 to 6500 feet): Increase first bake time to 12 to 14 minutes.

1 Serving: Calories 375 (Calories from Fat 180); Fat 20g (Saturated 11g); Cholesterol 85mg;
Sodium 260mg; Carbohydrate 45g (Dietary Fiber 1g); Protein 5g. **% Daily Value:** Vitamin A 14%;
Vitamin C 0%; Calcium 8%; Iron 6%.

Blueberry Cheesecake: Substitute 2 cans (21 ounces each) blueberry
pie filling for the cherry pie filling.

Betty's Tip Dusting your hands with a little bit of flour before patting
the crust into the pan keeps the dough from sticking to your hands.

Fabulous Finishing Touches

It's easy to turn a basic cake into a showstopper! Here are some irresistible ideas to make your cakes look as good as they taste.

Simple Additions

Create chocolate cutouts: Melt a 4-ounce bar of sweet cooking chocolate or 4 ounces of semisweet baking chocolate. Spread the melted chocolate over the outside bottom of an 8-inch square pan. Refrigerate until firm; bring to room temperature. Use cookie cutters in desired shapes and sizes to make cutouts. Refrigerate until ready to place on the cake.

Garnish with chocolate curls: Place a bar or block of chocolate on a sheet of waxed paper; let stand in a warm place for 15 minutes. Press a vegetable parer firmly against the bar of chocolate and pull the parer toward you in long, thin strokes to make curls. Transfer each curl carefully with a wooden pick to avoid breaking.

Dust with powdered sugar, cinnamon or cocoa: Place a paper doily or stencil on top of a frosted or unfrosted cake. Shake powdered sugar generously through a sieve over the doily; carefully remove doily. Try cocoa mixed with powdered sugar for added color variation.

Embellish with fresh flowers: Place fresh flowers in floral tubes. Poke the tubes right into the cake top. Remove the containers before slicing the cake.

Frosting Flourishes

Thread it: Frost the cake with a fluffy frosting. Dip a piece of white sewing thread in liquid food color; stretching it taut, press into frosting. Repeat, using a new thread for each color.

Go geometric: Pour melted chocolate or chocolate syrup over the top of a frosted layer cake, beginning with a small circle in the center and encircling with larger circles 1 inch apart. Alternately draw a spatula or knife from the center outward and from the outside inward 8 times.

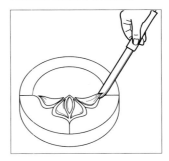

Make waves: Use the tines of a fork to make wave designs in the frosting.

On the wedge: Mark top and side of a frosted layered cake into 8 equal wedges and panels. Sprinkle candies over alternate wedges and press onto alternate side panels.

Pick your own pattern: Draw a design on a frosted cake, or dip a cookie cutter in food color and press it into the frosting. Fill in the design with crushed candies, colored sugar or chopped nuts.

Banana Split Dessert

Prep: 20 min * Bake: 38 min * Cool: 1 hr

15 SERVINGS

1 package Betty Crocker SuperMoist yellow cake mix

1 cup mashed very ripe bananas (about 2 medium)*

1/4 cup vegetable oil

3 eggs

1/4 cup baking cocoa

1/3 cup well-drained finely chopped maraschino cherries

1 quart vanilla ice cream, slightly softened

1/2 cup chocolate fudge topping, warmed

1 cup frozen (thawed) whipped topping or Sweetened Whipped Cream (page 243), if desired

Maraschino cherries with stems, if desired

*Do not use frozen bananas. Frozen bananas contain too much moisture and may cause the cake to sink and become gummy.

1 Heat oven to 350°. Grease bottom only of rectangular pan, 13 x 9 x 2 inches, with shortening.

2 Beat cake mix, bananas, oil and eggs in large bowl with electric mixer on low speed 30 seconds; beat on medium speed 2 minutes. Pour 1 1/2 cups of the batter into small bowl; stir in cocoa. Spread remaining batter in pan; sprinkle with chopped cherries. Drop cocoa batter by generous tablespoonfuls onto batter in pan. Cut through batters with knife or metal spatula several times for marbled design.

3 Bake 33 to 38 minutes or until toothpick inserted in center comes out clean. Run knife around side of pan to loosen cake. Cool completely, about 1 hour.

4 Cut cake into serving pieces. Split each serving of cake horizontally in half. Top bottom halves with ice cream; top with top halves of cake. Drizzle with fudge topping. Garnish with whipped topping and cherry. Serve immediately.

High Altitude (3500 to 6500 feet): Not recommended.

1 Serving: Calories 250 (Calories from Fat 80); Fat 9g (Saturated 3g); Cholesterol 40mg; Sodium 270mg; Carbohydrate 40g (Dietary Fiber 1g); Protein 3g. **% Daily Value:** Vitamin A 2%; Vitamin C 0%; Calcium 8%; Iron 6%.

Betty's Tip Just like an old-fashioned ice-cream parlor treat, this cake will bring back memories of days past. If you've had your fill of vanilla ice cream, get your licks in with chocolate, strawberry or Neapolitan.

Banana Split Dessert

Easy Fruit Crisp "Dump" Dessert

Prep: 5 min * Bake: 50 min * Cool: 30 min

12 SERVINGS

1 can (21 ounces) cherry
pie filling

1 can (8 ounces) crushed
pineapple, undrained

1 package Betty Crocker
SuperMoist yellow or butter
recipe yellow cake mix

1/2 cup butter or margarine,
melted

Vanilla ice cream, if desired

1 Heat oven to 350°. Spread pie filling and pineapple in ungreased
rectangular pan, 13 x 9 x 2 inches.

2 Stir cake mix and butter in large bowl, using spoon, until
crumbly. Sprinkle mixture evenly over fruit.

3 Bake 45 to 50 minutes or until deep golden brown. Cool
30 minutes. Serve warm or cool with ice cream. Store covered
in refrigerator.

High Altitude (3500 to 6500 feet): Heat oven to 375°.

1 Serving: Calories 300 (Calories from Fat 100); Fat 11g (Saturated 6g); Cholesterol 20mg; Sodium
320mg; Carbohydrate 50g (Dietary Fiber 1g); Protein 1g. **% Daily Value:** Vitamin A 6%; Vitamin C
2%; Calcium 8%; Iron 4%.

Betty's Tip Looking for some simple substitutions? If you have it on
hand, SuperMoist white cake mix can also be used instead of the yellow
cake mix. No pineapple lovers in your family? Use 2 cans of cherry pie
filling instead.

Easy Fruit Crisp "Dump" Dessert

Caramel-Apple Sundae Cake

Prep: 10 min * Bake: 50 min * Cool: 30 min

15 SERVINGS

1 package Betty Crocker SuperMoist yellow cake mix

1 cup chopped nuts

1/3 cup packed brown sugar

1/4 cup butter or margarine, softened

1 teaspoon ground cinnamon

1/3 cup water

2 tablespoons vegetable oil

2 eggs

3 medium cooking apples, peeled and sliced

1/2 cup caramel topping

Ice cream, if desired

Additional caramel topping, if desired

1 Heat oven to 350°. Grease bottom and sides of rectangular pan, 13 x 9 x 2 inches, with shortening; lightly flour.

2 Mix 1 cup of the cake mix, the nuts, brown sugar, butter and cinnamon in small bowl with fork until crumbly; set aside.

3 Mix remaining cake mix, 1/3 cup water, the oil and eggs in medium bowl with spoon (batter will be lumpy). Spread in pan. Arrange apple slices on top. Sprinkle with half of the crumbly mixture. Drizzle with 1/2 cup caramel topping. Sprinkle with remaining crumbly mixture.

4 Bake 45 to 50 minutes or until cake is golden brown and pulls away from sides of pan. Cool about 30 minutes. Serve warm with ice cream and additional caramel topping. Store covered in refrigerator.

High Altitude (3500 to 6500 feet): Bake 50 to 55 minutes.

1 Serving: Calories 310 (Calories from Fat 125); Fat 14g (Saturated 4g); Cholesterol 35mg; Sodium 290mg; Carbohydrate 45g (Dietary Fiber 1g); Protein 2g. **% Daily Value:** Vitamin A 2%; Vitamin C 0%; Calcium 8%; Iron 4%.

Betty's Tip Be picky when picking your apples for this recipe. Cooking apples, such as Rome Beauty, Granny Smith and Greening, have a firm texture and will hold their shape when baked in this dessert.

Betty had it caramel-covered in 1969 with an apple cake that was good to the core.

Fresh Fruit Tart

Prep: 15 min * Bake: 18 min * Cool: 30 min

12 SERVINGS

1 package Betty Crocker SuperMoist lemon cake mix

1/2 cup butter or margarine, softened

1 egg

3 containers (6 ounces each) vanilla yogurt (2 cups)

1 package (4-serving size) vanilla instant pudding and pie filling mix

1 cup sliced kiwifruit

1 cup sliced strawberries

3/4 cup fresh blueberries

3 tablespoons apricot preserves

1 cup fresh raspberries

1 Heat oven to 350°. Grease 12-inch pizza pan or rectangular pan, 13 x 9 x 2 inches, with shortening.

2 Mix cake mix, butter and egg until crumbly. Press on bottom of pan. Bake 15 to 18 minutes or until set. Cool completely, about 30 minutes.

3 Beat yogurt and pudding mix (dry) in medium bowl with electric mixer on medium speed until blended. Spoon over baked layer. Smooth surface with rubber spatula.

4 Arrange kiwifruit and strawberry slices around edge of yogurt mixture. Arrange blueberries around inside edge of fruit. Heat preserves over low heat until melted. Brush over fruit. Mound raspberries in center. Serve immediately, or refrigerate up to 24 hours. Store covered in refrigerator.

High Altitude (3500 to 6500 feet): Add 2 tablespoons all-purpose flour to dry cake mix. Bake 16 to 19 minutes.

1 Serving: Calories 350 (Calories from Fat 110); Fat 12g (Saturated 6g); Cholesterol 40mg; Sodium 470mg; Carbohydrate 59g (Dietary Fiber 2g); Protein 4g. **% Daily Value:** Vitamin A 6%; Vitamin C 44%; Calcium 16%; Iron 6%.

Betty's Tip In a pinch, a 21-ounce can of blueberry, cherry or apple pie filling can be substituted for the kiwifruit, strawberries, preserves and raspberries. Spoon pie filling to within 1 inch of edge of yogurt mixture.

Photo on page 175

Peachy Fruit Pizza

Prep: 15 min   *   Bake: 40 min   *   Cool: 1 hr

12 SERVINGS

1 package Betty Crocker
SuperMoist yellow cake mix

1/2 cup butter or margarine,
slightly softened

1/4 cup packed brown sugar

1 teaspoon ground cinnamon

1 cup sour cream

1 egg

1 can (29 ounces) sliced
peaches, drained and
patted dry

1/2 cup finely chopped nuts,
if desired

Cinnamon Glaze (below)

Cinnamon Glaze

1/2 cup powdered sugar

1/8 teaspoon ground cinnamon

2 teaspoons milk

1 Heat oven to 350°. Mix cake mix, butter, brown sugar and
cinnamon in large bowl with spoon until crumbly; reserve 1 cup
mixture. Press remaining crumbly mixture on bottom and side
of ungreased 12-inch pizza pan or on bottom only of ungreased
rectangular pan, 13 x 9 x 2 inches.

2 Beat sour cream and egg with spoon until blended; carefully
spread over crumbly mixture. Top with peaches. Sprinkle with
reserved crumbly mixture and the nuts.

3 Bake 35 to 40 minutes or until topping is light golden brown
and center is set. Cool completely, about 1 hour. Drizzle with
Cinnamon Glaze. Store covered in refrigerator.

Cinnamon Glaze

Stir all ingredients until consistency of thick syrup, adding
additional milk, 1 teaspoon at a time, if necessary.

High Altitude (3500 to 6500 feet): Heat oven to 375°. Bake 40 to 45 minutes.

1 Serving: Calories 355 (Calories from Fat 135); Fat 15g (Saturated 8g); Cholesterol 50mg; Sodium
340mg; Carbohydrate 53g (Dietary Fiber 1g); Protein 2g. **% Daily Value:** Vitamin A 18%; Vitamin
C 2%; Calcium 2%; Iron 2%.

Fresh Apple Pizza: Substitute 2 medium apples, thinly sliced,
for the peaches.

Betty's Tip For a sweet ending to any meal, serve this fruity pizza with
a scoop of vanilla, butter pecan or *dulce de leche* ice cream.

Peachy Fruit Pizza

Plum-Pear Cobbler

Prep: 15 min * Bake: 45 min

12 SERVINGS

2 cans (16 1/2 ounces each) purple plums in heavy syrup

1 package Betty Crocker SuperMoist white cake mix

1/2 cup milk

2 tablespoons butter or margarine, melted

2 eggs

4 pears, peeled and sliced (4 cups)

1 teaspoon grated lemon peel

1/4 teaspoon ground cinnamon

1/8 teaspoon ground nutmeg

1 tablespoon sugar

1 Heat oven to 375°. Grease bottom only of rectangular pan, 13 x 9 x 2 inches, with shortening. Drain plums, reserving syrup. Remove pits from plums.

2 Mix cake mix, milk, butter and eggs with spoon until moistened (batter will be slightly lumpy). Spread evenly in pan.

3 Mix plums (with syrup), pears, lemon peel, 1/4 teaspoon cinnamon and the nutmeg in large bowl; pour over batter.

4 Bake 40 to 45 minutes or until cake springs back when touched lightly in center.

5 Mix sugar and 1/4 teaspoon cinnamon; sprinkle over baked cobbler. Serve warm. Store covered in refrigerator.

High Altitude (3500 to 6500 feet): Heat oven to 400°. Bake 45 to 50 minutes.

1 Serving: Calories 320 (Calories from Fat 65); Fat 7g (Saturated 5g); Cholesterol 40mg; Sodium 330mg; Carbohydrate 62g (Dietary Fiber 2g); Protein 4g. **% Daily Value:** Vitamin A 4%; Vitamin C 2%; Calcium 10%; Iron 8%.

Betty's Tip Cobblers and crisps taste best the day they are baked. This one is especially good served warm from the oven with Sweetened Whipped Cream (page 243) or ice cream.

Strawberry Trifle

Prep: 15 min　*　Bake: 33 min　*　Cool: 1 hr　*　Chill: 2 hr

16 SERVINGS

1 package Betty Crocker
SuperMoist white cake mix

1 1/4 cups water

1/3 cup vegetable oil

3 egg whites

2 packages (4-serving size
each) vanilla instant pudding
and pie filling mix

4 cups milk

2 bags (16 ounces each) frozen
strawberries, thawed

1 1/2 cups frozen (thawed)
whipped topping or
Sweetened Whipped Cream
(page 243)

1/4 cup slivered almonds,
toasted (page 36)

1　Heat oven to 350°. Grease bottom only of rectangular pan,
13 x 9 x 2 inches, with shortening.

2　Make cake mix as directed on package, using water, oil and
egg whites. Pour into pan.

3　Bake 28 to 33 minutes or until toothpick inserted in center
comes out clean. Run knife around side of pan to loosen cake.
Cool completely, about 1 hour.

4　While cake is cooling, beat pudding mix into milk in large bowl
with wire whisk about 2 minutes or until blended.

5　Cut or tear cake into 1-inch pieces. Arrange half the pieces in
3 1/2-quart glass serving bowl, cutting pieces to fit shape of bowl.
Pour half the thawed strawberries (with syrup) over cake; spread
with 2 cups of the pudding. Place remaining cake pieces on pudding and around edge of bowl. Top with remaining strawberries
and pudding. Cover and refrigerate at least 2 hours until chilled.

6　Spread whipped topping over top of cake. Sprinkle with almonds.
Store covered in refrigerator up to 12 hours.

High Altitude (3500 to 6500 feet): Make cake mix following high-altitude
directions on package.

1 Serving: Calories 340 (Calories from Fat 100); Fat 11g (Saturated 3g); Cholesterol 5mg; Sodium
440mg; Carbohydrate 56g (Dietary Fiber 1g); Protein 5g. **% Daily Value:** Vitamin A 2%; Vitamin C
40%; Calcium 12%; Iron 4%.

Betty's Tip Also known as "punch bowl cake," this showy layered
dessert is just as delicious made with other fruits such as pineapple,
mango, blueberries, raspberries or a mixture of berries.

Photo on page 174

*In the 1970s, families didn't need
a special occasion to share this
elegant, middle-of-the-week treat.*

Pumpkin Pie Crunch

Prep: 10 min * Bake: 1 hr * Cool: 1 hr 30 min

12 SERVINGS

1 can (15 ounces) pumpkin
(not pumpkin pie mix)

1 can (12 ounces) evaporated
milk

3 eggs

1 cup sugar

4 teaspoons pumpkin pie spice

1 package Betty Crocker
SuperMoist white cake mix

1 1/2 cups chopped pecans or
walnuts

3/4 cup butter or margarine,
melted

1 Heat oven to 350°. Grease bottom and sides of rectangular pan,
13 x 9 x 2 inches, with shortening.

2 Stir pumpkin, milk, eggs, sugar and pumpkin pie spice until
smooth. Pour into pan. Sprinkle cake mix over pumpkin mixture.
Sprinkle with pecans. Pour melted butter evenly over top.

3 Bake 50 to 60 minutes or until knife inserted in center of dessert
comes out clean. Cool completely, about 1 hour 30 minutes.
Store covered in refrigerator.

High Altitude (3500 to 6500 feet): Heat oven to 375°.

1 Serving: Calories 515 (Calories from Fat 250); Fat 28g (Saturated 11g); Cholesterol 90mg;
Sodium 420mg; Carbohydrate 60g (Dietary Fiber 2g); Protein 8g. **% Daily Value:** Vitamin A 100%;
Vitamin C 2%; Calcium 20%; Iron 10%.

Betty's Tip For a fabulous taste treat, top this pumpkin dessert with
a scoop of butter pecan or cinnamon ice cream.

Pumpkin Pie Crunch

All-Time FAVORITE

Lemon Chiffon Dessert

Prep: 25 min * Bake: 47 min * Cool: 2 hr * Chill: 4 hr

15 SERVINGS

1 package Betty Crocker 1-step white angel food cake mix

1 1/4 cups cold water

2 cups boiling water

1 package (8-serving size) lemon-flavored gelatin

1 can (6 ounces) frozen lemon-ade concentrate, thawed

1 1/2 cups whipping (heavy) cream

1 Move oven rack to lowest position (remove other racks). Heat oven to 350°.

2 Beat cake mix and cold water in extra-large glass or metal bowl with electric mixer on low speed 30 seconds; beat on medium speed 1 minute. Pour into ungreased angel food cake pan (tube pan), 10 x 4 inches. (Do not use bundt cake pan or 9 x 3 1/2-inch angel food pan or batter will overflow.)

3 Bake 37 to 47 minutes or until top is dark golden brown and cracks feel very dry and not sticky. Do not underbake. Immediately turn pan upside down onto glass bottle until cake is completely cool, about 2 hours. Run knife around edges of cake; remove from pan.

4 Pour boiling water on gelatin in large bowl; stir until gelatin is dissolved. Refrigerate about 15 minutes or until thickened but not set. Add enough cold water to lemonade concentrate to measure 2 cups; stir into gelatin. Beat with electric mixer on medium speed until foamy; set aside. Beat whipping cream in chilled medium bowl on high speed until stiff; fold into gelatin.

5 Tear cake into about 1-inch pieces. Fold cake pieces into gelatin mixture. Spread in ungreased rectangular baking dish, 13 x 9 x 2 inches. Cover and refrigerate at least 4 hours until firm but no longer than 24 hours. Store covered in refrigerator.

High Altitude (3500 to 6500 feet): Make cake mix following high-altitude directions on package for angel food pan.

1 serving: Calories 240 (Calories from Fat 65); Fat 7g (Saturated 5g); Cholesterol 25mg; Sodium 330mg; Carbohydrate 40g (Dietary Fiber 0g); Protein 4g. **% Daily Value:** Vitamin A 6%; Vitamin C 4%; Calcium 8%; Iron 2%.

Betty's Tip This refreshing do-ahead dessert is perfect for a springtime lunch or bridal shower. Serve with small scoops of mango or raspberry sorbet and a garnish of fresh mint sprigs.

A dessert-time delight that's frosty, cool, delicious and perfect for a 1959 hot summer evening.

Frozen Angel Toffee Dessert

Prep: 20 min * Bake: 47 min * Cool: 2 hr * Freeze: 1 hr 30 min

15 SERVINGS

1 package Betty Crocker 1-step white angel food cake mix

1 1/4 cups cold water

6 bars (1.4 ounces each) chocolate-covered English toffee candy

1 container (8 ounces) frozen whipped topping, thawed, or 3 cups Sweetened Whipped Cream (page 243)

1 Move oven rack to lowest position (remove other racks). Heat oven to 350°.

2 Beat cake mix and water in extra-large glass or metal bowl with electric mixer on low speed 30 seconds; beat on medium speed 1 minute. Pour into ungreased angel food cake pan (tube pan), 10 x 4 inches. (Do not use bundt cake pan or 9 x 3 1/2-inch angel food pan or batter will overflow.)

3 Bake 37 to 47 minutes or until top is dark golden brown and cracks feel very dry and not sticky. Do not underbake. Immediately turn pan upside down onto glass bottle until cake is completely cool, about 2 hours. Run knife around edges of cake; remove from pan.

4 Crush or finely chop candy bars; reserve 1/3 cup. Fold remaining crushed candy into whipped topping.

5 Tear cake into about 1-inch pieces. Mix cake pieces and whipped topping mixture. Press lightly into ungreased rectangular pan, 13 x 9 x 2 inches. Sprinkle with reserved crushed candy. Freeze dessert about 1 hour 30 minutes or until firm. Cut into squares or spoon into dessert dishes. Store covered in freezer.

High Altitude (3500 to 6500 feet): Heat oven to 325°. Stir 1/3 cup cornstarch into dry cake mix. Increase water to 1 1/3 cups. Beat on low speed 30 seconds; beat on medium speed 3 minutes. Bake 53 to 58 minutes.

1 Serving: Calories 210 (Calories from Fat 65); Fat 7g (Saturated 3g); Cholesterol 4mg; Sodium 280mg; Carbohydrate 34g (Dietary Fiber 1g); Protein 4g. **% Daily Value:** Vitamin A 0%; Vitamin C 0%; Calcium 2%; Iron 2%.

Betty's Tip Get cracking on this cake—freeze the candy bars for easier crushing or chopping. Or if you're in a hurry, just buy chocolate-covered toffee bits.

Rainbow Sherbet Roll

Prep: 15 min * Bake: 45 min * Cool: 1 hr 10 min * Freeze: 6 hr

12 SERVINGS

1 package Betty Crocker 1-step white angel food cake mix

1 1/4 cups cold water

Powdered sugar

1 1/2 cups raspberry sherbet, softened

1 1/2 cups orange sherbet, softened

1 1/2 cups lime sherbet, softened

1 Move oven rack to lowest position (remove other racks). Heat oven to 350°. Line jelly roll pan, 15 1/2 x 10 1/2 x 1 inch, with waxed paper.

2 Beat cake mix and water in extra-large glass or metal bowl with electric mixer on low speed 30 seconds; beat on medium speed 1 minute. Spread half of the batter in jelly roll pan. Spread remaining batter in ungreased loaf pan, 9 x 5 x 3 inches.

3 Bake jelly roll pan 20 to 25 minutes, loaf pan 35 to 45 minutes, or until top springs back when touched lightly in center. Cool loaf cake and reserve for another use.

4 Cool jelly roll pan 10 minutes. Run knife around edge of pan to loosen cake; turn upside down onto towel sprinkled with powdered sugar. Carefully remove pan and waxed paper. Trim off stiff edges of cake if necessary. Carefully roll hot cake and towel from narrow end. Cool completely, about 1 hour.

5 Unroll cake; remove towel. Beginning at a narrow end, spread raspberry sherbet on one-third of cake, orange sherbet on next one-third of cake and lime sherbet on remaining cake. Roll up carefully. Place roll, seam side down, on 18 x 12-inch piece of aluminum foil. Wrap in foil; freeze at least 6 hours until firm. Remove from freezer 15 minutes before serving. Cut roll into 3/4-inch slices. Store covered in freezer.

High Altitude (3500 to 6500 feet): Make cake mix following high-altitude directions on package.

1 Serving: Calories 185 (Calories from Fat 10); Fat 1g (Saturated 1g); Cholesterol 5mg; Sodium 280mg; Carbohydrate 40g (Dietary Fiber 0g); Protein 4g. **% Daily Value:** Vitamin A 0%; Vitamin C 0%; Calcium 2%; Iron 4%.

Betty's Tip For a light and luscious treat, cut the leftover loaf cake into slices and serve with a dollop of whipped topping and fresh berries.

Rainbow Sherbet Roll

7

Easy Cookies
and Bars

**Chocolate Crinkle Cookies (page 202), Kissed Crinkle Cookies (variation, page 202),
Lollipop Cookies (page 212) and White Chocolate–Cranberry Bars (page 226)**

Chocolate Crinkle Cookies

Prep: 10 min ✳ Bake: 10 min per sheet ✳ Cool: 1 min

ABOUT 4 DOZEN COOKIES

1 package Betty Crocker
SuperMoist devil's food or
chocolate fudge cake mix

1/3 cup vegetable oil

2 eggs

Granulated sugar

1 Heat oven to 350°. Mix cake mix, oil and eggs in large bowl with spoon until dough forms.

2 Shape dough into 1-inch balls; roll in sugar. Place about 2 inches apart on ungreased cookie sheet.

3 Bake 8 to 10 minutes or until set. Cool 1 minute; remove from cookie sheet to wire rack.

High Altitude (3500 to 6500 feet): No changes.

1 Cookie: Calories 60 (Calories from Fat 20); Fat 2g (Saturated 1g); Cholesterol 10mg; Sodium 80mg; Carbohydrate 10g (Dietary Fiber 0g); Protein 0g. **% Daily Value:** Vitamin A 0%; Vitamin C 0%; Calcium 0%; Iron 0%.

Kissed Crinkle Cookies: Roll balls of dough in powdered sugar. Bake as directed, then immediately press a milk chocolate kiss or white chocolate kiss with milk chocolate stripes in the center of each cookie.

Betty's Tip For a soft and powdery look instead of a sparkly crystal one, try rolling your cookies in powdered sugar instead of granulated sugar.

Photo on page 200

Oatmeal-Raisin Cookies

Prep: 15 min * Bake: 12 min per sheet

ABOUT 4 DOZEN COOKIES

1 cup butter or margarine, softened

1/2 cup sugar

1 egg

1 teaspoon vanilla

1 package Betty Crocker SuperMoist yellow cake mix

2 cups quick-cooking oats

1 cup raisins

1 Heat oven to 350°. Stir butter, sugar, egg and vanilla in large bowl with spoon. Stir in cake mix and oats until blended. Stir in raisins.

2 Drop dough by rounded teaspoonfuls about 2 inches apart onto ungreased cookie sheet.

3 Bake about 12 minutes or until light brown. Immediately remove from cookie sheet to wire rack.

High Altitude (3500 to 6500 feet): No changes.

1 Cookie: Calories 115 (Calories from Fat 45); Fat 5g (Saturated 2g); Cholesterol 15mg; Sodium 95mg; Carbohydrate 16g (Dietary Fiber 0g); Protein 1g. **% Daily Value:** Vitamin A 2%; Vitamin C 0%; Calcium 2%; Iron 0%.

Betty's Tip Did you know that not all oats are the same? Quick-cooking oats are smaller than old-fashioned oats and absorb moisture better, which makes them especially good for holding these cookies together.

With Dad and the kids around, the cookie jar didn't stay full for long in 1972.

Old-Fashioned Peanut Butter Cookies

Prep: 10 min ✳ Bake: 12 min per sheet ✳ Cool: 1 min

ABOUT 4 1/2 DOZEN COOKIES

1 package Betty Crocker SuperMoist yellow or butter recipe yellow cake mix

1/3 cup water

1 cup creamy peanut butter

2 eggs

Sugar

1 Heat oven to 375°. Beat half of the cake mix, the water, peanut butter and eggs in large bowl with electric mixer on medium speed until smooth, or mix with spoon. Stir in remaining cake mix.

2 Drop dough by rounded teaspoonfuls about 2 inches apart onto ungreased cookie sheet. Flatten in crisscross pattern with fork dipped in sugar.

3 Bake 10 to 12 minutes or until golden brown. Cool 1 minute; remove from cookie sheet to wire rack.

High Altitude (3500 to 6500 feet): No changes.

1 Cookie: Calories 70 (Calories from Fat 25); Fat 3g (Saturated 1g); Cholesterol 10mg; Sodium 85mg; Carbohydrate 9g (Dietary Fiber 0g); Protein 2g. **% Daily Value:** Vitamin A 0%; Vitamin C 0%; Calcium 2%; Iron 2%.

Chocolate-Peanut Butter Sandwich Cookies: Spread 1 to 2 teaspoons chocolate frosting between bottoms of two cookies and press lightly.

Betty's Tip Give a new look to peanut butter cookies by pressing the bottom of a cut-crystal glass, a metal meat tenderizer, a potato masher or cookie stamp into cookies before baking. Whichever one you use, be sure to dip it in sugar each time you press a cookie.

Old-Fashioned Peanut Butter Cookies

Chocolate Chip Cookies

Prep: 10 min ✳ Bake: 12 min per sheet ✳ Cool: 1 min

ABOUT 3 1/2 DOZEN COOKIES

1 package Betty Crocker SuperMoist yellow cake mix

1/2 cup butter or margarine, softened

1 teaspoon vanilla

2 eggs

1/2 cup chopped nuts

1 bag (6 ounces) semisweet chocolate chips (1 cup)

1 Heat oven to 350°. Beat half of the cake mix, the butter, vanilla and eggs in large bowl with electric mixer on medium speed until smooth, or mix with spoon. Stir in remaining cake mix, the nuts and chocolate chips.

2 Drop dough by rounded teaspoonfuls about 2 inches apart onto ungreased cookie sheet.

3 Bake 10 to 12 minutes or until edges are set (centers will be soft). Cool 1 minute; remove from cookie sheet to wire rack.

High Altitude (3500 to 6500 feet): No changes.

1 Cookie: Calories 110 (Calories from Fat 55); Fat 6g (Saturated 3g); Cholesterol 15mg; Sodium 90mg; Carbohydrate 13g (Dietary Fiber 0g); Protein 1g. **% Daily Value:** Vitamin A 0%; Vitamin C 0%; Calcium 0%; Iron 0%.

Double-Chocolate Chip Cookies: Use SuperMoist chocolate fudge or devil's food cake mix instead of the yellow cake mix.

Ice-Cream Cookie Sandwiches: For each sandwich, place 1 heaping tablespoon of slightly softened ice cream between bottoms of 2 cookies and press sandwich in center to spread ice cream. Freeze uncovered on cookie sheet about 1 hour or until firm. Wrap each sandwich in plastic wrap, and store in the freezer in a plastic freezer bag.

Betty's Tip For best results, store these chewy cookies in a tightly covered container so they stay moist.

Chocolate Chip Cookies

Spicy Pumpkin Cookies

Prep: 15 min * Bake: 12 min per sheet * Cool: 30 min

ABOUT 2 1/2 DOZEN COOKIES

1 package Betty Crocker SuperMoist yellow cake mix

2 teaspoons pumpkin pie spice

1 cup canned pumpkin (not pumpkin pie mix)

1/4 cup butter or margarine, softened

1/2 cup raisins, if desired

1 cup Betty Crocker Rich & Creamy vanilla ready-to-spread frosting or 1/2 recipe Vanilla Buttercream Frosting (page 236)

Ground nutmeg or cinnamon, if desired

1 Heat oven to 375°. Lightly grease cookie sheet with shortening. Mix cake mix and pumpkin pie spice in large bowl. Stir in pumpkin and butter until well blended. Stir in raisins.

2 Drop dough by generous tablespoonfuls about 2 inches apart onto cookie sheet.

3 Bake 11 to 12 minutes or until set and light golden brown around edges. Cool 1 to 2 minutes; remove from cookie sheet to wire rack. Cool completely, about 30 minutes. Frost with frosting. Sprinkle with nutmeg.

High Altitude (3500 to 6500 feet): Bake 12 to 13 minutes.

1 Cookie: Calories 85 (Calories from Fat 35); Fat 4g (Saturated 2g); Cholesterol 5mg; Sodium 120mg; Carbohydrate 22g (Dietary Fiber 0g); Protein 0g. **% Daily Value:** Vitamin A 26%; Vitamin C 0%; Calcium 2%; Iron 2%.

Betty's Tip If pumpkin pie spice isn't handy, use 1 teaspoon ground cinnamon, 1/2 teaspoon ground nutmeg and 1/2 teaspoon ground ginger instead. If you prefer nuts to raisins, substitute 1/2 cup of chopped pecans or walnuts for the raisins.

Spicy Pumpkin Cookies

Lemon Cookies

Prep: 15 min ✳ Bake: 12 min per sheet ✳ Cool: 30 min

ABOUT 2 1/2 DOZEN COOKIES

1 package Betty Crocker SuperMoist lemon cake mix

1/3 cup shortening

1/3 cup butter or margarine, softened

1 egg

1 tub Betty Crocker Whipped or Rich & Creamy lemon ready-to-spread frosting or Lemon Buttercream Frosting (page 236)

1 Heat oven to 375°. Stir half of the cake mix, the shortening, butter and egg in medium bowl until well mixed. Stir in remaining cake mix.

2 Drop dough by rounded teaspoonfuls about 2 inches apart onto ungreased cookie sheet.

3 Bake 10 to 12 minutes or until light brown around edges. Cool 1 minute; remove from cookie sheet to wire rack. Cool completely, about 30 minutes. Frost with frosting.

High Altitude (3500 to 6500 feet): No changes.

1 Cookie: Calories 145 (Calories from Fat 65); Fat 7g (Saturated 2g); Cholesterol 5mg; Sodium 160mg; Carbohydrate 21g (Dietary Fiber 0g); Protein 0g. **% Daily Value:** Vitamin A 2%; Vitamin C 0%; Calcium 8%; Iron 4%.

Betty's Tip If you really love lemon, add 1 teaspoon grated lemon peel to the dough and stir 1 teaspoon grated lemon peel into the frosting.

Snickerdoodles

Prep: 10 min * Bake: 12 min per sheet

ABOUT 3 DOZEN COOKIES

1 package Betty Crocker
SuperMoist white cake mix

1/4 cup vegetable oil

2 eggs

2 tablespoons sugar

1 teaspoon ground cinnamon

1 Heat oven to 350°. Mix cake mix, oil and eggs in large bowl with spoon until dough forms (some dry mix will remain).

2 Shape dough into 1-inch balls. Mix sugar and cinnamon in small bowl. Roll balls in cinnamon-sugar mixture. Place about 2 inches apart on ungreased cookie sheet.

3 Bake 10 to 12 minutes or until set. Remove from cookie sheet to wire rack.

High Altitude (3500 to 6500 feet): No changes.

1 Cookie: Calories 70 (Calories from Fat 25); Fat 3g (Saturated 1g); Cholesterol 10mg; Sodium 100mg; Carbohydrate 12g (Dietary Fiber 0g); Protein 1g. **% Daily Value:** Vitamin A 0%; Vitamin C 0%; Calcium 2%; Iron 0%.

Betty's Tip Size up your snickerdoodles! Shape dough into 1 1/2-inch balls and place them about 3 inches apart on baking sheet; bake 12 to 14 minutes. You'll get about 20 cookies.

Holiday baking made easy in the 1950s. Now you can have your cake and cookies, too!

Lollipop Cookies

Prep: 20 min * Bake: 11 min per sheet * Cool: 30 min

ABOUT 2 DOZEN COOKIES

1 package Betty Crocker
SuperMoist white cake mix

1/3 cup vegetable oil

2 eggs

About 24 wooden sticks with
rounded ends

1 tub Betty Crocker Rich & Creamy
ready-to-spread frosting (any
flavor) or Vanilla Buttercream
Frosting (page 236)

Candy sprinkles, if desired

1 Heat oven to 375°. Mix cake mix, oil and eggs, using spoon.

2 Drop dough by rounded tablespoonfuls about 3 inches apart onto ungreased cookie sheet. Insert wooden stick into edge of dough until tip reaches the center.

3 Bake 8 to 11 minutes or until puffed and almost no indentation remains when touched. Cool 1 minute; remove from cookie sheet to wire rack. Cool completely, about 30 minutes. Frost with frosting and decorate with sprinkles.

High Altitude (3500 to 6500 feet): Add 2 tablespoons all-purpose flour to dry cake mix. Bake 10 to 13 minutes.

1 Cookie: Calories 195 (Calories from Fat 70); Fat 8g (Saturated 2g); Cholesterol 20mg; Sodium 180mg; Carbohydrate 30g (Dietary Fiber 0g); Protein 1g. **% Daily Value:** Vitamin A 0%; Vitamin C 0%; Calcium 6%; Iron 2%.

Betty's Tip Need an easy cookie to make for a bake sale? This one is it! When cookies are completely cooled, frosted and decorated, wrap them with colorful plastic wrap and tie the sticks with ribbon. They can be priced and sold individually or in small bouquets.

Photo on page 200

Chocolate Chip–Coconut Macaroons

Prep: 15 min * Bake: 14 min per sheet * Cool: 30 min

ABOUT 6 DOZEN COOKIES

1 package Betty Crocker SuperMoist white cake mix

1 cup water

1/3 cup vegetable oil

3 egg whites

1 bag (12 ounces) miniature semisweet chocolate chips

2 bags (14 ounces each) flaked coconut

Easy Chocolate Glaze (page 241) or Chocolate Glaze (page 241), if desired

1 Heat oven to 350°. Lightly grease cookie sheet with shortening.

2 Make cake mix as directed on package, using 1 cup water, oil and egg whites. Stir in chocolate chips until well mixed. Stir in coconut.

3 Drop dough by rounded tablespoonfuls about 2 inches apart onto cookie sheet. Bake 12 to 14 minutes or until edges are golden brown. Remove from cookie sheet to wire rack. Cool completely, about 30 minutes. Drizzle with Easy Chocolate Glaze.

High Altitude (3500 to 6500 feet): No changes.

1 Cookie: Calories 140 (Calories from Fat 70); Fat 8g (Saturated 6g); Cholesterol 0mg; Sodium 80mg; Carbohydrate 17g (Dietary Fiber 1g); Protein 1g. **% Daily Value:** Vitamin A 0%; Vitamin C 0%; Calcium 0%; Iron 2%.

Betty's Tip Keep your cookies from spreading too much by scooping cookie dough onto completely cooled cookie sheets. You can cool cookie sheets quickly by popping them in the refrigerator or freezer or by running cold water over them (dry completely and grease again if needed).

Rolled Sugar Cookies

Prep: 25 min ✳ Bake: 7 min per sheet ✳ Cool: 1 min

ABOUT 4 DOZEN 2 1/2-INCH COOKIES

1 package Betty Crocker SuperMoist white or yellow cake mix

1/2 cup shortening

1/3 cup butter or margarine, softened

1 teaspoon vanilla, almond extract or lemon extract

1 egg

Sugar

1 tub Betty Crocker Rich & Creamy vanilla ready-to-spread frosting or Vanilla Buttercream Frosting (page 236)

1 Heat oven to 375°. Beat half of the cake mix, the shortening, butter, vanilla and egg in large bowl with electric mixer on medium speed until smooth, or mix with spoon. Stir in remaining cake mix.

2 Divide dough into 4 equal parts. Roll each part 1/8-inch thick on lightly floured surface. Cut into desired shapes; sprinkle with sugar. Place 2 inches apart on ungreased cookie sheet.

3 Bake 5 to 7 minutes or until light brown. Cool 1 minute; remove from cookie sheet to wire rack. Microwave frosting in microwavable bowl uncovered on High 20 to 30 seconds or until melted; stir. Spread frosting on cookies.

High Altitude (3500 to 6500 feet): No changes.

1 Cookie: Calories 110 (Calories from Fat 55); Fat 6g (Saturated 3g); Cholesterol 5mg; Sodium 80mg; Carbohydrate 14g (Dietary Fiber 0g); Protein 0g. **% Daily Value:** Vitamin A 0%; Vitamin C 0%; Calcium 0%; Iron 0%.

Betty's Tip To give a special look to your cookies, marble frosting with Food Color Paint. Stir together small amounts of water and food color. Paint different colors on freshly frosted cookies, using a fine-tip brush, then swirl the colors with a clean brush or toothpick to create marbled designs. (Do not allow frosting to dry or harden before marbling or this technique won't work.) Dry completely before storing.

Rolled Sugar Cookies

Toasted Coconut–Almond Biscotti

Prep: 15 min ✳ Bake: 37 min ✳ Cool: 50 min ✳ Stand: 30 min

2 DOZEN COOKIES

1 package Betty Crocker SuperMoist white cake mix

1 tablespoon vegetable oil

2 eggs

1 cup coconut, toasted*

1/2 cup chopped slivered almonds, toasted*

1 bag (6 ounces) semisweet chocolate chips (1 cup)

1 tablespoon shortening

To toast coconut and almonds: Spread coconut and almonds in an ungreased shallow pan. Bake uncovered in 350° oven 5 to 8 minutes, stirring frequently, until coconut is golden brown. Cool completely, about 15 minutes.

1 Heat oven to 350°. Mix cake mix, oil and eggs in large bowl with spoon until dough forms (some dry mix will remain). Stir in coconut and almonds, using hands if necessary.

2 Shape dough into 15 x 4-inch rectangle on cookie sheet with greased hands. Bake 20 to 25 minutes or until golden brown. Cool on cookie sheet on wire rack 15 minutes.

3 Cut dough crosswise into 1/2-inch slices. Place slices, cut sides down, on cookie sheet. Bake 10 to 12 minutes or until edges are deep golden brown. Cool 5 minutes; remove from cookie sheet to wire rack. Cool completely, about 30 minutes.

4 Heat chocolate chips and shortening in 1-quart saucepan over low heat, stirring constantly, until chocolate is melted. Drizzle chocolate over cookies, or dip one end of each cookie into chocolate. Let stand about 30 minutes or until chocolate is set.

High Altitude (3500 to 6500 feet): Increase second bake to 12 to 14 minutes. When toasting coconut and almonds, bake 7 to 10 minutes.

1 Biscotti: Calories 170 (Calories from Fat 70); Fat 8g (Saturated 3g); Cholesterol 20mg; Sodium 160mg; Carbohydrate 23g (Dietary Fiber 1g); Protein 2g. **% Daily Value:** Vitamin A 0%; Vitamin C 0%; Calcium 4%; Iron 4%.

Betty's Tip If using almonds that have been frozen, make sure they are room temperature before toasting so that the coconut and almonds toast evenly.

Cookie Baking Clues

What's more welcoming than a cookie jar brimming with treats? Baking cookies and bars from a cake mix is super-easy and super-tasty, and cleanup is a breeze. For best results, follow these tips.

Confident Baking

* **Measure liquids,** like water and vegetable oil, in a liquid measuring cup instead of a "nested" or dry-ingredient measuring cup for an accurate amount.

* **Use shiny aluminum** cookie sheets. There are many types of cookie sheets to choose from, but shiny aluminum ones will give the best results.

* **Scoop cookie dough** onto completely cooled cookie sheets. Cookies will spread too much if put on a hot, or even warm, cookie sheet. You can quickly cool a cookie sheet by popping it in the refrigerator or freezer, or by running cold water over it, drying it completely and greasing again if needed.

* **Dip edges** of plastic cookie cutters, if using, in vegetable oil to get a sharper, more defined edge on cookies.

* **Shape cookie dough** into balls by using a level measuring tablespoon of dough. It's just the right amount to create a perfect 1-inch ball.

* **Bake cookies** on the middle oven rack. For even baking, bake one cookie sheet at a time. If you decide to bake two sheets at once, switch the placement of the sheets halfway through baking to help the cookies bake more evenly.

* **Cool cookies** on wire cooling racks so air can flow around the cookies, which will keep them from getting soggy. Cool pans of bars in the pan on a wire cooling rack. Cool cookies and bars completely before frosting them unless the recipe tells you to frost them while they are warm.

* **Line baking pans** with aluminum foil for super-quick cleanup. Let some foil overhang the edges of the pan. Then, when the bars or brownies are cool, just lift them out of the pan by the "handles," peel back the foil and cut as directed.

* **Cool bars** completely before cutting so they don't fall apart.

* **Use a plastic knife** to cut soft and sticky bars or brownies.

Clever Cookies

* **Dress up white or light-colored cookies** by sprinkling them with colored sugar before baking. To make your own colored sugar, put 1/4 to 1/2 cup granulated sugar into a resealable plastic food-storage bag and add 1 to 3 drops of desired food color; seal bag. "Smoosh" or knead bag until all of the sugar is tinted.

* **Add extra crunch** to cookies by rolling dough in chopped nuts or cereal before baking.

* **Create a lunch-box treat!** Make sandwich cookies by putting baked cookies together in pairs with about 1 tablespoon ready-to-spread frosting, marshmallow creme or peanut butter.

* **Embellish baked cookies** by dipping them in melted chocolate or candy coating. After dipping cookies, place them on a wire cooling rack until chocolate is set.

German Chocolate Bars

Prep: 15 min ✳ Bake: 40 min ✳ Cool: 1 hr ✳ Chill: 2 hr

48 BARS

1/2 cup butter or margarine, softened

1 package Betty Crocker SuperMoist German chocolate cake mix

1 tub Betty Crocker Rich & Creamy coconut pecan ready-to-spread frosting or Coconut-Pecan Topping (page 244)

1 bag (6 ounces) semisweet chocolate chips (1 cup)

1/4 cup milk

1 Heat oven to 350°. Lightly grease bottom and sides of rectangular pan, 13 x 9 x 2 inches, with shortening. Cut butter into cake mix in medium bowl, using pastry blender or crisscrossing 2 knives, until crumbly. Press half of the mixture (2 1/2 cups) in bottom of pan. Bake 10 minutes.

2 Carefully spread frosting over baked layer; sprinkle evenly with chocolate chips. Stir milk into remaining cake mixture. Drop by teaspoonfuls onto chocolate chips.

3 Bake 25 to 30 minutes or until cake portion is slightly dry to the touch. Cool completely, about 1 hour. Cover and refrigerate about 2 hours or until firm. For bars, cut into 8 rows by 6 rows. Store covered in refrigerator.

High Altitude (3500 to 6500 feet): No changes.

1 Bar: Calories 135 (Calories from Fat 70); Fat 8g (Saturated 4g); Cholesterol 15mg; Sodium 100mg; Carbohydrate 15g (Dietary Fiber 0g); Protein 1g. **% Daily Value:** Vitamin A 2%; Vitamin C 0%; Calcium 2%; Iron 2%.

Betty's Tip For an easy dessert with restaurant style, place 2 bars on individual serving plates. Top with whipped cream and grated milk chocolate from a candy bar.

German Chocolate Bars

Triple-Chocolate Cherry Bars

Prep: 10 min ✳ Bake: 30 min ✳ Cool: 1 hr

48 BARS

1 package Betty Crocker SuperMoist chocolate fudge cake mix

1 can (21 ounces) cherry pie filling

2 eggs, beaten

1/2 bag (12-ounce size) miniature semisweet chocolate chips (1 cup)

1 tub Betty Crocker Whipped chocolate ready-to-spread frosting or Creamy Chocolate Frosting (page 238)

1 Heat oven to 350°. Grease bottom and sides of jelly roll pan, 15 1/2 x 10 1/2 x 1 inch, with shortening; lightly flour.

2 Mix cake mix, pie filling, eggs and chocolate chips in large bowl with spoon. Pour into pan.

3 Bake 20 to 30 minutes or until toothpick inserted in center comes out clean. Cool completely, about 1 hour. Frost with frosting. For bars, cut into 8 rows by 6 rows.

High Altitude (3500 to 6500 feet): Heat oven to 375°.

1 Bar: Calories 110 (Calories from Fat 35); Fat 4g (Saturated 2g); Cholesterol 10mg; Sodium 80mg; Carbohydrate 18g (Dietary Fiber 1g); Protein 1g. **% Daily Value:** Vitamin A 0%; Vitamin C 0%; Calcium 0%; Iron 2%.

Triple-Chocolate Strawberry Bars: Substitute strawberry pie filling for the cherry.

Betty's Tip Shiny metal pans are preferred for making bars because they reflect the heat away from the bars, preventing the crust from getting too brown and dark. If using dark nonstick or glass baking pans, follow the manufacturer's directions, usually reducing the oven temperature 25°.

Triple-Chocolate Cherry Bars

Rocky Road Bars

Prep: 15 min * Bake: 35 min * Cool: 1 hr

24 BARS

1 package Betty Crocker
SuperMoist chocolate fudge
or devil's food cake mix

1/2 cup butter or margarine,
melted

1/3 cup water

1/4 cup packed brown sugar

2 eggs

1 cup chopped nuts

3 cups miniature marshmallows

Easy Chocolate Glaze (page 241)
or Chocolate Glaze (page 241)

1 Heat oven to 350°. Grease bottom and sides of rectangular pan,
13 x 9 x 2 inches, with shortening.

2 Mix half of the cake mix, the butter, water, brown sugar and eggs
in large bowl with spoon until blended. Stir in remaining cake
mix and the nuts (some dry mix might remain). Spread in pan.

3 Bake 20 minutes; sprinkle with marshmallows. Bake 10 to 15
minutes longer or until marshmallows are puffed and golden.
Drizzle Easy Chocolate Glaze over bars. Cool completely,
about 1 hour. For bars, cut into 6 rows by 4 rows.

High Altitude (3500 to 6500 feet): Add 2 tablespoons all-purpose flour to dry cake
mix. Decrease butter to 1/4 cup; increase water to 1/2 cup. Bake 30 minutes; sprinkle with marshmallows. Bake 8 to 10 minutes longer.

1 Bar: Calories 210 (Calories from Fat 90); Fat 10g (Saturated 4g); Cholesterol 30mg; Sodium
200mg; Carbohydrate 28g (Dietary Fiber 0g); Protein 2g. **% Daily Value:** Vitamin A 2%; Vitamin C
0%; Calcium 2%; Iron 4%.

Betty's Tip If you line the pan with aluminum foil, you can lift out the
bars for easy cutting and cleanup. To make bar cutting a breeze, use a
plastic knife dipped in hot water.

Chocolate-Caramel-Oatmeal Bars

Prep: 15 min ✳ Bake: 40 min ✳ Cool: 1 hr

24 BARS

1 package Betty Crocker SuperMoist yellow cake mix

1/2 cup butter of margarine, softened

1 egg

2 cups quick-cooking or old-fashioned oats

1 1/2 cups semisweet chocolate chips

1 cup chopped walnuts or pecans

2/3 cup caramel topping

1 tablespoon all-purpose flour

1 Heat oven to 350°. Grease bottom only of rectangular pan, 13 x 9 x 2 inches, with shortening.

2 Mix cake mix, butter and egg in large bowl with electric mixer on low speed until crumbly. Stir in oats, using hands if necessary. Reserve 1 1/2 cups crumb mixture. Press remaining crumb mixture in pan. Bake 12 to 15 minutes or until light golden brown.

3 Sprinkle crust with chocolate chips and walnuts. Mix caramel topping and flour in small bowl; drizzle evenly over nuts. Sprinkle reserved crumb mixture over caramel.

4 Bake 20 to 25 minutes or until golden brown. Run knife around sides of pan to loosen. Cool completely, about 1 hour. For bars, cut into 6 rows by 4 rows.

High Altitude (3500 to 6500 feet): Heat oven to 375°.

1 Bar: Calories 250 (Calories from Fat 110); Fat 12g (Saturated 5g); Cholesterol 20mg; Sodium 200mg; Carbohydrate 34g (Dietary Fiber 2g); Protein 3g. **% Daily Value:** Vitamin A 2%; Vitamin C 0%; Calcium 6%; Iron 6%.

Betty's Tip It's best to bake bars in the exact pan size called for in a recipe. Bars baked in a pan that is too large will overbake and be hard. Those baked in a pan that's too small can be doughy in the center and hard on the edges.

Lemon Cheesecake Bars

Prep: 15 min ✳ Bake: 25 min ✳ Cool: 1 hr ✳ Chill: 3 hr

48 BARS

1 package Betty Crocker
SuperMoist lemon cake mix

1/3 cup butter or margarine,
softened

3 eggs

1 package (8 ounces) cream
cheese, softened

1 cup powdered sugar

2 teaspoons grated lemon peel

2 tablespoons lemon juice

1 Heat oven to 350°. Beat cake mix, butter and 1 of the eggs in large bowl with electric mixer on low speed until crumbly. Press in bottom of ungreased rectangular pan, 13 x 9 x 2 inches.

2 Beat cream cheese in medium bowl with electric mixer on medium speed until smooth. Gradually beat in powdered sugar on low speed. Stir in lemon peel and lemon juice until smooth. Reserve 1/2 cup cream cheese mixture; refrigerate. Beat remaining 2 eggs into remaining cream cheese mixture on medium speed until blended. Spread over cake mixture.

3 Bake about 25 minutes or until set. Cool completely, about 1 hour. Spread with reserved cream cheese mixture. Refrigerate about 3 hours or until firm. For bars, cut into 8 rows by 6 rows. Store covered in refrigerator.

High Altitude (3500 to 6500 feet): Decrease butter to 1/4 cup.

1 Bar: Calories 85 (Calories from Fat 35); Fat 4g (Saturated 2g); Cholesterol 20mg; Sodium 95mg; Carbohydrate 11g (Dietary Fiber 0g); Protein 1g. **% Daily Value:** Vitamin A 2%; Vitamin C 0%; Calcium 2%; Iron 2%.

Betty's Tip How many lemons do you need for this recipe? One lemon will be fine. One lemon yields 1 1/2 to 3 teaspoons of grated peel and 2 to 3 tablespoons of juice.

This 1974 ad proves just how easy it is to bring in sunshine and smiles with these lemony bars.

Lemon Cheesecake Bars

White Chocolate–Cranberry Bars

Prep: 10 min * Bake: 25 min * Cool: 1 hr

24 BARS

1 package Betty Crocker
SuperMoist white cake mix

1/3 cup butter or margarine,
melted

2 tablespoons water

2 eggs

1 1/2 cups dried cranberries

1 cup white baking chips

1 Heat oven to 350°. Grease bottom only of rectangular pan, 13 x 9 x 2 inches, with shortening; lightly flour.

2 Mix cake mix, butter, water and eggs in large bowl with spoon until dough forms (some dry mix will remain). Stir in cranberries and white baking chips. Spread evenly in pan.

3 Bake 20 to 25 minutes or until toothpick inserted in center comes out clean. Cool completely, about 1 hour. For bars, cut into 6 rows by 4 rows.

High Altitude (3500 to 6500 feet): Bake 25 to 30 minutes. When melting white baking chips and chocolate chips with shortening as directed in Betty's Tip, use 1 1/2 teaspoons to 1 tablespoon shortening so melted mixture is thin enough to drizzle.

1 Bar: Calories 210 (Calories from Fat 80); Fat 9g (Saturated 5g); Cholesterol 25mg; Sodium 180mg; Carbohydrate 30g (Dietary Fiber 0g); Protein 2g. **% Daily Value:** Vitamin A 2%; Vitamin C 0%; Calcium 6%; Iron 2%.

Betty's Tip These bars look especially festive when topped with white chocolate. To make white chocolate drizzle, melt 1/3 cup white baking chips and 1 1/2 teaspoons shortening in 1-quart saucepan over low heat, stirring frequently, until melted and smooth. Drizzle melted white baking chip mixture over cooled bars. Let stand 30 minutes or until set.

Photo on page 200

Chocolate Chip–Pecan Bars

Prep: 15 min ✳ Bake: 32 min ✳ Cool: 1 hr

32 BARS

1/2 cup butter or margarine, softened

1 package Betty Crocker SuperMoist white or yellow cake mix

2 cups pecan halves

2/3 cup butter or margarine

2/3 cup packed brown sugar

1 bag (6 ounces) semisweet chocolate chips (1 cup)

1 Heat oven to 350°. Cut 1/2 cup butter into cake mix in medium bowl, using pastry blender or crisscrossing 2 knives, until crumbly. Press firmly in bottom of ungreased rectangular pan, 13 x 9 x 2 inches. Bake 10 to 12 minutes or until crust is dry.

2 Sprinkle pecan halves evenly over baked layer. Heat 2/3 cup butter and the brown sugar to boiling in 2-quart saucepan over medium heat, stirring occasionally; boil and stir 1 minute. Spoon mixture evenly over pecans.

3 Bake about 20 minutes or until bubbly and light brown. Sprinkle chocolate chips over warm bars. Cool completely, about 1 hour. For bars, cut into 8 rows by 4 rows.

High Altitude (3500 to 6500 feet): Grease bottom and sides of pan with shortening. Heat butter and brown sugar until butter is melted, but do not boil.

1 Bar: Calories 220 (Calories from Fat 125); Fat 14g (Saturated 6g); Cholesterol 20mg; Sodium 160mg; Carbohydrate 22g (Dietary Fiber 1g); Protein 2g. **% Daily Value:** Vitamin A 4%; Vitamin C 0%; Calcium 4%; Iron 2%.

Betty's Tip A pastry blender is a very efficient, easy-to-use tool to have on hand. It blends butter or shortening into dry ingredients without much effort. Pastry blenders are inexpensive and can be found in the cooking- and baking-utensil section of most discount stores and supermarkets.

Carrot-Raisin Bars

Prep: 10 min ✳ Bake: 20 min ✳ Cool: 1 hr

48 BARS

1 package Betty Crocker SuperMoist carrot cake mix

1/2 cup vegetable oil

1/4 cup water

2 eggs

3/4 cup raisins

1/2 cup chopped nuts

1 tub Betty Crocker Rich & Creamy cream cheese frosting or Cream Cheese Frosting (page 234)

Ground cinnamon, if desired

1 Heat oven to 350°. Grease bottom and sides of jelly roll pan, 15 1/2 x 10 1/2 x 1 inch, with shortening; lightly flour.

2 Mix cake mix, oil, water and eggs in large bowl with spoon. Stir in raisins and nuts. Spread evenly in pan.

3 Bake 15 to 20 minutes or until toothpick inserted in center comes out clean. Cool completely, about 1 hour. Frost with frosting. Sprinkle with cinnamon. For bars, cut into 8 rows by 6 rows. Store covered in refrigerator.

High Altitude (3500 to 6500 feet): Bake 22 to 27 minutes.

1 Bar: Calories 115 (Calories from Fat 45); Fat 5g (Saturated 1g); Cholesterol 10mg; Sodium 90mg; Carbohydrate 17g (Dietary Fiber 0g); Protein 1g. **% Daily Value:** Vitamin A 2%; Vitamin C 0%; Calcium 2%; Iron 2%.

Carrot-Raisin-Coconut Bars: Stir in 1 cup flaked coconut with the raisins and nuts.

Betty's Tip Decorate your bars with cookie-cutter designs. Dip a small cookie cutter into ground cinnamon and lightly press onto the top of frosted bars; remove cookie cutter. Or for a super-speedy finish, simply sprinkle frosted bars with chopped nuts.

Carrot-Raisin Bars

8

Fabulous Frostings and Glazes

Layered Boston Cream Pie (page 70) with Chocolate Glaze (page 241) and May Day Baskets (page 129) with Vanilla Buttercream Frosting (page 236)

All "Dec'ed" Out

You can make a great number of shapes and designs with frostings when you use a decorating bag fitted with a variety of tips. The thickness of the frosting is important; if it becomes too thick, add water or milk to thin it to a consistency that is easy to pipe. Use steady pressure when pressing out the frosting. The amount of pressure will determine the size and evenness of any design. Be sure to cover the frosting while working with it to keep it from drying out.

How to Use a Decorating Bag

1 If you are not using a coupler or if the decorating bag is large, simply place the tip in the bag. If you are using a coupler, place the desired decorating tip on the coupler base and screw the coupler ring into place over the tip to hold it securely.

2 To fill the bag with frosting or whipped cream, fold down the open end of the bag to form a cuff approximately 2 inches wide. Holding the bag beneath the cuff and using a spatula, fill the bag half full with frosting. (Don't fill the bag too full or frosting will back up out of the bag.)

3 To close the bag, unfold the cuff and twist the top of the bag, forcing the frosting down into the tip. Continue to twist the end of the bag as you decorate.

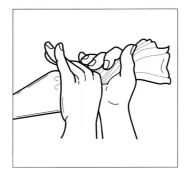

4 To change decorating tips, unscrew the coupler ring, remove the tip, replace it with another tip and screw the ring on again.

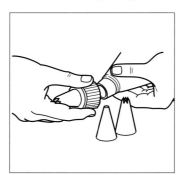

How to Make Rosettes

Using a star tip, press out frosting or whipped cream, using steady, even pressure, into a circle. Then, without stopping, spiral the frosting on top in a smaller circle, finally ending the swirl in a peak as you decrease the pressure.

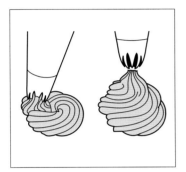

How to Make Drop Flowers

Using a drop flower tip, hold the decorating bag perpendicular to the cake with the tip touching the surface. Squeeze the bag, keeping the tip in frosting until petals are formed. Stop pressure and pull away.

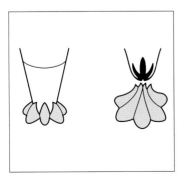

✳ Decorating Tips ✳

Drop Flower Tip: Makes easy flowers

Leaf Tip: Makes plain, ruffled or stand-up leaves

Petal Tip: Makes roses and flower petals. Also used for making ribbons, bows, swags and ruffles.

Star Tip: Makes shells and small borders. Also used for making stars, rosettes and simple flowers

Writing Tip: Makes dots, beads and balls and is used for writing

Creamy White Frosting

Prep: 10 min

12 TO 16 SERVINGS, ABOUT 2 CUPS

3 cups powdered sugar

1/3 cup shortening

1/4 cup milk

1/2 teaspoon clear vanilla or almond extract

1 Mix powdered sugar and shortening in medium bowl with spoon or with electric mixer on low speed.

2 Stir in milk and vanilla until smooth. If necessary, stir in additional milk, a few drops at a time, until smooth and spreadable. **Generously frosts a 13 x 9-inch cake, or fills and frosts an 8- or 9-inch two-layer cake.**

Betty's Tip This frosting is perfect when you want a topping that's white as snow. Clear vanilla or almond extract adds a nice flavor but won't change the color of the frosting.

Cream Cheese Frosting

Prep: 10 min

12 TO 16 SERVINGS, ABOUT 2 1/2 CUPS

1 package (8 ounces) cream cheese, softened

1/4 cup butter or margarine, softened

2 to 3 teaspoons milk

1 teaspoon vanilla

4 cups powdered sugar

1 Beat cream cheese, butter, milk and vanilla in medium bowl with electric mixer on low speed until smooth.

2 Gradually beat in powdered sugar, 1 cup at a time, on low speed until smooth and spreadable. Store frosted cake or any remaining frosting covered in refrigerator. **Generously frosts a 13 x 9-inch cake, or fills and frosts an 8- or 9-inch two-layer cake.**

Chocolate–Cream Cheese Frosting: Add 2 ounces unsweetened baking chocolate, melted and cooled, with the butter.

Betty's Tip This fresh, delicious cream cheese frosting will spoil if left out at room temperature, so be sure to refrigerate the frosted cake or any leftover frosting.

Ultimate Carrot Cake (page 86) with
Cream Cheese Frosting

Vanilla Buttercream Frosting

Prep: 10 min

12 TO 16 SERVINGS, ABOUT 1 3/4 CUPS

3 cups powdered sugar

1/3 cup butter or margarine, softened

1 1/2 teaspoons vanilla

1 to 2 tablespoons milk

1 Mix powdered sugar and butter in medium bowl with spoon or with electric mixer on low speed. Stir in vanilla and 1 tablespoon of the milk.

2 Gradually beat in just enough remaining milk to make frosting smooth and spreadable. If frosting is too thick, beat in more milk, a few drops at a time. If frosting becomes too thin, beat in a small amount of powdered sugar. **Generously frosts a 13 x 9-inch cake, or fills and frosts an 8- or 9-inch two-layer cake.**

Lemon Buttercream Frosting: Omit vanilla. Substitute lemon juice for the milk. Stir in 1/2 teaspoon grated lemon peel.

Cherry Buttercream Frosting: 2 tablespoons drained, chopped maraschino cherries and 2 drops red food color.

Orange Buttercream Frosting: Omit vanilla. Substitute orange juice for the milk. Stir in 2 teaspoons grated orange peel.

Peanut Butter Frosting: Substitute creamy peanut butter for the butter. Increase milk to 1/4 cup, adding more if necessary, a few drops at a time.

Betty's Tip **Make waves in your frosting by pressing the back of a spoon in and out of the frosting around the top and sides of the cake.**

Whipped Cream Cheese Frosting

Prep: 10 min

12 TO 16 SERVINGS, ABOUT 3 CUPS

2 ounces cream cheese, softened

2 teaspoons milk

1 1/2 cups whipping (heavy) cream

1/2 cup powdered sugar

1 Stir cream cheese and milk in chilled large bowl until smooth.

2 Beat in whipping cream and powdered sugar with electric mixer on high speed, scraping bowl occasionally, until soft peaks form. Store frosted cake or any remaining frosting covered in refrigerator. **Generously frosts a 13 x 9-inch cake, or fills and frosts an 8- or 9-inch two-layer cake.**

Betty's Tip **It's best to frost your cake with this fluffy frosting just before you're going to serve it. If you make it too far ahead, the frosting may break down.**

Strawberries and Cream Cake (page 41) with Whipped Cream Cheese Frosting

Chocolate Ganache

Prep: 5 min * Cook: 5 min * Stand: 5 min

12 TO 16 SERVINGS, ABOUT 1 1/4 CUPS

2/3 cup whipping (heavy) cream

6 ounces semisweet baking chocolate, chopped

1 Heat whipping cream in 1-quart saucepan over low heat until hot but not boiling; remove from heat.

2 Stir in chocolate until melted. Let stand about 5 minutes. Ganache is ready to use when it mounds slightly when dropped from a spoon. It will become firmer the longer it cools.

3 Pour ganache carefully onto top center of cake; spread with large spatula so it flows evenly over top and down to cover side of cake. **Glazes a 13 x 9-inch cake or top and side of an 8- or 9-inch two-layer cake.**

Betty's Tip If you glaze the cake on a cooling rack with waxed paper underneath the rack, the ganache will flow over the side of the cake and the extra drips will fall onto the waxed paper. When the ganache hardens, you can easily and neatly transfer the cake to your serving plate.

Creamy Chocolate Frosting

Prep: 15 min

12 TO 16 SERVINGS, ABOUT 2 CUPS

3 cups powdered sugar

1/3 cup butter or margarine, softened

2 teaspoons vanilla

3 ounces unsweetened baking chocolate, melted and cooled

3 to 4 tablespoons milk

1 Mix powdered sugar and butter in medium bowl with spoon or with electric mixer on low speed. Stir in vanilla and chocolate.

2 Gradually beat in just enough milk to make frosting smooth and spreadable. If frosting is too thick, beat in more milk, a few drops at a time. If frosting becomes too thin, beat in a small amount of powdered sugar. **Generously frosts a 13 x 9-inch cake, or fills and frosts an 8- or 9-inch two-layer cake.**

Creamy Cocoa Frosting: Substitute 1/3 cup baking cocoa for the chocolate.

Creamy Mocha Frosting: Add 2 1/2 teaspoons instant coffee (dry) with the powdered sugar.

Creamy White Chocolate Frosting: Substitute 3 ounces chopped white baking bar, melted and cooled, for the chocolate.

Betty's Tip For the ultimate time-saver, place all ingredients in a food processor. Cover and process, stopping occasionally to scrape sides, until frosting is smooth and spreadable.

Halloween Black Cat Cake (page 132) with Creamy Chocolate Frosting

Browned Butter Frosting

Prep: 15 min

12 TO 16 SERVINGS, ABOUT 1 3/4 CUPS

1/3 cup butter

3 cups powdered sugar

1 1/2 teaspoons vanilla

1 to 2 tablespoons milk

1 Heat butter in 1-quart saucepan over medium heat until just light brown. Watch carefully because butter can brown then burn quickly. Remove saucepan from heat.

2 Stir in powdered sugar, vanilla and 1 tablespoon of the milk. Stir in just enough remaining milk to make frosting smooth and spreadable. If frosting is too thick, stir in more milk, a few drops at a time. If frosting becomes too thin, beat in a small amount of powdered sugar. **Generously frosts a 13 x 9-inch cake, or fills and frosts an 8- or 9-inch two-layer cake.**

Betty's Tip The rich and caramel-like flavor and creamy texture of this frosting comes from using real butter. Margarine just won't give you the same delicious results.

Caramel Frosting

Prep: 10 min * Cook: 5 min

12 TO 16 SERVINGS, ABOUT 2 CUPS

1/2 cup butter or margarine

1 cup packed brown sugar

1/4 cup milk

2 cups powdered sugar

1 Melt butter in 2-quart saucepan over medium heat. Stir in brown sugar. Heat to boiling, stirring constantly; reduce heat to low. Boil and stir 2 minutes. Remove from heat; stir in milk.

2 Gradually stir in powdered sugar. Beat with spoon until smooth and spreadable. If frosting becomes too stiff, stir in additional milk, 1 teaspoon at a time, or heat over low heat, stirring constantly. **Generously frosts a 13 x 9-inch cake, or fills and frosts an 8- or 9-inch two-layer cake.**

Betty's Tip You'll love this soft and smooth caramel frosting spread on apple, banana, carrot or chocolate cake.

Chocolate Glaze

Prep: 5 min * Cook: 5 min * Cool: 10 min

12 TO 16 SERVINGS, ABOUT 1/2 CUP

1/2 cup semisweet chocolate chips

2 tablespoons butter or margarine

2 tablespoons corn syrup

1 to 2 teaspoons hot water

1 Heat chocolate chips, butter and corn syrup in 1-quart saucepan over low heat, stirring frequently, until chocolate chips are melted. Cool about 10 minutes.

2 Stir in hot water, 1 teaspoon at a time, until consistency of thick syrup. **Glazes top of one 12-cup bundt cake, 10-inch angel food cake, 13 x 9-inch cake or 8- or 9-inch layer cake.**

Chocolate Cappuccino Glaze: Stir in 2 teaspoons instant espresso coffee (dry) with the chocolate chips.

Milk Chocolate Glaze: Substitute milk chocolate chips for the semisweet chocolate chips.

Mint Chocolate Glaze: Substitute mint chocolate chips for the semisweet chocolate chips.

White Chocolate Glaze: Substitute white baking chips for the chocolate chips.

Betty's Tip Glaze is a perfect topper for cakes that would be too rich if frosted. It's also great for drizzling decoratively over the top of cake, bars or cookies. To save some time, place chocolate chips, butter and corn syrup in a 2-cup microwavable measure. Microwave uncovered on Medium (50%) 1 to 2 minutes or until chocolate can be stirred smooth. Don't add the water.

Easy Chocolate Glaze

Prep: 5 min

12 TO 16 SERVINGS, 1/2 CUP

1/2 cup Betty Crocker Rich & Creamy chocolate ready-to-spread frosting

Spoon frosting from tub into microwavable bowl. Microwave uncovered on High about 15 seconds or until frosting can be stirred smooth and is thin enough to drizzle. (Or spoon frosting into 1-quart saucepan and heat over low heat, stirring constantly, until thin enough to drizzle.) **Glazes top of one 12-cup bundt cake, 10-inch angel food cake, 13 x 9-inch cake or 8- or 9-inch layer cake.**

Betty's Tip Be careful if you're heating the frosting in a saucepan. The saucepan retains its heat longer than a microwavable bowl.

Vanilla Glaze

Prep: 5 min

12 TO 16 SERVINGS, ABOUT 1/2 CUP

1 cup powdered sugar

1 to 2 tablespoons milk

1/2 teaspoon vanilla or clear vanilla

Mix powdered sugar, 1 tablespoon milk and the vanilla. Stir in additional milk, 1 teaspoon at a time, until smooth and consistency of thick syrup. **Glazes top of one 12-cup bundt cake, 10-inch angel food cake or 13 x 9-inch cake.**

Betty's Tip White glazes and frostings that call for milk will look whiter and less translucent if you use whole milk, half-and-half or cream.

Easy Vanilla Glaze

Prep: 5 min

12 TO 16 SERVINGS, 1/2 CUP

1/2 cup Betty Crocker Rich & Creamy vanilla ready-to-spread frosting

Spoon frosting from tub into microwavable bowl. Microwave uncovered on High about 15 seconds or until frosting can be stirred smooth and is thin enough to drizzle. (Or spoon frosting into 1-quart saucepan and heat over low heat, stirring constantly, until thin enough to drizzle.) **Glazes top of one 12-cup bundt cake, 10-inch angel food cake, 13 x 9-inch cake or 8- or 9-inch layer cake.**

Easy Cinnamon Glaze: Stir in 1/2 teaspoon ground cinnamon.

Betty's Tip When you just want a drizzle for cookies and bars, you can make a smaller amount of this glaze. Place 1/4 cup frosting in a microwavable bowl and microwave on High 5 to 10 seconds or until thin enough to drizzle.

Sweetened Whipped Cream

Prep: 5 min

For 1 Cup: Beat 1/2 cup whipping (heavy) cream and 1 tablespoon granulated or powdered sugar in chilled small bowl with electric mixer on high speed until soft peaks form.

For 1 1/2 Cups: Beat 3/4 cup whipping (heavy) cream and 2 tablespoons granulated or powdered sugar in chilled medium bowl with electric mixer on high speed until soft peaks form.

For 2 Cups: Beat 1 cup whipping (heavy) cream and 3 tablespoons granulated or powdered sugar in chilled medium bowl with electric mixer on high speed until soft peaks form.

For 3 Cups: Beat 1 1/2 cups whipping (heavy) cream and 1/4 cup granulated or powdered sugar in chilled large bowl with electric mixer on high speed until soft peaks form.

Almond-Flavored Whipped Cream: Beat 1 cup whipping (heavy) cream, 3 tablespoons granulated or powdered sugar and 1/2 teaspoon almond extract in chilled medium bowl with electric mixer on high speed until soft peaks form.

Citrus-Flavored Whipped Cream: Beat 1 cup whipping (heavy) cream, 3 tablespoons granulated or powdered sugar and 1 teaspoon grated lemon or orange peel in chilled medium bowl with electric mixer on high speed until soft peaks form.

Maple-Flavored Whipped Cream: Beat 1 cup whipping (heavy) cream, 3 tablespoons granulated or powdered sugar and 1/4 teaspoon maple extract in chilled medium bowl with electric mixer on high speed until soft peaks form.

Peppermint-Flavored Whipped Cream: Beat 1 cup whipping (heavy) cream, 3 tablespoons granulated or powdered sugar and 1/2 teaspoon peppermint extract in chilled medium bowl with electric mixer on high speed until soft peaks form.

Rum-Flavored Whipped Cream: Beat 1 cup whipping (heavy) cream, 3 tablespoons granulated or powdered sugar and 1/2 teaspoon rum extract in chilled medium bowl with electric mixer on high speed until soft peaks form.

Spiced Whipped Cream: Beat 1 cup whipping (heavy) cream, 3 tablespoons granulated or powdered sugar and 1/2 teaspoon ground cinnamon, ground ginger or ground nutmeg in chilled medium bowl with electric mixer on high speed until soft peaks form.

Vanilla Whipped Cream: Beat 1 cup whipping (heavy) cream, 3 tablespoons granulated or powdered sugar and 1 teaspoon vanilla in chilled medium bowl with electric mixer on high speed until soft peaks form.

Betty's Tip Well-chilled cream will whip the best, so keep it refrigerated until ready to use. It also helps to chill the bowl and beaters before you begin. When the cream begins to thicken as you beat it, reduce the mixer speed so you can watch carefully and beat just until soft peaks form. Overbeaten cream will look curdled.

Coconut-Pecan Topping

Prep: 10 min * Cook: 12 min * Cool: 30 min

12 TO 16 SERVINGS, ABOUT 3 CUPS

1 cup sugar

1/2 cup butter or margarine

1 cup evaporated milk

3 egg yolks

1 1/3 cups flaked coconut

1 cup chopped pecans

1 teaspoon vanilla

1 Mix sugar, butter, milk and egg yolks in 2-quart saucepan. Cook over medium heat about 12 minutes, stirring occasionally, until thick.

2 Stir in coconut, pecans and vanilla. Cool about 30 minutes, beating occasionally with spoon, until spreadable. **Generously frosts a 13 x 9-inch cake, or fills and frosts an 8- or 9-inch two- or three-layer cake.**

Betty's Tip Though this filling is traditionally used for German chocolate cake, it is also delicious on other cakes, including your favorite chocolate or white cake. Frost layer cakes only between the layers and on top, leaving the sides unfrosted.

Chocolate Whipped Cream Topping

Prep: 10 min

12 TO 16 SERVINGS, ABOUT 2 CUPS

1 cup whipping (heavy) cream

3/4 cup powdered sugar

1/4 cup Dutch process baking cocoa

1/2 teaspoon vanilla

Beat all ingredients in chilled medium bowl with electric mixer on high speed until soft peaks form. **Generously frosts a 13 x 9-inch cake, or fills and frosts an 8- or 9-inch two-layer cake.**

Betty's Tip Dutch process baking cocoa is a darker cocoa with a more mellow chocolate flavor than regular baking cocoa, but regular cocoa also works fine in this recipe.

**Mocha Mousse Cake (page 66) with
Chocolate Whipped Cream Topping**

Helpful Nutrition and Cooking Information

Nutrition Guidelines

We provide nutrition information for each recipe that includes calories, fat, cholesterol, sodium, carbohydrate, fiber and protein. Individual food choices can be based on this information. The recommended intake for a daily diet of 2,000 calories as set by the Food and Drug Administration.

Total Fat	Less than 65g
Saturated Fat	Less than 20g
Cholesterol	Less than 300mg
Sodium	Less than 2,400mg
Total Carbohydrate	300g
Dietary Fiber	25g

Criteria Used for Calculating Nutrition Information

* The first ingredient was used wherever a choice is given (such as 1/3 cup sour cream or plain yogurt).
* The first serving number was used wherever a range is given (such as 4 to 6 servings).
* "If desired" ingredients and recipe variations were not included (such as sprinkle with brown sugar, if desired).

Ingredients Used in Recipe Testing and Nutrition Calculations

* Ingredients used for testing represent those that the majority of consumers use in their homes: large eggs and 2% milk.
* Fat-free, low-fat or low-sodium products were not used, unless otherwise indicated.
* Solid vegetable shortening (not butter, margarine, nonstick cooking sprays or vegetable oil spread as they can cause sticking problems) was used to grease pans, unless otherwise indicated.

Equipment Used in Recipe Testing

We use equipment for testing that the majority of consumers use in their homes. If a specific piece of equipment (such as a wire whisk) is necessary for recipe success, it is listed in the recipe.

* Cookware and bakeware without nonstick coatings were used, unless otherwise indicated.
* No dark-colored, black or insulated bakeware was used.
* When a pan is specified in a recipe, a metal pan was used; a baking dish or pie plate means ovenproof glass was used.
* An electric hand mixer was used for mixing only when mixer speeds are specified in the recipe directions. When a mixer speed is not given, a spoon or fork was used.

Index

Note: *Italicized* page references indicate photographs.

Complete your cookbook library
with these *Betty Crocker* titles

Betty Crocker's A Passion for Pasta

Betty Crocker's Best Bread Machine Cookbook

Betty Crocker's Best Chicken Cookbook

Betty Crocker's Best Christmas Cookbook

Betty Crocker's Best of Baking

Betty Crocker's Best of Healthy and Hearty Cooking

Betty Crocker's Best-Loved Recipes

Betty Crocker's Bisquick® Cookbook

Betty Crocker's Bread Machine Cookbook

Betty Crocker's Cook It Quick

Betty Crocker's Cookbook, 9th Edition - *The* BIG RED *Cookbook*®

Betty Crocker's Cookbook, Bridal Edition

Betty Crocker's Cookie Book

Betty Crocker's Cooking Basics

Betty Crocker's Cooking for Two

Betty Crocker's Cooky Book, Facsimile Edition

Betty Crocker's Easy Slow Cooker Dinners

Betty Crocker's Eat and Lose Weight

Betty Crocker's Entertaining Basics

Betty Crocker's Flavors of Home

Betty Crocker's Great Grilling

Betty Crocker's Healthy New Choices

Betty Crocker's Indian Home Cooking

Betty Crocker's Italian Cooking

Betty Crocker's Kids Cook!

Betty Crocker's Kitchen Library

Betty Crocker's Living with Cancer

Betty Crocker's Low-Fat Low-Cholesterol Cooking Today

Betty Crocker's New Cake Decorating

Betty Crocker's New Chinese Cookbook

Betty Crocker's Picture Cook Book, Facsimile Edition

Betty Crocker's Quick & Easy Cookbook

Betty Crocker's Slow Cooker Cookbook

Betty Crocker's Ultimate Cake Mix Cookbook

Betty Crocker's Vegetarian Cooking